Merry Christmas 1962

defer

# I QUOTE

# I QUOTE

## A Collection of
## Ancient & Modern
## Wisdom & Inspiration

EDITED BY

## Virginia Ely

*Instead of a gem or a flower, cast the gift of
a lovely thought into the heart of a friend.*
—George MacDonald

FLEMING H. REVELL CO.

DEDICATED

*With tenderest devotion*

*To My Parents*

Franklin Pierce Ely and Susan Coleman Ely

# ACKNOWLEDGMENTS

I wish to express my gratitude and to acknowledge my obligation to the following individuals and publishers by whose inspiration and assistance the publication of I QUOTE has been made possible:

To my aunt, Cora Virginia Coleman, who, by her own example, taught me, as a little child, to read with a pencil in my hand;

To my teachers—in grade school, high school, college and seminary—who painstakingly directed my love toward the beautiful in literature;

To the following authors who have graciously granted me permission to employ their poems: Faye Carr Adams, Sybil Leonard Armes; Zula Evelyn Coon, and Martha Snell Nicholson;

To the following publishers for permission to reprint extracts or whole poems from copyrighted material by authors listed here:

THE BAPTIST STANDARD, for *Think on Big Things,* by Faye Carr Adams; THE BAPTIST SUNDAY SCHOOL BOARD, for *This is my Father's World,* by Faye Carr Adams, and my own poem, *The Conquering Christ;* BOBBS-MERRILL COMPANY, for permission to use James Whitcomb Riley's poem, *Away,* taken from *Afterwhiles;* WILLIAM CAMELFORD, for *Companions,* by Henrietta Heron; COKESBURY PUBLISHING COMPANY, for the quotation by Leslie D. Weatherhead; W. B. CONKEY COMPANY, for quotations from Ella Wheeler Wilcox's poems; THE DIAL PRESS, for *Yes, Thou Art Ever Present,* by Hannah More; DODD, MEAD & COMPANY, for *De Darkest Hour,* by Paul Lawrence Dunbar, and *I Watched Them Tearing a Building Down,* by G. K. Chesterton; THE EVANGELICAL PRESS, Toronto, Canada, for quotations by Annie Johnson Flint; MRS. MARJORIE (ROBERT) FREEMAN, for quotations by Robert Freeman; HOUGHTON-MIFFLIN COMPANY, for quotations from Bret Harte, John Burroughs and Lizette W. Reese; HARPER & BROTHERS, for *Keep Love in Your Life,* by Thomas Curtis Clark, and *So Long as There are Homes,* by Grace Noll Crowell, from *The Light of the Years;* LONE STAR SCHOOL BOOK PUBLISHERS, for *Let Me Grow Lovely Growing Old,* from *Dreamers on Horse-*

# ACKNOWLEDGMENTS

*back,* by Karle Wilson Baker; THE MACMILLAN COMPANY, for quotations by Richard Lovelace, William A. Percy and John Richard Moreland; FLEMING H. REVELL COMPANY, for *The Evangel,* from *The Romance of Evangelism,* by Roland Q. Leavell, and for quotations by Eliza M. Hickok, Clyde McGee, Ruby T. Weyburn, taken from *Best Beloved Religious Poems,* edited by J. G. Lawson; CHARLES SCRIBNER'S SONS, for *God Send us Men,* by F. J. Gillman, from *Modern Religious Verse and Prose,* edited by Fred Merrifield, and for quotations from Henry Van Dyke and M. B. Babcock; VIRGIL MARKHAM, for permission to quote from poems by Edwin Markham; WILLETT, CLARKE & COMPANY, for quotations by Phillip James Bailey, Clinton Scollard, Horatius Bomar, F. B. Mayer, G. A. Studdart Kennedy, and Washington Gladden.

I have made diligent effort to identify authorship and ownership of all other poetry employed, and so far as my knowledge extends, it is all in public domain.

THE AUTHOR

# CONTENTS

# CONTENTS

# CONTENTS

# CONTENTS

# ABILITY

Without me, ye can do nothing.—JOHN 15:5.

My God shall supply all your needs according to His riches in glory in Christ Jesus.—PHIL. 4:19.

No man's abilities are so remarkably shining as not to stand in need of a proper opportunity, a patron, and even the praises of a friend to recommend them to the notice of the world.—PLINY.

Although men are accused of not knowing their own weakness, yet perhaps a few know their own strength. It is in man as in soils, where sometimes there is a vein of gold which the owner knows not of.—JONATHAN SWIFT.

The winds and waves are always on the side of the ablest navigators.—EDWARD GIBBON.

The king is the man who can.—THOMAS CARLYLE.

Genius does what it must; talent does what it can.—OWEN MEREDITH.

There is something that is much more scarce, something finer far, something rarer than ability. It is the ability to recognize ability.—ELBERT HUBBARD.

The ablest men in all the walks of life are men of faith.—BRUCE BARTON.

A buried talent is never a buried treasure. Talents become treasures only through use.—H. RUPERT.

Ability is the poor man's wealth.—M. WREN.

I believe if a man is willing to surrender his will to God, he can do anything within the circle of God's will for him.—JOHN W. RALEY.


# AFFLICTION

And the Lord said, I have surely seen the affliction of my people which are in Egypt, and have heard their cry by reason of their taskmasters; for I know their sorrows;

# AFFLICTION

And I am come down to deliver them out of the hand of the Egyptians, and to bring them up out of the land unto a good land and a large, unto a land flowing with milk and honey. —Exo. 3:7-8.

Many are the afflictions of the righteous: but the Lord delivereth him out of them all.—Psa. 34:19.

Before I was afflicted I went astray, but now I have kept thy Word.—Psa. 119:67.

Behold, I have refined thee, but not with silver; I have chosen thee in the furnace of affliction.—Isa. 48:10.

God had one son on earth without sin, but never one without suffering.—St. Augustine.

A truly virtuous person is like good metal—the more he is fired, the more he is refined; the more he is opposed, the more he is approved. Wrongs may well try him and touch him, but they cannot imprint on him any false stamp.—Cardinal Richelieu.

Why should I start at the plow of my Lord, that maketh the deep furrows on my soul? I know He is no idle husbandman; He purposeth a harvest.—Samuel Rutherford..

God hath many sharp cutting instruments and rough files for the polishing of his jewels; and those He especially loves and means to make the most resplendent, He hath oftenest His tools upon.—Robert Leighton.

Among my list of blessings infinite stands this the foremost—that my heart has bled.—Edward Young.

God washes the eyes by tears until they can behold the invisible land where tears shall come no more.—Henry Ward Beecher.

There are no crown-wearers in heaven that were not cross-bearers here below.—Charles Haddon Spurgeon.

As sure as God puts his children in the furnace, he will be in the furnace with them.—Charles Haddon Spurgeon.

# AFFLICTION

As in nature and in the arts, so in grace: it is rough treatment that gives souls, as well as stones, their luster. The more the diamond is cut, the brighter it sparkles, and in what seems hard dealings God has no end in view but to perfect our graces. He sends tribulations, but tells us their purpose—that "tribulation worketh patience, and patience experience, and experience hope."
—Thomas Anstey Guthrie.

Man is never helped in his suffering by what he thinks for himself, but only by revelation of a wisdom greater than his own. It is this which lifts him out of his distress.—Carl Jung.

It lightens the stroke to draw near to Him who handles the rod.—Tryon Edwards.

Great trials seem to be necessary preparation for great duties.
—E. Thompson.

When a founder has cast a bell he does not presently fix it in the steeple, but tries it with his hammer, and beats it on every side to see if there be any flaw in it. So Christ doth not presently after he hath converted a man, convey him to heaven; but suffers him first to be beaten upon by many temptations and then exalts him to his crown.—Richard Cecil.

It is the easiest thing in the world to obey God when He commands us to do what we like, and to trust Him when the path is all sunshine. The real victory of faith is to trust God in the dark and through the dark.—Theodore L. Cuyler.

In the time of Jesus, the Mount of Transfiguration was on the way to the cross. In our day the cross is on the way to the Mount of Transfiguration. If you would be on the mountain, you must consent to pass over the road to it.—H. C. Trumbull.

The brightest crowns that are worn in heaven have been tried and smelted and polished and glorified through the furnace of tribulation.—E. H. Chapin.

> Shut in with a trio of angels sweet:
> Patience and Grace all pain to meet,
> With Faith that can suffer and stand and wait,
> And lean on the promises strong and great.

3

# AFFLICTION

Shut in with Christ, O wonderful thought;
Shut in with the peace his suffering brought;
Shut in with the love that wields the rod;
O company blest, shut in with God.

A. AUGUSTA RYDER.

# AGE

Thou shalt rise up before the hoary head, and honor the face of the old man.—LEV. 19:32.

Rebuke not an elder, but entreat him as a father.—I TIM. 5:1.

But speak thou the things which become sound doctrine; that aged men be sober, grave, temperate, sound in faith, in love, in patience; the aged women likewise, that they be in behavior as becometh holiness . . . teachers of good things.—TITUS 1:2.

A graceful and honorable old age is the childhood of immortality.—PINDAR.

And He that doth the ravens feed,
Yea, providently caters for the sparrow,
Be comfort to my age!
—WILLIAM SHAKESPEARE.

He who would pass his declining years with honor and comfort, should, when young, consider that he may one day become old, and remember when he is old that he has once been young.—JOSEPH ADDISON.

The evening of a well spent life brings its lamps with it.
—JOSEPH JOUBERT.

Heaven gives our years of failing strength
Indemnifying fleetness;
And those of youth a seeming length
Proportioned to their sweetness.
—THOMAS CAMPBELL.

I have often thought what a melancholy world this would be without children, and what an inhuman world without the aged.
—SAMUEL TAYLOR COLERIDGE.

4

# AGE

To be happy we must be true to nature and carry our age along with us.—WILLIAM HAZLITT.

Childhood itself is scarcely more lovely than a cheerful, kindly, sunshiny old age.—LYDIA MARIA CHILD.

We do not count a man's years until he has nothing else to count.—RALPH WALDO EMERSON.

How beautiful can time with goodness make an old man look. —DOUGLAS WILLIAM JERROLD.

A comfortable old age is the reward of a well spent youth. —RAY PALMER.

Grow old along with me!
The best is yet to be,
The last of life, for which the first was made.
Our times are in His hand,
Who saith: "A whole I planned,
Youth shows but half; trust God; see all, nor be afraid."
—ROBERT BROWNING.

To have known one good old man—one man who, through the chances and mischances of a long life, has carried his heart in his hand, like a palm branch, waving all discords into peace— helps our faith in God, in ourselves and in each other, more than many sermons.—GEORGE WILLIAM CURTIS.

If wrinkles must be written upon our brow, let them not be written upon our heart. The spirit should not grow old.—JAMES A. GARFIELD.

To be seventy years young is sometimes far more cheerful and hopeful than to be forty years old.—OLIVER WENDELL HOLMES.

As soon as you feel too old to do a thing, do it.—MARGARET DELAND.

If you take all the experience and judgment of men over fifty out of the world, there wouldn't be enough left to run it. —HENRY FORD.

5

# AGE

Growing old is more like a bad habit which a busy man has no time to form.—ANDRÉ MAUROIS.

To resist the frigidity of old age, one must combine the body, the mind and the heart;—and to keep these in parallel vigor one must exercise, study and love.—CHARLES VICTOR DE BONSTETTEN.

Age does not depend upon years, but upon temperament and health. Some men are born old and some never grow old.—TRYON EDWARDS.

Age is a quality of the mind:
If you have left your dreams behind,
    If hope is cold;
If you no longer look ahead,
If your ambition's fires are dead—
    Then you are old.

But if from life you take the best,
And if in life you keep the jest,
    If love you hold;
No matter how the years go by,
No matter how the birthdays fly—
    You are not old.
                    —EDWARD TUCK.

An aged Christian, with the snow of time upon his head, may remind us that those points of earth are whitest which are nearest to heaven.—E. H. CHAPIN.

Let me grow lovely growing old,
    So many fine things do;
Laces, ivory or gold,
    And silks need not be new.
There is healing in old trees,
    Old streets a glamor hold—
Why may not I, as well as these
    Grow lovely growing old?
                —KARLE WILSON BAKER.

Age without cheerfulness is a Lapland without a sun—ANONYMOUS.

6

# ANCESTRY

Honor thy father and thy mother. . . .—Exo. 20:12.

It is indeed a desirable thing to be well descended, but the glory belongs to our ancestors.—PLUTARCH.

It is a shame for a man to desire honor only because of his noble progenitors, and not to deserve it by his own virtue.—SAINT JOHN CHRYSOSTOM.

I am no herald to inquire after men's pedigree; it sufficeth me if I know of their virtues.—SIR PHILIP SIDNEY.

The happiest lot for a man, as far as birth is concerned, is that it should be such as to give him but little occasion to think much about it.—ARCHBISHOP RICHARD WHATELY.

The man of the true quality is not he who labels himself with genealogical tables, and lives on the reputation of his fathers, but he in whose conversation and behavior there are references and characteristics positively unaccountable except on the hypothesis that his descent is pure and illustrious.—THEODORE PARKER.

Consider whether we ought not to be more in the habit of seeking honor from our descendants than from our ancestors; thinking it better to be nobly remembered than nobly born; and striving so to live, that our sons, and our sons' sons, for ages to come, might still lead their children reverently to the doors out of which we had been carried to the grave, saying, "Look, this was his house, this was his chamber."—JOHN RUSKIN.

Thought and deed, not pedigree, are the passports to enduring fame.—MIKHAIL SKOBELEFF.

It would be more honorable to our distinguished ancestors to praise them in words less, but in deeds to imitate them more.—HORACE MANN.

The inheritance of a distinguished and noble name is a proud inheritance to him who lives worthily of it.—C. C. COLTON.

# APPEARANCE

The Lord seeth not as man seeth; for man looketh on the outward appearance, but the Lord looketh on the heart.—I SAM. 16:7.

Judge not according to the appearance, but judge righteous judgment.—JOHN 7:24.

The shortest and surest way to live with honor in the world is to be in reality what we would appear to be.—SOCRATES.

The apparel oft proclaims the man.—WILLIAM SHAKESPEARE.

How little do they see what is, who frame their hasty judgment upon that which seems.—ROBERT SOUTHEY.

The world is governed more by appearances than by realities, so that it is fully as necessary to seem to know something as to know it.—DANIEL WEBSTER.

Do not judge from mere appearance; for the light laughter that bubbles on the lip often mantles over the depths of a sadness, and the serious look may be the sober veil that covers a divine peace and joy.—E. H. CHAPIN.

A good appearance is at a premium everywhere.—ANONYMOUS.

Clothes don't make the man, but good clothes have got many a man a good job.—ANONYMOUS.

# APPRECIATION

There came unto him a woman having an alabaster box of very precious ointment, and poured it on his head.—MATT. 26:7.

Can there any good thing come out of Nazareth?—JOHN 1:46.

Cleave to that which is good.—ROM. 12:9b.

We must never undervalue any person. The workman loves not to have his work despised in his presence. Now God is present everywhere, and every person is His work.—SAINT FRANCIS DE SALES.

8

# APPRECIATION

To love one that is great is almost to be great one's self.—MME. SUZANNE NECKER.

He is incapable of truly a good action who finds not a pleasure in contemplating the good actions of others.—JOHANN KASPAR LAVATER.

You will find poetry nowhere unless you bring some with you. —JOSEPH JOUBERT.

When a nation gives birth to a man who is able to produce a great thought, another is born who is able to understand and admire it.—JOSEPH JOUBERT.

We never know a greater character unless there is in ourselves something congenial to it.—WILLIAM ELLERY CHANNING.

One of the Godlike things of this world is the veneration done to human worth by the hearts of men.—THOMAS CARLYLE.

Next to beauty is the power of appreciating it.—MARGARET FULLER.

Next to excellence is the appreciation of it.—WILLIAM MAKEPEACE THACKERAY.

The more sympathies we gain or awaken for what is beautiful, by so much deeper will be our sympathy for that which is most beautiful, the human soul.—JAMES RUSSELL LOWELL.

If my friends have alabaster boxes laid away full of fragrant perfumes or sympathy and affection that they intend to break over my dead body, I would rather they would bring them in my weary and troubled hours and open them that I might be cheered and refreshed by them when I need them. I would rather have a plain coffin without a flower, a funeral without an eulogy, than a life without the fragrance of love and sympathy.
We should learn to prepare ourselves before for the burial. Post mortem kindness does not cheer the burdened spirit, and flowers upon the coffin cast no fragrance backward o'er the weary way. If, therefore, there is any kind thing I can say or any good thing I can do, let me do it now. Let me not defer it nor neglect it, for I shall not pass this way again.—HENRY W. WATTERSON.

# APPRECIATION

To feel exquisitely is the lot of very many; but to appreciate belongs to the few.—C. AUCHESTER.

If you want to live more you must master the art of appreciating the little, everyday blessings of life. This is not altogether a golden world, but there are countless gleams of gold to be discovered in it if we give our minds to them.—HENRY ALFORD PORTER.

A work of real merit finds favor at last.—ANONYMOUS.

# ART

Blessed be the Lord God of our fathers, which hath put such a thing in the king's heart, to beautify the house of the Lord.—EZRA 7:27.

Art, as far as it has the ability, follows nature, as a pupil imitates his master, so that art must be, as it were, a descendant of God.—DANTE ALIGHIERI.

A true work of art is but a shadow of divine perfection.—MICHELANGELO.

The highest problem in any art is to cause by appearance the illusion of a higher reality.—JOHANN WOLFGANG VON GOETHE.

Since I have known God in a saving manner, painting, poetry and music have had charms unknown to me before. I have either received what I suppose is a taste for them, or religion has refined my mind and made it susceptible of new impressions from the sublime and beautiful. . . . Oh, how religion secures the heightened enjoyment of these pleasures which keep so many from God by their being a source of pride.—HENRY MARTYN.

> In the elder days of Art
> Builders wrought with greatest care
> Each minute and unseen part
> For the gods see everywhere.
> —HENRY WADSWORTH LONGFELLOW.

# ART

Some have eyes
That see not; but in every block of marble
I see a statue—see it as distinctly
As if it stood before me shaped and perfect
In attitude and action. I have only
To hew away the stone wall that imprisons
The lovely apparition, and reveal it
To other eyes as mine already see it.
—HENRY WADSWORTH LONGFELLOW.

The object of art is to crystalize emotion into thought, and then to fix it in form.—FRANCOIS ALEXANDRE DELSARTE.

For, don't you mark? We're made so that we love
First when we see them painted, things we have passed
Perhaps a hundred times nor cared to see;
And so they are better, painted— better to us,
Which is the same thing. Art was given for that.
—ROBERT BROWNING.

Very sacred is the vocation of the artist, who has to do directly with the works of God, and interpret the teaching of creation to mankind. All honor to the man who treats it sacredly; who studies, as in God's presence, the thoughts of God which are expressed to Him; and makes all things according to the pattern which he is ever ready to show to earnest and reverent genius on the mount.—JOHN GEORGE BROWN.

Fine art is that in which the hand, the head and the heart go together.—JOHN RUSKIN.

All that is good in art is the expression of one soul talking to another, and is precious according to the greatness of the soul that utters it.—JOHN RUSKIN.

All great art is the expression of man's delight in God's work, not his own.—JOHN RUSKIN.

The highest art is always the most religious, and the greatest artist is always a devout man. A scoffing Raphael, or an irreverent Michael Angelo is not conceivable.—WILLIAM G. BLAIKIE.

11

# ART

Art is a human activity having for its purpose the transmission to others of the highest and best feelings to which men have risen.—LEO TOLSTOI.

The artist needs but a roof, a crust of bread and his easel, and all the rest God gives him in abundance.—ALBERT PINKHAM RYDER.

A building is not merely a sight. It is an experience. And one who knows architecture only by photographs does not know it at all.—LEWIS MUMFORD.

The mission of art is to present nature; not to imitate her. —W. M. HUNT.

Never judge a work of art by its defects.—WASHINGTON ALLSTON.

# ASPIRATION

Give me this mountain.—JOSH. 14:12.

I press toward the mark for the prize of the high calling of God in Christ Jesus.—PHIL. 3:14.

The true worth of a man is to be measured by the objects he pursues.—MARCUS AURELIUS.

In great attempts it is glorious even to fail.—CASSIUS LONGINUS.

He who would not be frustrate of his hope to write well hereafter in laudable things ought himself to be a true poem.—JOHN MILTON.

What are the aims which are at the same time duties? They are the perfection of ourselves and the happiness of others.—IMMANUEL KANT.

What we truly and earnestly aspire to be, that in some sense we are. The mere aspiration, by changing the frame of the mind, for the moment realizes itself.—ANNA JAMESON.

# ASPIRATION

Out of the lowest depths there is a path to the loftiest heights.
—THOMAS CARLYLE.

> Make my mortal dreams come true,
> with the work I fain would do;
> Clothe with life the weak intent,
> let me be the thing I meant;
> Let me find in Thy employ,
> peace that dearer is than joy.
> —JOHN GREENLEAF WHITTIER.

> Aspire, break bonds, I say;
> Endeavor to be good and better still,
> And best! Success is naught, endeavor's all.
> —ROBERT BROWNING.

> 'Tis not what a man does which exalts him,
> But what a man would do!
> —ROBERT BROWNING.

> I know this earth is not my sphere,
> For I cannot so narrow me but that
> I still exceed it.
> —ROBERT BROWNING.

> Ah, but a man's reach should exceed his grasp
> Else what's a heaven for?
> —ROBERT BROWNING.

There is not a heart but has its moments of longing, yearning for something better, nobler, holier than it knows now.—HENRY WARD BEECHER.

> Greatly begin! though thou have time
> But for a line, be that sublime—
> Not failure, but low aim is crime.
> —JAMES RUSSELL LOWELL.

It seems to me we can never give up longing and wishing while we are thoroughly alive. There are certain things we feel to be beautiful and good, and we must hunger after them.—GEORGE ELIOT.

# ASPIRATION

I find the great thing in this world is not so much where we stand as in what direction we are moving.—OLIVER WENDELL HOLMES.

It is a sad thing to begin life with low conceptions of it. It may not be possible for a young man to measure life; but it is possible to say, I am resolved to put life to its noblest and best use.—T. T. MUNGER.

> Be High, O soul! scorn what is low and base;
>     "Child of a King" they call thee; be a king,
>     And troops of vassals will their tribute bring
> To crown thee heir of glory, child of grace.
>                                     —HENRY BURTON.

There are glimpses of heaven to us in every act, or thought, or word, that raises us above ourselves.—A. F. STANLEY.

>         If I can live
> To make some pale face brighter, and to give
> A second luster to some tear-dimmed eye,
>         Or e'en impart,
> One throb of comfort to an aching heart,
> Or cheer some way-worn soul in passing by—
>         If I can lend
> A strong hand to the fallen, or defend
> The right against a single envious strain,
>         My life, though bare,
> Perhaps, of much that seemeth dear and fair
> To us of earth, will not have been in vain.
>         The purest joy—
> Most near to heaven—far from earth's alloy,
> Is bidding cloud give way to sun and shine;
>         And 'twill be well
> If on that day of days the angels tell
> Of me: "She did her best for one of Thine."
>                                 —MILDRED McNEAL.

The desires and longings of man are vast as eternity, and they point him to it.—TRYON EDWARDS.

# ASPIRATION

May every soul that touches mine,
Be it the slightest contact, get therefrom some good,
Some little grace, one kindly thought,
One aspiration yet unfelt, one bit of courage;
For the darkening sky, one gleam of faith
To brave the thickening ills of life,
One gleam of brighter skies beyond the gathering mist,
To make this life worth while,
And heaven a surer heritage.

—ANONYMOUS.

God has never ceased to be the one true aim of all human aspirations.—ANONYMOUS.

Lord, give me not just words to say,
Tho' I need right words too;
But strength to live in such a way
My life will make my words come true.

—ANONYMOUS.

# ASSURANCE

I know that my Redeemer liveth.—JOB 19:25.

I will both lay me down in peace and sleep: for thou, Lord, only makest me dwell in safety.—PSALM 4:8.

Behold, He that keepeth Israel shall neither slumber nor sleep.—PSALM 121:4.

Lo, I am with you alway, even unto the end of the world. —MATT. 28:20.

If God be for us, who can be against us?—ROM. 8:31.

Who shall separate us from the love of Christ? shall tribulation, or distress, or persecution, or famine, or nakedness, or peril, or sword? . . .
Nay in all these things we are more than conquerors through him that loved us.

# ASSURANCE

For I am persuaded that neither death, nor life, nor angels, nor principalities, nor powers, nor things present, nor things to come, nor height, nor depth, nor any other creature, shall be able to separate us from the love of God, which is in Christ Jesus our Lord.—ROM. 8:35, 37, 38, 39.

I know whom I have believed, and am persuaded that He is able to keep that which I have committed unto Him against that day.—II TIM. 1:12.

They can conquer who believe they can.—JOHN DRYDEN.

> The Lord my pasture shall prepare,
> And feed me with a shepherd's care;
> His presence shall my wants supply,
> And guard me with a watchful eye.
> —JOSEPH ADDISON.

> Though waves and storms go o'er my head,
>     Though strength, and health and friends be gone,
> Though joys be withered all and dead,
>     Though every comfort be withdrawn,
>         On this my steadfast soul relies—
>         Father, thy mercy never dies!
> Fixed on this ground will I remain,
>     Though my heart fail and flesh decay:
> This anchor shall my soul sustain,
>     When earth's foundations melt away:
>         Mercy's full power I then shall prove,
>         Loved with an everlasting love.
> —JOHN WESLEY.

> I know not where His islands lift
>     Their fronded palms in air;
> I only know I cannot drift
>     Beyond His love and care.
> —JOHN GREENLEAF WHITTIER.

> I see my way as birds their trackless way.
> I shall arrive,—what time, what circuit first,
> I ask not; but unless God sends his hail

# ASSURANCE

Or blinding fire-balls, sleet or stifling snow,
In some time, His good time, I shall arrive:
He guides me and the bird.
—ROBERT BROWNING.

Fields are won by those who believe in winning.—THOMAS
WENTWORTH HIGGINSON.

My bark is wafted to the strand
By breath divine,
And on its helm there rests a hand
Other than mine.
One who was known in storms to sail
I have on board;
Above the roaring of the gale
I hear my Lord.
Safe to the land! safe to the land!
The end is this,
And then with him go hand in hand
Far into bliss.
—WASHINGTON GLADDEN.

When I cannot enjoy the faith of assurance, I live by the faith
of adherence.—MATTHEW HENRY.

My hope is built on nothing less
Than Jesus' blood and righteousness.
I dare not trust the sweetest frame
But wholly lean on Jesus' name.
When darkness veils His lovely face,
I rest in His unchanging grace;
In every high and stormy gale
My anchor holds within the veil.
On Christ the Solid Rock I stand;
All other ground is sinking sand.
—EDWARD MOTE.

The assurance that the child of God is secure in his salvation
gives strong encouragement and furnishes a basis for Christian
service in gratitude rather than in fear. Such service must be
more pleasing to our Lord and more effective in moving the

world toward God. Furthermore, since hope causes rejoicing, the hope that is based on God's promises as set forth in the Scriptures must make an exceeding happy Christian and therefore must add greatly to the comfort and power of the Christian life. —J. W. CROWDER.

"The Lord is my shepherd," not was, not maybe, not will be. "The Lord is my shepherd"—is on Sunday, is on Monday, and is through every day of the week; is in January, is in December, and every month of the year; is at home, and is in China; is in peace, and is in war; in abundance and in penury.—J. HUDSON TAYLOR.

Two things will never happen to me—the thing that is too much for me, and the thing that is not best for me.—A. R. BROWN.

> I know not when I go or where
>   From this familiar scene;
> But He is here and He is there,
>   And all the way between;
> And when I leave this life, I know,
>   For that dim vast unknown,
> Though late I stay, or soon I go,
>   I shall not go alone.
>                           —ANONYMOUS.

We are never without a pilot when we know not how to steer. —ANONYMOUS.

## BEAUTY

So shall the King greatly desire thy beauty: for He is thy Lord. —PSALM 45:11.

Let the beauty of the Lord our God be upon us.—PSALM 90:17.

He hath made everything beautiful in His time.—ECC. 3:11.

How beautiful upon the mountains are the feet of him that bringeth good tidings, that publisheth peace; that bringeth good tidings of good, that publisheth salvation; that saith unto Zion, thy God reigneth!—ISA. 52:7.

# BEAUTY

I pray thee, O God, that I may be beautiful within.—SOCRATES.

Whatever is in anyway beautiful hath its source of beauty in itself, and is complete in itself; praise forms no part of it. So is none the worse nor the better for being praised.—MARCUS AURELIUS.

If I give you a rose you won't doubt God anymore.—FLORENS TERTULLIAN.

The hand that hath made you fair, hath made you good. —WILLIAM SHAKESPEARE.

He hath a daily beauty in his life.—WILLIAM SHAKESPEARE.

The best part of beauty is that which no picture can express. —FRANCIS BACON.

The serene, silent beauty of a holy life is the most powerful influence in the world, next to the might of God.—BLAISE PASCAL.

When beauty fires the blood, how love exalts the mind.—JOHN DRYDEN.

Loveliness
Needs not the foreign aid of ornament,
But is when unadorn'd, adorn'd the most.
—JAMES THOMSON.

True beauty dwells in deep retreats
Whose veil is unremoved.
—WILLIAM WORDSWORTH.

A thing of beauty is a joy forever;
Its loveliness increases; it will never
Pass into nothingness. . . .
—JOHN KEATS.

Tho' we travel the world over to find the beautiful, we must have it in us or find it not.—RALPH WALDO EMERSON.

Never lose an opportunity of seeing anything that is beautiful; for beauty is God's handwriting—a wayside sacrament. Welcome it in every fair face, in every fair sky, in every fair flower, and thank God for it as a cup of blessing.—RALPH WALDO EMERSON.

# BEAUTY

Glorious indeed is the world of God around us, but more glorious the world of God within us. There lies the land of song; there lies the poet's native land.—HENRY WADSWORTH LONGFELLOW.

The beautiful are never desolate: someone always loves them —God or man. If man abandons, God takes them.—PHILIP JAMES BAILEY.

Every man feels instinctively that all the beautiful sentiments in the world weigh less than a single lovely action.—JAMES RUSSELL LOWELL.

To cultivate a sense of the beautiful is one of the most effectual ways of cultivating an appreciation of the divine goodness. —C. N. BOVEE.

Beauty seen is partly in him who sees it.—C. N. BOVEE.

Instead of a gem or a flower, cast the gift of a lovely thought into the heart of a friend.—GEORGE MCDONALD.

> Beautiful hands are those that do
> Work that is earnest, brave and true,
> Moment by moment the whole day through.
> —ELLEN ALLERTON.

Beautiful thoughts make a beautiful soul, and a beautiful soul makes a beautiful face.—ANONYMOUS.

# BENEDICTION

The Lord watch between me and thee, while we are absent, one from the other.—GEN. 31:49.

The Lord bless thee, and keep thee:
The Lord make his face to shine upon thee, and be gracious
　　unto thee:
The Lord lift up his countenance upon thee, and give thee peace.
　　　　　　　　　　　　　　　　　　　—NUM. 6:24-26.

# BENEDICTION

The grace of our Lord, Jesus Christ, and the love of God, and the communion of the Holy Ghost, be with you all. Amen.—II COR. 13:14.

Grace be unto you, and peace, from God our Father, and from the Lord Jesus Christ. I thank my God upon every remembrance of you, always in every prayer of mine for you all making request with joy, for your fellowship in the gospel, from the first day until now; being confident of this very thing, that he which hath begun a good work in you will perform it until the day of Jesus Christ.—PHIL. 1:3-6.

Now unto him that is able to keep you from falling, and to present you faultless before the presence of his glory with exceeding joy; to the only wise God, our Saviour, be glory and majesty, dominion and power, both now and ever. Amen.—JUDE 1:24-25.

> Be thou the rainbow to the storm of life,
> The evening beam that smiles the clouds away,
> And tints tomorrow with prophetic ray!
> —GEORGE GORDON, LORD BYRON.

> Calm on the bosom of thy God
> Fair spirit, rest thee now!
> —FELICIA HEMANS.

Let every dawn of the morning be to you as the beginning of life. And let every setting of the sun be to you as its close. Then let every one of these short lives leave its sure record of some kindly thing done for others; some good strength or knowledge gained for yourself.—JOHN RUSKIN.

May hope ever be a bright part of your life's equipment.—GRACE NOLL CROWELL.


# BENEVOLENCE

It is more blessed to give than to receive.—ACTS 20:35.

Every good and perfect gift is from above and cometh down from the Father of lights, with whom is no variableness, neither shadow of turning.—JAS. 1:17.

# BENEVOLENCE

Loving kindness is greater than laws; and the charities of life are more than all ceremonies.—THE TALMUD.

He who wishes to secure the good of others has already secured his own.—CONFUCIUS.

It is another's fault if he be ungrateful, but it is mine if I do not give.—SENECA.

If our virtues did not go forth from us
'Twere all alike as if we had them not.
—WILLIAM SHAKESPEARE.

I will chide no heathen in the world but myself
Against whom I know most faults.
—WILLIAM SHAKESPEARE.

Rich gifts prove poor when givers prove unkind.—WILLIAM SHAKESPEARE.

For his bounty, there was no winter to it;
An autumn it was that grew more by reaping.
—WILLIAM SHAKESPEARE.

The luxury of doing good surpasses every other personal enjoyment.—JOHN GAY.

There cannot be a more glorious object in creation than a human being replete with benevolence, meditating in what manner he may render himself most acceptable to the Creator by doing good to his creatures.—HENRY FIELDING.

Beneficence is a duty; and he who frequently practices it and sees his benevolent intentions realized, at length comes to love him to whom he has done good.—IMMANUEL KANT.

Do not wait for extraordinary circumstances to do good actions; try to use ordinary situations.—JEAN PAUL RICHTER.

The best portion of a good man's life—
His little, nameless, unremembered acts
Of kindness and love.
—WILLIAM WORDSWORTH.

# BENEVOLENCE

Charities that soothe and heal and bless lie scattered at the feet of men like flowers.—WILLIAM WORDSWORTH.

We are rich only through what we give; and poor only through what we refuse to keep.—MME. SOYMONOFF SWETCHINE.

Benevolent feeling ennobles the most trifling actions.—WILLIAM MAKEPEACE THACKERAY.

> God, who registers the cup
>     Of mere cold water for His sake
> To a disciple rendered up,
>     Disdains not His own thirst to slake
>     At the poorest love was ever offered
>                     —ROBERT BROWNING.

In this world it is not what we take up but what we give up that makes us rich.—HENRY WARD BEECHER.

How often it is difficult to be wisely charitable—to do good without multiplying the sources of evil. To give alms is nothing unless you give thought also. It is written, not "blessed is he that feedeth the poor," but "blessed is he that considereth the poor." A little thought and a little kindness are often worth more than a great deal of money.—JOHN RUSKIN.

A noble deed is a step toward God.—JOHN G. HOLLAND.

We enjoy thoroughly only the pleasures that we give.—ALEXANDRE DUMAS.

Give as though you love to give—as the flower pours forth its perfume.—CHARLES HADDON SPURGEON.

Be good; get good, and do good. Do all the good you can, to all the people you can, in all ways you can, as often as ever you can, as long as you can.—CHARLES HADDON SPURGEON.

It is well for us to think that no grace or blessing is truly ours until God has blessed some one else with it through us.—PHILLIPS BROOKS.

23

# BENEVOLENCE

The disposition to give a cup of cold water to a disciple is a far nobler property than the finest intellect.—WILLIAM DEAN HOWELLS.

It is not enough to do good; one must do it in the right way. —JOHN MORLEY.

Give pleasure; lose no chance of giving pleasure.—HENRY DRUMMOND.

He that turneth from the road to rescue another, turneth toward his goal; he shall arrive by the footpath of mercy; God will be his guide.—HENRY VAN DYKE.

To tolerate misery among men without feeling the call to remedy it, is to fall under the reprobation—"Inasmuch as ye did it not—ye did it not unto Me."—BISHOP CHARLES GORE.

I gave a beggar from my little store
Of well earned gold.
He spent the shining ore, and came again and yet again
Still cold and hungry as before.
I gave a thought, and through that thought of mine
He found himself, the man, supreme, divine!
Fed, clothed and crowned with blessings manifold,
And now he begs no more.
—ELLA WHEELER WILCOX.

There are two kinds of charity, remedial and preventive.—The former is often injurious in its tendency; and latter is always praiseworthy and beneficial.—THOMAS CHARLES EDWARDS.

God has so constituted our nature that we cannot be happy unless we are, or think we are, the means of good to others. We can scarcely conceive of greater wretchedness than must be felt by him who knows he is wholly useless in the world.—ERSKINE MASON.

Posthumous charities are the very essence of selfishness when bequeathed by those who, while alive, would part with nothing. —C. C. COLTON.

Charity is injurious unless it helps the recipient to become independent of it.—JOHN D. ROCKEFELLER, JR.

# BENEVOLENCE

Money spent on ourselves may be a millstone about the neck; spent on others it may give us wings like an eagle's.—R. D. HITCH-COCK.

The truly generous is truly wise, and he who loves not others, lives unblest.—ANONYMOUS.

One act of charity will teach us more of the love of God than a thousand sermons.—ANONYMOUS.

# BIBLE

Stand thou still awhile, that I may show thee the word of God. —I SAM. 9:27.

Thy word have I hid in mine heart that I might not sin against thee.—PSALM 119:11.

Thy word is a lamp unto my feet, and a light unto my path. —PSALM 119:105.

Let the word of God dwell in you richly in all wisdom.—COL. 3:16.

All scripture is given by inspiration of God and is profitable. —II TIM. 3:16.

But the word of the Lord endureth forever.—I PET. 1:25.

For I testify unto every man that heareth the words of the prophecy of this book, If any man shall add unto the things, God shall add unto him the plagues that are written in this book:
And if any man shall take away from the words of the book of this prophecy, God shall take away his part out of the book of life, and out of the holy city, and from the things which are written in this book.—REV. 22: 18-19

The highest earthly enjoyments are but a shadow of the joy I find in reading God's word.—LADY JANE GREY.

# BIBLE

It is the wonderful property of the Bible, though the authorship is spread over a long list of centuries, that it never withdraws any truth once advanced, and never adds new without giving fresh force to the old.—ANDREW MELVILLE.

There never was found, in any age of the world, either religion or law, that did so highly exalt the public good as the Bible.—FRANCIS BACON.

The Bible is one of the greatest blessings bestowed by God on the children of men. It has God for its author; salvation for its end, and truth without any mixture of error for its matter. It is all pure, all sincere; nothing too much; nothing wanting.—JOHN LOCKE.

We count the Scripture of God to be the most sublime philosophy.—SIR ISAAC NEWTON.

The majesty of Scripture strikes me with admiration, as the purity of the Gospel has its influence on my heart. Peruse the works of our philosophers: with all their pomp of diction, how mean, how contemptible, are they, compared with the Scripture! Is it possible that a book at once so simple and sublime should be merely the work of man? The Jewish authors were incapable of the diction, and strangers to the morality contained in the Gospel, the marks of whose truths are so striking and inimitable that the inventor would be a more astonishing character than the hero.—JEAN JACQUES ROUSSEAU.

It is a belief in the Bible, the fruit of deep meditation, which has served me as the guide of my moral and literary life. I have found it a capital safely invested, and richly productive of interest.—JOHANN WOLFGANG VON GOETHE.

I speak as a man of the world to men of the world, and I say to you: Search the Scriptures. The Bible is the Book of all others to read at all ages and in all conditions of human life; not to be read once or twice or thrice through, and then laid aside; but to be read in small portions of one or two chapters a day and never to be omitted by some overwhelming necessity.—JOHN QUINCY ADAMS.

# BIBLE

The Gospel is not merely a book—it is a living power—a book surpassing all others. I never omit to read it, and every day with the same pleasure. Nowhere is to be found such a series of beautiful ideas, and admirable moral maxims, which pass before us like the battalions of a celestial army. . . . The soul can never go astray with this book for its guide.—NAPOLEON BONAPARTE, *on St. Helena.*

I know the Bible is inspired because it finds me at a greater depth of my being than any other book.—SAMUEL TAYLOR COLERIDGE.

The incongruity of the Bible with the age of its birth; its freedom from earthly mixtures; its original unborrowed, solitary greatness; the suddenness with which it broke forth amidst the general gloom; these, to me, are strong indications of Divine descent: I cannot reconcile them with human origin.—WILLIAM ELLERY CHANNING.

If religious books are not widely circulated among the masses in this country, and the people do not become religious, I do not know what is to become of us as a nation. And the thought is one to cause solemn reflection on the part of every patriot and Christian. If truth be not diffused, error will be; if God and His Word are not known and received, the devil and his works will gain the ascendancy; if the evangelical volume does not reach every hamlet, the pages of a corrupt and licentious literature will; if the power of the gospel is not felt through the length and breadth of the land, anarchy and misrule, degradation and misery, corruption and darkness, will reign without mitigation or end. —DANIEL WEBSTER.

The Bible is a book of faith and a book of doctrine, and a book of morals, and a book of religion, of special revelation from God.—DANIEL WEBSTER.

If we abide by the principles taught in the Bible, our country will go on prospering and to prosper, but if we and our posterity neglect its instruction and authority, no man can tell how sudden a catastrophe may overwhelm us and bury our glory in profound obscurity.—DANIEL WEBSTER.

# BIBLE

All human discoveries seem to be made only for the purpose of confirming more and more strongly the truths that come from on high and are contained in the sacred writings.—SIR JOHN FREDERIC HERSCHEL.

The book wherein, for thousands of years, the spirit of man has found light and nourishment, and the response to whatever was deepest in his heart.—THOMAS CARLYLE.

A noble book! All men's Book! It is our first, oldest statement of the never-ending problem—man's destiny, and God's ways with him here on earth; and all in such free, flowing outlines—grand in its sincerity; in its simplicity and its epic melody.—THOMAS CARLYLE.

> In teaching me the way to live,
> It taught me how to die.
> —GEORGE POPE MORRIS.

After reading the doctrine of Plato, Socrates, or Aristotle, we feel that the specific difference between their words and Christ's is the difference between an inquiry and a revelation.—JOSEPH PARKER.

If I am asked what is the remedy for the deeper sorrows of the human heart, I must point to something which in the well known hymn is called "The old, old story," told of an old, old Book and taught with the old, old teaching which is the greatest and best guide ever given to mankind.—WILLIAM EWART GLADSTONE.

It is impossible to mentally or socially enslave a Bible reading people. The principles of the Bible are the ground work of human freedom.—HORACE GREELEY.

The answer to the Shastas is India; the answer to Confucianism is China; the answer to the Koran is Turkey; the answer to the Bible is the Christian civilization of Protestant Europe and America.—WENDELL PHILLIPS.

The book to read is not the one which thinks for you, but the one that makes you think. No book in the world equals the Bible for that.—JAMES McCOSH.

# BIBLE

All that I am I owe to Jesus Christ revealed to me in His divine Book.—DAVID LIVINGSTONE.

The grand old Book of God still stands, and, this old earth, the more its leaves are turned over and pondered, the more it will sustain and illustrate the sacred Word.—JAMES DWIGHT DANA.

The Bible, thoroughly known, is a literature in itself—the rarest and richest in all departments of thought and imagination which exists.—JAMES ANTHONY FROUDE.

Make it the first morning business of your life to understand some part of the Bible clearly, and make it your daily business to obey it in all that you do understand.—JOHN RUSKIN.

Hold fast to the Bible as the sheet anchor to your liberties. Write its precepts in your hearts and practice them in your lives. To the influence of this Book we are indebted for all the progress made in true civilization and to this we look as our guide in the future.—ULYSSES S. GRANT.

There are some old things we cannot dispense with, and among these are God's Word and truth, and those religious influences by which He brings the heart of man into subjection to moral law. Do not be ashamed to confess yourselves Christians. To me, one all-important thing is that we should have a freer flow of conversation relating to nature, God and eternity. I have always had a sort of compassion for those who think they are wiser than the Creator. There is a God, and if a God, then a governor. He has not created us and flung us out to be the mere sport of chance and time. But I will not dwell upon the relation of science to religion. I will only add that he is as cruel who attempts to scorn away and overthrow religion as he who knocks the crutches from beneath a lame man. In the observances of the laws of God and in the promise of the Gospel of Jesus Christ there is the best guarantee of peace upon earth and the only hope of eternal life.—BENJAMIN HARRISON.

Nobody ever outgrows Scripture; the book widens and deepens with our years.—CHARLES HADDON SPURGEON.

# BIBLE

I cannot too greatly emphasize the importance and value of Bible study—more important than ever before in these days of uncertainties, when men and women are apt to decide questions from the standpoint of expediency rather than on the eternal principles laid down by God Himself.—John Wanamaker.

The empire of Caesar is gone; the legions of Rome are smouldering in the dust; the avalanches that Napoleon hurled upon Europe have melted away; the prince of the Pharaohs is fallen; the Pyramids they raised to be their tombs are sinking every day in the desert sands; Tyre is a rock for bleaching fisherman's nets; Sidon has scarcely left a wreck behind; but the Word of God still survives. All things that threatened to extinguish it have only aided it; and it proves every day how transient is the noblest monument that men can build, how enduring is the least word that God has spoken. Tradition has dug for it a grave, intolerance has lighted for it many a fagot; many a Judas has betrayed it with a kiss; many a Peter has denied it with an oath! Many a Demas has forsaken it, but the Word of God still endures.—Albert Baird Cummings.

Born in the East and clothed in Oriental form and imagery, the Bible walks the ways of all the world with familiar feet and enters land after land to find its own everywhere. It has learned to speak in hundreds of languages to the heart of man. It comes into the palace to tell the monarch that he is a servant of the Most High, and into the cottage to assure the peasant that he is a son of God. Children listen to its stories with wonder and delight, and wise men ponder them as parables of life. It has a word of peace for the time of peril, a word of comfort for the day of calamity, a word of light for the hour of darkness. Its oracles are repeated in the assembly of the people, and its counsels whispered in the ear of the lonely. The wicked and the proud tremble at its warning, but to the wounded and the penitent it has a mother's voice. The wilderness and the solitary place have been made glad by it, and the fire on the hearth has lit the reading of its well-worn page. It has woven itself into our deepest affections and colored our dearest dreams so that love and friendship, sympathy and devotion, memory and hope, put on the beautiful garments of its treasured speech, breathing of frankincense and myrrh.—HENRY VAN DYKE.

After all, the Bible must be its own argument and defense. The power of it can never be proved unless it is felt. The authority of it can never be supported unless it is manifest. The light of it can never be demonstrated unless it shines.—HENRY VAN DYKE.

When you have read the Bible you will know it is the Word of God because you will have found it the key to your own heart, your own happiness and your own duty.—WOODROW WILSON.

Do you know a book that you are willing to put under your head for a pillow when you lie dying? Very well: that is the book you want to study while you are living. There is but one such book in the world.—SIR JOSEPH COOK.

I have always believed in the inspiration of the Holy Scriptures, whereby they have become the expression to man of the Word and Will of God.—WARREN G. HARDING.

Just as all things upon earth represent and image forth all the realities of another world, so the Bible is one mighty representative of the whole spiritual life of humanity.—HELEN KELLER.

An enlightened knowledge of the Word of God will greatly contribute to the exercise of sanctified common sense. There can be no shifting of authority from the Scripture to the opinion of man. Opinions must be formed from the action taken in accord with the Word given.—J. C. MASSEE.

> Generations follow generations—yet it lives.
> Nations rise and fall—yet it lives.
> Kings, dictators, presidents come and go—yet it lives.
> Torn, condemned, burned,—yet it lives
> Doubted, suspected, criticized—yet it lives.
> Damned by atheists— yet it lives.
> Exaggerated by fanatics— yet it lives.
> Misconstrued and misstated— yet it lives.
> Ranted and raved about— yet it lives.
> Its inspiration denied— yet it lives.

# BIBLE

Yet it lives as — a lamp to our feet,
a light to our paths,
a standard for childhood,
a guide for youth
a comfort for the aged,
food for the hungry,
water for the thirsty,
rest for the weary,
light for the heathen,
salvation for the sinner,
grace for the Christian.
To know it is to love it;
To love it is to accept it;
To accept it means life eternal.
—WILLARD L. JOHNSON.

Its majesty of style combined with simplicity of statement make it a book for the philosopher and yet for the humblest believer.—DEAN C. DUTTON.

If God is a reality and the soul is a reality, and you are an immortal being, what are you doing with your Bible shut!—HERRICK JOHNSON.

A loving trust in the Author of the Bible is the best preparation for a wise and profitable study of the Bible itself.—H. C. TRUMBULL.

The Bible contains more true sublimity, more exquisite beauty, more pure morality, more important history, and finer strains of poetry and eloquence than can be collected from all other books, in whatever age or language they may have been written.—SIR WILLIAM JAMES.

The Scriptures teach us the best way of living, the noblest way of suffering and the most comfortable way of dying.—JOHN FLAVEL.

Science flourishes best in a land where the Bible is honored, for there alone is the guarantee of liberty and its attendant blessings.—DR. HOWARD KELLY.

# BIBLE

**To say** nothing of its holiness or authority, the Bible contains more specimens of genius and taste than any other volume in existence.—WILLIAM LANDOR.

**God's Word** has been challenged all down the ages, but the nearer we come to the time of our Lord's return, the clearer does fulfilled prophecy bear witness to the Bible as the infallible Word of the loving God. God has overruled that two champions should enter the field—archaeology and fulfilled prophecy, and before these two champions a whole army of infidel objections have been overturned. The "unanswerable criticisms" of yesterday have become the "exploded assumptions" of today. Many a "last word in scholarship" would be regarded as "the first word in foolishness" were it to be repeated as sober fact.—J. B. ROWELL.

**When Dr.** Johnson was asked why so many literary men were infidels, he replied, "Because they are ignorant of the Bible. Were they truly acquainted with its contents, they must acknowledge it to be from God." And the truth of the remark is confirmed by the fact that some of the most distinguished advocates of Christianity took up the Bible to oppose, but ended by believing and defending it.—W. R. WILLIAMS.

**Travel** wherever you may in the world, you will find the civilization of the people ranks in keeping with their belief in the teachings of the Bible. No other book has played such an important part in the making of civilization as the Bible. It deals with the terrestrial as well as the celestial affairs of life. It proclaims the past and foretells the future. It is the only book that gives man a place and a purpose in the world. It furnishes to him a code, fixes for him a goal, and bids him "subdue the earth." It is no common book. It bears the Divine imprint on every page.—PAT M. NEFF, *President Baylor University.*

> Just use me— I am the Bible.
> I am God's wonderful library.
> I am always— and above all— The Truth.
> To the weary pilgrim, I am a good strong staff.
> To the one who sits in gloom, I am a glorious light.

# BIBLE

To those who stoop beneath heavy burdens, I am sweet
 rest.
To him who has lost his way, I am a safe guide.
To those who have been hurt by sin, I am healing
 balm.
To the discouraged, I whisper glad messages of hope.
To those who are distressed by the storms of life, I
 am an anchor.
To those who suffer in lonely solitude, I am a cool,
 soft hand resting on a fevered brow.
O, child of man, to best defend me, just use me!
—ANONYMOUS.

Wilmot, the infidel, when dying, laid his trembling hand on
the Bible and solemnly said: "The only objection against this
book is a bad life."—ANONYMOUS.

This Book, this holy Book, on every line
Marked with the seal of high divinity,
On every leaf bedewed with drops of love;
This lamp from off the everlasting throne,
Mercy took down, and in the night of Time
Stood, casting in the dark her gracious bow;
And evermore beseeching men with tears
And earnest sighs, to read, believe and live.
—ANONYMOUS.

Liberty without the Bible is either dead or delirious.—
ANONYMOUS.

Last eve I paused beside a blacksmith's door
 And heard the anvil ring the vesper chime;
Then, looking in, I saw upon the floor
 Old hammers worn with beating years of time.

"How many anvils have you had?" said I,
 "To wear and batter all these hammers, so?"
"Just one," said he; then said, with twinkling eye,
 "The anvil wears the hammers out, you know."

# BIBLE

And so, I thought, the anvil of God's Word
For ages skeptic blows have beat upon:
Yet, though the noise of falling blows was heard
The anvil is unharmed— the hammers, gone!
—ANONYMOUS.

## FAMOUS TEXTS OF FAMOUS MEN:

The text from which John Bunyan preached to multitudes: "All that the Father giveth me shall come to me; and him that cometh to me I will in no wise cast out."—JOHN 6:37.

The text that saved William Cowper from suicide: "Being justified freely by his grace through the redemption that is in Christ Jesus: Whom God hath set forth to be a propitiation through faith in his blood, to declare his righteousness for the remission of sins that are past, through the forbearance of God."—ROM. 3:24,25.

The text that made Martin Luther the hero of the Reformation: "For therein is the righteousness of God revealed from faith to faith: as it is written, The just shall live by faith."—ROM. 1:17.

The text that comforted the troubled soul of John Wesley: "And when Jesus saw that he answered discreetly, he said unto him, Thou art not far from the kingdom of God."—MARK 12:34.

The text that made David Livingstone a missionary: "Go ye, therefore, and teach all nations, baptizing them in the name of the Father, and of the Son, and of the Holy Ghost: Teaching them to observe all things whatsoever I have commanded you; and, lo, I am with you always, even unto the end of the world. Amen." MATT. 28:19-20.

The text to which John Knox anchored his soul: "And this is life eternal, that they might know thee, the only true God, and Jesus Christ, whom thou hast sent.—JOHN 17:3.

The text that led to the conversion of B. H. Carroll: "If any man will do his will, he shall know of the doctrine, whether it be of God, or whether I speak of myself."—JOHN 7:17.

# BROTHERHOOD

Am I my brother's keeper?—GEN. 4:9.

He that loveth his brother abideth in the light.—I JOHN 2:10.

We know that we have passed from death unto life because we love the brethren.—I JOHN 3:14.

If anyone says, I love God, and hateth his brother, he is a liar.—I JOHN 4:20.

The universe is but one great city, full of beloved ones, divine and human by nature, endeared to each other.—EPICTITUS.

We are members of one great body, planted by nature in a mutual love, and fitted for a social life. We must consider that we were born for the good of the whole.—SENECA.

However wretched a fellow mortal may be, he is still a member of our common species.—SENECA.

We must love men ere they will seem worthy of our love.—WILLIAM SHAKESPEARE.

The race of mankind would perish from the earth did they cease to aid each other.—SIR WALTER SCOTT.

Of a truth men are mystically united; a mysterious bond of brotherhood makes all men one.—THOMAS CARLYLE.

> Affliction's sons are brothers in distress;
> A brother to relieve—how exquisite the bliss!
> ROBERT BURNS.

> The Romans were like brothers
> In the brave days of old
> —THOMAS BABINGTON MACAULAY.

It is through fraternity that liberty is saved.—VICTOR HUGO.

> All your strength is in your union;
> All your danger in discord
> Therefore be at peace henceforward
> And as brothers live together.
> —HENRY WADSWORTH LONGFELLOW.

# BROTHERHOOD

The time shall come
When man to man shall be a friend and brother.
—WILLIAM ALLINGHAM.

We must not only affirm the brotherhood of man; we must live it.—BISHOP HENRY CODMAN POTTER.

Jesus throws down the dividing prejudices of nationality, and teaches universal love, without distinction of race, merit or rank. A man's neighbor is every one that needs help.—JAMES GEIKIE.

There is a destiny that makes us brothers;
None goes his way alone:
All that we send into the lives of others
Comes back into our own.
—EDWIN MARKHAM.

The crest and crowning of all good
Life's final star, is Brotherhood!
—EDWIN MARKHAM.

God, what a world if man in street and mart,
Felt that same kinship of the human heart
Which makes them, in the face of fire and flood,
Rise to the true meaning of Brotherhood.
—ELLA WHEELER WILCOX.

You can't hold a man down without staying down with him.
—BOOKER T. WASHINGTON.

Our doctrine of equality and liberty and humanity comes from our belief in the brotherhood of man and the fatherhood of God.—CALVIN COOLIDGE.

Devotion to common principles eliminates differences in race, and identity of ideals is the strongest possible solvent of racial dissimilarities.—MME. CHIANG KAI-SHEK.

The working man must not lose sight of the fact that the principles of brotherhood are applicable to all men, regardless of capital or poverty.—JOHN LEWIS ZACKER.

# BROTHERHOOD

Blow wind of God and set us free
from hate and want of charity;
Strip off the trappings of our pride,
and give us to our brother's side.
—WILLIAM CHARLES BRAITHWAITE.

A jeweled pivot on which our lives must turn is the deep
realization that every person we meet in the course of a day is a
dignified, essential human soul and that we are being guilty of
gross inhumanity when we snub or abuse him.—JOSHUA LOTH
LIEBMAN.

I met a little maid
A rosy burden bearing;
"Is he not heavy?" I said
As past me she was hurrying.
She looked at me with grave, sweet eyes,
This fragile little mother,
And answered in swift surprise:
"Oh, no Sir. He's my brother."
—ANONYMOUS.

# BUILDING

What man is there that hath built a new house and hath not
dedicated it?—DEUT. 20:5.

Let us rise up and build.—NEH. 2:18.

I watched them tearing a building down,—
A gang of men in a busy town—
With a yo-heave-ho and a lusty yell,
They swung a beam and the side wall fell.

I asked the foreman: "Are these men skilled—
The kind you would hire if you wanted to build?"
He laughed and said: "Why no indeed.
Just common labor is all I need;
They can easily wreck in a day or two
What builders have taken years to do."

# BUILDING

I asked myself, as I went my way,
"Which of these roles have I tried today?
Am I a builder who works with care,
    Measuring life by the rule and square,
Shaping my deeds by a well made plan,
    Patiently doing the best I can?
Or am I a wrecker who walks the town,
    Content with the labor of tearing down?"
                    —Gilbert Keith Chesterton.

The price of a bridge is often measured in the lives of its
builders. For he who would build a bridge must be ready to pay
for it with his life.—Pen Lyle Pittard.

Build it well whate'er you do;    ,
Build it straight and strong and true;
Build it thick and high and broad;
Build it for the eye of God.
                    —Anonymous.

Isn't it strange that princes and kings
And clowns that caper in sawdust rings,
And common folks, like you and me
Are builders for Eternity.

To each is given a bag of tools,
A shapeless mass and a book of rules
And each must make, ere life be flown
A stumbling block or a stepping stone.
                    —Anonymous.

We all are blind until we see
    That in the human plan
Nothing is worth the making if
    It does not make the man.

Why build these cities glorious
    If man unbuilded goes?
In vain we build the world, unless
    The builder also grows.
                    —Anonymous.

# CHARACTER

As he thinketh in his heart, so is he.—PROV. 23:7.

The shallows murmur, but the deeps are dumb.—SIR WALTER RALEIGH.

His words are bonds, his oaths are oracles;
His love sincere, his thoughts immaculate;
His tears, pure messages sent from his heart;
His heart, as far from fraud as heaven from earth.
—WILLIAM SHAKESPEARE.

A habitation giddy and unsure
Hath he that buildeth on the vulgar heart.
—WILLIAM SHAKESPEARE.

This above all—to thine own self be true,
And it must follow, as the night the day,
Thou can'st not then be false to any man.
—WILLIAM SHAKESPEARE.

He that has light within his own clear breast
May sit i' the centre, and enjoy bright day:
But he that hides a dark soul and foul thoughts,
Benighted walks under the mid-day sun;
Himself is his own dungeon.
—JOHN MILTON.

All men that are ruined, are ruined on the side of their natural propensities.—EDMUND BURKE.

A noble nature can alone attract the noble, and alone knows how to retain them.—WOLFGANG JOHANN VON GOETHE.

Character is perfectly educated will.—NOVALIS (pseud. of GEORG FRIEDRICH VON HARDENBURG).

The great hope of society is the individual character.—WILLIAM ELLERY CHANNING.

Grandeur of character lies in force of soul—that is, in the force of thought, moral principles, and love; and this may be found in the humblest conditions of life.—WILLIAM ELLERY CHANNING.

# CHARACTER

The measure of a man's real character is what he would do if he knew he would never be found out.—THOMAS BABINGTON MACAULAY.

Characters do not change. Opinions alter, but characters are only developed.—BENJAMIN DISRAELI.

In character, in manner, in style, in all things, the supreme excellence is simplicity.—HENRY WADSWORTH LONGFELLOW.

The noblest contribution any man can make for the benefit of posterity is that of a good character. The richest bequest which any man can leave to the youth of his native land is that of a shining, spotless example.—ROBERT CHARLES WINTHROP.

Fame is vapor; popularity an accident; riches take wings. Only one thing endures, and that is character.—HORACE GREELEY.

Nature has written a letter of credit upon some men's faces which is honored wherever presented. You cannot help trusting such men. Their very presence gives confidence.—WILLIAM MAKEPEACE THACKERAY.

The plain rule is to do nothing in the dark, and to be a party to nothing underhand or mysterious.—CHARLES DICKENS.

Men of character are not only the conscience of society, but in every well governed state they are the best motive power; for it is moral qualities which, in the main, rule the world.—SAMUEL SMILES.

To be worth anything character must be capable of standing firm upon its feet in the world of daily work, temptation and trial; and able to bear the wear and tear of actual life. Cloistered virtues do not count for much.—SAMUEL SMILES.

You cannot dream yourself into a character; you must hammer and forge yourself one.—JAMES ANTHONY FROUDE.

Not education but character is man's greatest need and man's greatest safeguard.—HERBERT SPENCER.

Let us be silent about things which are a discredit to Christian character. Remember, you may yourself deserve rebuke one of

# CHARACTER

these days; and as you would like this to be done gently and privately, so keep your remarks upon others within the happy circle of love.—CHARLES HADDON SPURGEON.

The truth for us to remember at all times, and especially in these times, is the truth that the hope of the nation is not in its forms of government, not in the wisdom and equity of its executive, nor in the justice and purity of its administration, so much as in the elevation and redemption of individual character among its people.—BISHOP HENRY CODMAN POTTER.

Our character is but the stamp on our souls of the free choices of good and evil we have made through life.—ARCHIBALD GEIKIE.

Familiarity does not breed contempt except of contemptible things or in contemptible people.—PHILLIPS BROOKS.

A man who lives right and is right has more power in his silence than many another has by his words. Character is like bells which ring out sweet notes, and which, when touched—accidentally even—resound with sweet music.—PHILLIPS BROOKS.

If I take care of my character, my reputation will take care of itself.—DWIGHT L. MOODY.

> The heart that is soonest awake to the flowers
> Is always the first to be touch'd by the thorns.
> —VISCOUNT JOHN MORLEY.

Unless there is a predominating and overmastering purpose to which all the accessories and incidents of life contribute, the character will be weak, irresolute, uncertain.—FRANCES E. WILLARD.

The most important thing for a young man is to establish credit, a reputation and character.—JOHN D. ROCKEFELLER.

We want the spirit of America to be efficient; we want American character to be efficient; we want American character to display itself in what I may, perhaps, be allowed to call spiritual efficiency—clear, disinterested thinking and fearless action along the right lines of thought.—WOODROW WILSON.

# CHARACTER

Be good at the depths of you, and you will discover that those who surround you will be good even to the same depths. Therein lies a force that has no name; a spiritual rivalry that has no resistance.—MAURICE MAETERLINCK.

There is nothing so fatal to character as half finished tasks. —DAVID LLOYD GEORGE.

I would like to see a state of society in which every man and woman preferred the old Scottish Sunday to the modern French one. We should then find solid and eternal foundations of character and self-command.—RAMSAY MACDONALD.

Character building begins in our infancy and continues until death.—ELEANOR ROOSEVELT.

Man's mettle is tested both in adversity and in success. Twice is this true of the soul of a nation.—MME. CHIANG KAI-SHEK.

Character is the product of daily, hourly actions and words and thoughts; daily forgiveness, unselfishness, kindness, sympathies, charities, sacrifices for the good of others, struggles against temptations, submissiveness under trial. Oh, it is these, like the blending of colors in a picture or the blending of notes of music which constitutes the man.—J. R. MACDUFF.

Only what we have wrought into our characters during life can we take away with us.—KARL WILLIAM HUMBOLT.

We shall never wander from Christ while we make character the end and aim of all our intellectual discipline; and we shall never misconceive character while we hold fast to Christ, and keep him first in our motto and our hearts.—S. F. SCOVEL.

Truthfulness is a corner-stone of character, and if it be not firmly laid in youth, there will ever after be a weak spot in the foundation.—JACKSON DAVIS.

The greatest affair in life is the creation of character, and this can be accomplished as well in a cottage as in a palace.—ALEXANDER MACLAREN.

The character is like white paper: if once blotted, it can hardly ever be made to appear white as before.—J. HAWES.

# CHARACTER

Change is an easy panacea. It takes character to stay in one place and be happy.—ELIZABETH DUNN.

In the great battles of life, no brilliancy of intellect, no perfection of bodily movement will count when weighed in the balance against that assemblage of virtues, active and passive, of moral qualities which we group together under the name of character.—ANONYMOUS.

No nation can rise higher than the character of its people.
—ANONYMOUS.

Snarling at other folks is not the best way of showing the superior quality of your own character.—ANONYMOUS.

Characters are achieved—not received. They grow out of the substance of the man's soul. They are not put on as a beggar might put on a stolen coat. They grow with use.—ANONYMOUS.

When the late J. P. Morgan was asked what he considered the best bank collateral, he replied, "Character."—ANONYMOUS.

There never did and there never will exist anything permanently noble and excellent in character which is a stranger to the exercise of resolute self-denial.—ANONYMOUS.

No quality of Christian character can be essential that is not possible to every man.—ANONYMOUS.

Every man gages us by himself. A rogue believes all men are rascals; and moral weakness excuses mankind on the same ground. But a Parsival sees no rascality in any one, for the pure see all things purely.—ANONYMOUS.

# CHASTENING

He knoweth the way that I take; and when He has tried me, I will come through as gold.—JOB 23:10.

My son, despise not thou the chastening of the Lord, nor faint when thou art rebuked of Him:

44

# CHASTENING

For whom the Lord loveth He chasteneth, and scourgeth every son whom He receiveth.—HEB. 12:5, 6.

Now no chastening for the present seemeth to be joyous, but grievous: nevertheless, afterward it yieldeth the peaceable fruit of righteousness unto them which are exercised thereby.—HEB. 12:11.

If a man suffer as a Christian, let him not be ashamed; but let him glorify God on this behalf.—I PET. 4:16.

As many as I love I rebuke and chasten.—REV. 3:19.

Better a little chiding than a great deal of heartbreak.—WILLIAM SHAKESPEARE.

We ought as much to pray for a blessing upon our daily rod as upon our daily bread.—JOHN OWEN.

> The gods in bounty work up storms about us,
> That give mankind occasion to exert
> Their hidden strength, and throw out into practice
> Virtues which shun the day.
> > —JOSEPH ADDISON.

Who hath not known ill fortune, never knew himself, or his own virtue.—DAVID MALLET.

> Aromatic plants bestow
> No spicy fragrance while they grow;
> But crushed or trodden to the ground
> Diffuse their sweetness all around.
> > —OLIVER GOLDSMITH.

He that wrestles with us strengthens our nerves and sharpens our skill.—EDMUND BURKE.

> Behind a frowning Providence
> He hides a shining face.
> > —WILLIAM COWPER.

It requires greater virtue to sustain good fortune than bad.—FRANCOIS DE LA ROCHEFOUCAULD.

# CHASTENING

Tho losses and crosses be lessons right severe,
There's wit there ye'll get there
You'll find no other where.
—ROBERT BURNS.

It is only great periods of calamity that reveal to us our great men, as comets are revealed by total eclipses of the sun.—JEAN PAUL RICHTER.

Those who have suffered much are like those who know many languages: they have learned to understand all and be understood by all.—MME. SOYMONOFF SWETCHINE.

Those who inflict must suffer, for they see
The work of their own hearts, and this must be
Our chastisement or recompense.
—PERCY BYSSHE SHELLEY.

When Christ brings His cross, He brings His presence; and where He is none is desolate, and there is no room for despair. As He knows His own, so He knows how to comfort them, using sometimes the very grief itself, and straining it to a sweetness of peace unattainable by those ignorant of sorrow.—ELIZABETH BARRETT BROWNING.

Then welcome each rebuff
That turns earth's smoothness rough,
Each sting that bids not sit nor stand, but go!
Be our joys three-parts pain!
Strive, and hold cheap the strain;
Learn, nor account the pang; dare, never grudge the throe!
—ROBERT BROWNING.

Put pain from out the world, what
room were left
For thanks to God, for love to man?
—ROBERT BROWNING.

I have lived, seen God's hand through a lifetime, and all was for best.—ROBERT BROWNING.

But all God's angels come to us disguised;
Sorrow and sickness, poverty and death,

# CHASTENING

One after other lift their frowning masks
And we behold the seraph's face beneath
All radiant with the glory and the calm
Of having looked upon the front of God.
—JAMES RUSSELL LOWELL.

'Tis sorrow builds the shining ladder up
Whose golden rounds are our calamities
Whereon our firm feet planting, nearer God
The spirit climbs, and hath its eyes unsealed.
— JAMES RUSSELL LOWELL.

Organs mean melody and beauty, but organ factories mean din and dirt. The instrument is built for music, and music it will ultimately bring, but the building where it is fashioned resounds with more racket than rhythm. The world is such a factory. In it the Master Builder is creating and completing new men in Christ Jesus; making them mete for the inheritance of the saints in light. The process, however, by which the author and finisher of faith prosecutes and perfects his plans will often be misunderstood. Many of the operations will appear hard and rough, and will hit as heavily and hurt as badly as the raps of the hammer in the shop.—T. A. VASSAR.

Waiting is a common instrument of providential discipline for those to whom exceptional work has been assigned.—JAMES STALKER.

Many a man has thought himself broken up, when he has merely been made ready for the sowing.—HUGH REDWOOD.

Heaven is not always angry when He strikes
But most chastises those whom most He likes
—JOHN POMFRET.

Let us accept affliction as the boon we are most unworthy of. We may rest assured that the day is coming when the bitterest dealing shall be to us the sweetest.—LADY POWERSCOURT.

God would not test the quality of wood with fire. The fierceness of the fire points to gold.—LESLIE D. WEATHERHEAD.

# CHASTENING

As there can be no height where there is no depth, so there can be no triumph where there is no trouble, no smile where there are no tears, no roses where there are no thorns, no hope where there is no fear, and no crown where there is no cross.—ANONYMOUS.

Turn your face to the sun and the shadows will fall behind you.—ANONYMOUS.

The soul would have no rainbow had the eyes no tears.—ANONYMOUS.

The greatest affliction of life is never to be afflicted.—ANONYMOUS.

Not they who have studied much but they who have suffered much are the deliverers of mankind.—ANONYMOUS.

God's grace is sufficient for us anywhere his providence places us.—ANONYMOUS.

There is frequently more love in a frown than there could be in a smile.—ANONYMOUS.


# CHEERFULNESS

A merry heart doeth good like a medicine.—PROV. 17:22.

Son, be of good cheer; thy sins be forgiven thee.—MATT. 9:2.

When the disciples saw him walking on the sea, they were troubled . . . and they cried out in fear, but straightaway Jesus spake unto them saying, Be of good cheer; it is I; be not afraid. —MATT. 14:26, 27.

In the world ye shall have tribulation, but be of good cheer, I have overcome the world.—JOHN 16:33.

Burdens become light when cheerfully borne.—OVID.

A face that cannot smile is never good.—MARTIAL.

# CHEERFULNESS

The highest wisdom is continual cheerfulness; such a state, like the region above the moon, is always clear and serene.—MICHEL DE MONTAIGNE.

> Frame your mind to mirth and merriment
> Which bar a thousand harms and lengthen life.
> —WILLIAM SHAKESPEARE.

If good people would but make their goodness agreeable, and smile instead of frowning in their virtue, how many would they win to the good cause.—ARCHBISHOP JAMES USHER.

I wonder many times that ever a child of God should have a sad heart, considering what the Lord is preparing for him.—SAMUEL RUTHERFORD.

> The mind is its own place, and in itself
> Can make a heaven of hell, and hell of heaven.
> —JOHN MILTON.

An ounce of cheerfulness is worth a pound of sadness to serve God with.—THOMAS FULLER.

Gloom and sadness are poison to us, the origin of hysteria, which is a disease of the imagination caused by vexation and supported by fear.—MME. MARIE DE SÉVIGNÉ.

'Tis impious in a good man to be sad.—EDWARD YOUNG.

A propensity to hope and joy is real riches; one to fear and sorrow is real poverty.—DAVID HUME.

A careless song, with a little nonsense now and then, does not misbecome the monarch.—HORACE WALPOLE.

If the soul be happily disposed everything becomes capable of affording entertainment, and distress will almost want a name.—OLIVER GOLDSMITH.

Cheerfulness is the atmosphere under which all things thrive.—JEAN PAUL RICHTER.

A laugh is worth a hundred groans in any market.—CHARLES LAMB.

# CHEERFULNESS

The gloomy soul aggravates misfortune while a cheerful smile often dispels those mists that portend a storm.—LYDIA HUNTLEY SIGOURNEY.

You find yourself refreshed by the presence of cheerful people. Why not make earnest effort to confer that pleasure on others. Half the battle is gained if you never allow yourself to say anything gloomy.—LYDIA MARIE CHILD.

The sun shines after every storm; there is a solution for every problem, and the soul's highest duty is to be of good cheer.—RALPH WALDO EMERSON.

To be amiable is more certainly a duty, but it is not to be exercised at the expense of any virtue. . . . He who seeks to do the amiable always can at times be successful only by the sacrifice of his manhood.—WILLIAM G. SIMMS.

Laughter is day, and sobriety is night; a smile is the twilight that hovers gently between both, more bewitching than either.—HENRY WARD BEECHER.

God is glorified, not by our groans but by our thanksgiving; and all good thought and good action claim a natural alliance with good cheer.—EDWIN P. WHIPPLE.

Let us be of good cheer, remembering that the misfortune hardest to bear is the one which never comes.—JAMES RUSSELL LOWELL.

Cheerfulness is as natural to the heart of a man in strong health, as color to his cheek; and wherever there is habitual gloom, there must be either bad air, unwholesome food, improperly severe labor, or erring habits of life.—JOHN RUSKIN.

> If the world seems cold to you,
>   Kindle fires to warm it;
> Let their comfort hide from view
>   Winters that deform it.
> Hearts as frozen as your own
>   To that radiance gather;
> You will soon forget to moan:
>   "Oh, the cheerless weather."
>             —LUCY LARCOM.

# CHEERFULNESS

When a bit of kindness hits ye
  After passing of a cloud;
When a bit of laughter gits ye,
  And yer spine is feeling proud,
Don't forget to up and fling it
  As at a soul that's feeling blue
For the moment that you sling it,
  It's a boomerang to you.
                    —CAPTAIN JACK.


A happy man or woman is a radiant focus of good will, and their entrance into a room is as though another candle had been lighted.—ROBERT LOUIS STEVENSON.


It's easy enough to be pleasant,
  When life flows by like a song,
    But the man worth while
    Is the one who can smile,
  When everything goes dead wrong.
For the test of the heart is trouble
And it always comes with the years,
    And the smile that is worth
    The praises of earth
  Is the smile that shines through tears.
                    —ELLA WHEELER WILCOX


Cheerfulness is a friend to grace; it puts the heart in tune to praise God and so honors religion by proclaiming to the world that we serve a good master.—SIR WILLIAM WATSON.


Laughter is one of the best things that God has given us, and with hearty laughter neither malice nor indecency can exist.—STANLEY BALDWIN.


It is quite deplorable to see how many rational creatures mistake suffering for sanctity, and think a sad face and a gloomy habit of mind propitious offerings to that Deity whose works are all light and lustre and harmony and loveliness.—LADY SYDNEY MORGAN.

# CHEERFULNESS

It was only a glad "Good morning,"
As she passed along the way,
But it spread the morning's glory
Over the livelong day.
—CHARLOTTE PERRY.

A sunny disposition is the very soul of success.—CHARLES MATTHEWS.

Amiable people, are often subject to imposition in their contact with the world, yet radiate so much of sunshine that they are reflected in all appreciative hearts.—MADAM DEULZY.

We ask God to forgive us for our evil thoughts and evil temper, but rarely, if ever, ask Him to forgive us for our sadness. —R. W. DALE.

Cheerfulness is health; its opposite, melancholy, is disease.— THOMAS C. HALLIBURTON.

You have not fulfilled every duty unless you have fulfilled that of being cheerful and pleasant.—CHARLES BURTON.

Something of a person's character may be discovered by observing how he smiles. Some people never smile—they only grin. —C. N. BOVEE.

If I can put one thought of rosy sunset into the life of any man or woman, I shall feel that I have worked with God.— GEORGE McDONALD.

Get into the habit of looking for the silver lining of the cloud, and when you have found it, continue to look at it, rather than at the leaden gray in the middle. It will help you over many hard places.—A. A. WILLITTS.

Oh, what a little thing can turn
A heavy heart from sighs to song!
A smile can make the world less stern,
A word can cause the soul to burn
With glow of heaven, all night long.
—ANONYMOUS.

# CHEERFULNESS

A happy, joyful spirit spreads joy everywhere; a fretful spirit is a trouble to ourselves and to all around us.—ANONYMOUS.

If pansies, with their dark impassioned faces
   Had but been given the power of human speech,
What is the lesson that from lowly places
   Each tender, fragrant voice to me would teach?
Perchance in tones like tinkling dewdrops sighing,
   What their lives tell, their voice lips would say:
"Forget life's trials that are 'round thee lying
   And be the brightest in the darkest day."
                    —ANONYMOUS.

A cheerful temper joined with innocence will make beauty attractive, knowledge delightful, and will good natured. It will lighten sickness, poverty, and affliction; convert ignorance into an amiable simplicity; and render deformity itself agreeable.—ANONYMOUS.

There is no argument equal to a happy smile.—ANONYMOUS.

It's everybody's business
   In this old world of ours,
To pull up all the weeds we find
   To make room for the flowers,
So that every little garden
   No matter where it lies
Will look like one God made
   And called it Paradise.
                  —ANONYMOUS.

A smile creates happiness in the home, fosters good will in business, and is the countersign of friends.—ANONYMOUS.

# CHILDREN

Children are an heritage of the Lord.—PSALM 127:3.

Children's children are the crown of old men, and the glory of children are their fathers.—PROV. 17:6.

# CHILDREN

Suffer the little children to come unto me and forbid them not, for of such is the kingdom of heaven.—LUKE 18:16.

Children generally hate to be idle. All the care then should be that their busy humor should be constantly employed in something that is of use to them.—JOHN LOCKE.

If I were asked what single qualification was necessary for one who has the care of children, I should say patience—patience with their tempers, with their understandings, with their progress. It is not brilliant parts or great acquirements which are necessary for teachers, but patience to go over first principles again and again; steadily to add a little every day; never to be irritated by wilful or accidental hinderances.—FRANCOIS DE LA FENELON.

Never fear spoiling children by making them too happy. Happiness is the atmosphere in which all good affections grow.—THOMAS BRAY.

Children have more need of models than of critics.—JOSEPH JOUBERT.

The clew to our destiny, wander where we will, lies at the foot of the cradle.—JEAN PAUL RICHTER.

The future destiny of a child is always the work of the mother. —NAPOLEON BONAPARTE.

Where children are, there is the golden age.—NOVALIS.

Call not that man wretched, who, whatever ills he suffers, has a child to love.—ROBERT SOUTHEY.

The little child is the only true democrat.—HARRIET BEECHER STOWE.

I love these little people; and it is not a slight thing when they, who are so fresh from God, love us.—CHARLES DICKENS.

You cannot teach a child to take care of himself unless you will let him try to take care of himself. He will make mistakes; and out of these mistakes will come his wisdom.—HENRY WARD BEECHER.

# CHILDREN

In the man whose childhood has known caresses and kindness, there is always a fiber of memory that can be touched to gentle issues.—GEORGE ELIOT.

With children we must mix gentleness with firmness. They must not always have their own way, but they must not always be thwarted. If we never have headaches through rebuking them, we shall have plenty of heartaches when they grow up. Be obeyed at all costs; for if you yield up your authority once, you will hardly get it again.—CHARLES HADDON SPURGEON.

Every child born into the world is a new thought of God, an ever-fresh and radiant possibility.—KATE DOUGLAS WIGGIN.

The child's grief throbs against its little heart as heavily as the man's sorrow; and the one finds as much delight in his kite or drum as the other in striking the springs of enterprise or soaring on the wings of fame.—E. H. CHAPIN.

The first duty to children is to make them happy. If you have not made them so, you have wronged them. No other good they may get can make up for that.—SIR THOMAS BUXTON.

The interests of childhood and youth are the interests of mankind.—E. S. JANES.

When a child can be brought to tears, not from fear of punishment, but from repentance for his offence, he needs no chastisement. When the tears begin to flow from grief at one's own conduct, be sure there is an angel nestling in the bosom.—ALEXANDER MANN.

Children need love, especially when they do not deserve it.—HAROLD S. HULBERT.

I believe in little children as the most precious gift of Heaven to earth. I believe that they have immortal souls created in the image of God, coming forth from him and to return to him. I believe that in every child are infinite possibilities for good or evil and that the kind of influence with which he is surrounded in early childhood largely determines whether or not the budding life shall bloom in fragrance and beauty with the fruits thereof, a noble Godlike character.—RANDALL J. CONDON.

# CHILDREN

Words of praise, indeed, are almost as necessary to warm a child into congenial life as acts of kindness and affection. Judicious praise is to children what sun is to flowers.—C. N. BOVEE.

The only way you will ever solve the problem of reaching the masses is by getting hold of the children.—W. A. ("BILLY") SUNDAY.

If telling were teaching my child would be perfect.—WILLIAM L. HOWSE.

# CHRIST

And I will put enmity between thee and the woman, and between thy seed and her seed; it shall bruise thy head, and thou shalt bruise his heel.—GEN. 3:15.

A virgin shall conceive and bear a son, and shall call his name Immanuel.—ISA. 7:14.

For unto us a child is born, unto us a son is given: and the government shall be upon his shoulder: and his name shall be called Wonderful, Counsellor, The Mighty God, The everlasting Father, The Prince of Peace.—ISA. 9:6.

He is despised and rejected of men; a man of sorrows, and acquainted with grief. . . .
Surely he hath borne our griefs, and carried our sorrows: . . .
But he was wounded for our transgressions, he was bruised for our iniquities: the chastisement of our peace was upon him; and with his stripes we are healed.
All we like sheep have gone astray; we have turned every one to his own way; and the Lord hath laid on him the iniquity of us all.
He was oppressed, and he was afflicted, yet he opened not his mouth: he is brought as a lamb to the slaughter, and as a sheep before her shearers is dumb, so he openeth not his mouth. . . .
And he made his grave with the wicked, and with the rich in his death; because he had done no violence, neither was any deceit in his mouth.—ISA. 53:3, 4, 5, 6, 7, 9.

# CHRIST

But thou, Bethlehem Ephratah, though thou be little among the thousands of Judah, yet out of thee shall he come forth unto me that is to be ruler in Israel; whose goings forth have been from of old, from everlasting.—MIC. 5:2.

So they weighed for my price thirty pieces of silver.—ZECH. 11:12.

And one shall say unto him, What are these wounds in thine hands? Then he shall answer, Those with which I was wounded in the house of my friends.—ZECH. 13:6.

Thou art the Christ, the son of the living God.— (SIMON PETER) MATT. 16:16.

This is my beloved Son in whom I am well pleased; hear ye him.— (THE HEAVENLY FATHER) MATT. 17:5b.

What think ye of Christ?— (JESUS) MATT. 22:42.

I have sinned in that I have betrayed the innocent blood.— (JUDAS ISCARIOT) MATT. 27:4.

What shall I do then with Jesus which is called the Christ?— (PILATE) MATT. 27:22.

Truly, this man was the Son of God.— (ROMAN CENTURION) MARK 15:39.

Unto you is born this day in the City of David a Savior, which is Christ, the Lord.— (ANGELS) LUKE 2:11.

For mine eyes have seen thy salvation,
Which thou hast prepared before the face of all people;
A light to lighten the Gentiles, and the glory of thy people Israel.— (SIMEON) LUKE 2:30,31,32.

The Holy One of God.— (UNCLEAN SPIRIT) LUKE 4:34.

And the Word was made flesh, and dwelt among us (and we beheld his glory, the glory as of the only begotten of the Father) full of grace and truth.— (JOHN, THE BELOVED APOSTLE) JOHN 1:14.

# CHRIST

Behold the Lamb of God which taketh away the sin of the world.— (JOHN THE BAPTIST) JOHN 1:29.

Whatsoever He saith unto you, do it.— (MARY, HIS MOTHER) JOHN 2:5.

We know that thou art a teacher come from God.— (NICO-DEMUS) JOHN 3:2.

I find no fault in him.— (PILATE) JOHN 19:6.

My Lord, and my God.— (THOMAS) JOHN 20:28.

I count all things but loss for the excellency of the knowledge of Christ Jesus my Lord: for whom I have suffered the loss of all things.— (PAUL) PHIL. 3:8.

Jesus Christ, the same yesterday and today and forever.— (WRITER TO THE HEBREWS) HEB. 13:8.

With whom is no variableness, neither shadow of turning.— (JAMES) JAS. 1:17b.

Jesus Christ, perfect in deity, perfect in humanity, truly God and truly man, of reasonable soul and body; of the same substance with the Father as to His divinity, of the same substance with us as to his humanity; in all things like to us, except sin.— COUNCIL OF CHALCEDON A.D. 451.

Too late I loved Thee, O Beauty of Ancient Days! Yet ever new! And, lo! Thou were with me and I abroad searching for Thee! Thou were with me, but I was not with Thee.—SAINT AUGUSTINE.

In his life Christ is an example showing us how to live; in his death, he is a sacrifice satisfying for our sins; in his resurrection, a conqueror; in his ascension, a king; in his intercession, a high priest.—MARTIN LUTHER.

> In those holy fields
> Over whose acres walk'd those blessed feet
> Which fourteen hundred years ago were nail'd
> For our advantage on the bitter cross.
> —WILLIAM SHAKESPEARE.

# CHRIST

Tho' Christ a thousand times in Bethlehem be born,
If He's not born in thee, thy soul is still forlorn.
—JOHANNES SCHEFFLER.

Love divine, all love excelling,
   Joy of heav'n to earth come down!
Fix in us Thy humble dwelling;
   All Thy faithful mercies crown.
Jesus, Thou art all compassion,
   Pure unbounded love Thou art;
Visit us with Thy salvation;
   Enter every trusting heart.
—JOHN WESLEY.

The nature of Christ's existence is mysterious, I admit; but this mystery meets the wants of man. Reject it and the world is an inexplicable riddle; believe it, and the history of our race is satisfactorily explained.—NAPOLEON BONAPARTE.

I know men, and I tell you that Jesus is not a man. The religion of Christ is a mystery which subsists by its own force, and proceeds from a mind which is not a human mind. We find it in a marked individuality, which originated a train of words and actions unknown before. Jesus is not a philosopher, for His proofs are miracles, and from the first His disciples adored Him. Alexander, Caesar, Charlemagne and myself founded empires; but on what foundation did we rest the creatures of our genius? Upon force. But Jesus Christ founded an empire upon love; and at this hour millions of men would die for Him.

I die before my time, and my body will be given back to the earth to become food for worms. Such is the fate of him who has been called the "great Napoleon." What an abyss between my deep misery and the eternal kingdom of Christ, which is proclaimed, loved, adored and is still existing over the whole earth.

(Turning to General Bertrand, the emperor added:) If you do not perceive that Jesus Christ is God, I did wrong in appointing you general.—NAPOLEON BONAPARTE.

A sense o'er all my soul imprest
That I am weak but not unblest,

# CHRIST

Since in me, round me, everywhere
Eternal Strength and Wisdom are.
—SAMUEL TAYLOR COLERIDGE.

I believe Plato and Socrates. I believe in Jesus Christ.—SAMUEL
TAYLOR COLERIDGE.

If I might comprehend Jesus Christ, I could not believe on
him. He would be no greater than myself. Such is my consciousness of sin and inability that I must have a super-human Saviour.—DANIEL WEBSTER.

The name of Jesus is not so much written as plowed into the
history of the world.—RALPH WALDO EMERSON.

So . . . comes a human voice,
Saying: "O heart I made, a heart beats here;
Face my hands fashioned see it in myself;
Thou hast no strength, nor mayst conceive of mine;
But love I gave thee, with myself to love,
And thou must love me who have died for thee."
—ROBERT BROWNING.

It fortifies my soul to know
That tho' I perish, Truth is so;
That howso'er I stray and range,
What'er I do, Thou dost not change.
I steadier step when I recall
That if I slip, Thou dost not fall.
—ARTHUR HUGH CLOUGH.

All history is incomprehensible without Christ.—ERNEST
RENAN.

Jesus Christ, the condescension of divinity and the exaltation
of humanity.—PHILLIPS BROOKS.

You may go the world over, and you will not find a single
believer who is disappointed in the once crucified, now glorified,
soon coming King. This is the best answer to the skepticism of the
day. Take any class of society, the highest or the lowest, and
there is not an instance of one who trusted in the Lord and was
confounded.—WILLIAM PENNEFEATHER.

# CHRIST

He was allowed less than three years in which to do his work; little more than a year in his public ministry, and a year in retirement training his pathetic remnant. He was cut off in his young manhood, a little past the age of thirty. Socrates had taught for forty years, Plato for fifty, Aristotle had lived long and filled libraries with his learning, Budda and Confucius had fulfilled their three-score years and ten. He was among a crushed people, under an oppressive legalism, zealously opposed and hated by Scribes and Pharisees, betrayed by Jews and crucified by Gentiles. He left no book, no tract, or written page behind him. He bequeathed no system, no philosophy, no theology, no legislation. He raised no armies, held no office, sought no influence, turned his back forever on might, magic and cheap miracle . . . , (yet he was) to transform the bigoted Jew and universalize his religion; to show the philosophizing Greek the highest truth; to win the proud Roman to plant the cross on his standard instead of the eagle; to stretch out his hand to the great continents and transform them—to Asia, to savage Europe, to darkest Africa and to America.—SHERWOOD EDDY.

Christ has outlasted the empire that crucified Him nineteen centuries ago. He will outlast the dictators who defy him now.—RALPH W. SOCKMAN.

The human body of Christ is the veil which hides the glory of God, on which we could not look with unveiled face.—G. RODGERS.

The most destructive criticism has not been able to dethrone Christ as the incarnation of perfect holiness. The waves of a tossing and restless sea of unbelief break at His feet, and He stands still the supreme model, the inspiration of great souls, the rest of the weary, the fragrance of all Christendom, the one divine flower in the garden of God.—HERRICK JOHNSON.

This is part of the glory of Christ as compared with the chiefest of His servants that He alone stands at the absolute center of humanity, the one completely harmonious man, unfolding all which was in humanity, equally and fully on all sides, the only one in whom the real and ideal met and were absolutely

one. He is the absolute and perfect truth, the highest that humanity can reach; at once its perfect image and supreme Lord.—
NICHOLAS FRENCH.

All the world's joy comes from the grave of our risen Lord.—
J. R. MILLER.

There is one, and only one, term to tell of the relation of our blessed Saviour to humanity as far as his birth is concerned, and that is the Virgin Birth. . . . The denial of the Virgin Birth bespeaks neither a sound mind nor a Bible-based theology. If there be no virgin birth there could be no blood atonement and much of the Bible is a deliberate falsehood. To deny the Virgin Birth is to deny the necessity of faith, the necessity of Christ dying and shedding his blood, the necessity of the truth of the Bible. Indeed, it denies that man has ever sinned and been away from God, for there is no other plan that God has ever had save the plan of man's redemption through his Son, Jesus Christ.—FRED H. PORTER.

"Jesus." It was the voice of one of the robbers. "Jesus," he says painfully, "remember me, when thou comest into thy kingdom!"
Read that, oh, men and bow your heads. You who have let yourself picture him as weak, as a man of sorrows, uninspiring, glad to die. There have been leaders who could call forth enthusiasm when their fortunes ran high. But he, when his enemies had done their worst, so bore himself that a crucified felon looked into his dying eyes and saluted him as king.—BRUCE BARTON.

He was himself forsaken that none of his children might ever need to utter his cry of loneliness.—J. H. VINCIENT.

Our great High Priest is in glory, exalted above all created angels. But he is the same Jesus we knew in the days of his flesh. He is the same Jesus in heaven as he was on earth, as he was before the world began. The face shining above the brightness of the sun is the face that drew sinners to his feet. The hand that holds the seven stars is the hand that was laid in blessing upon little children. The breast girt about with a golden girdle is the breast upon which the beloved disciple laid his head at the last supper. He is the same Jesus.—A. D. FOREMAN, JR.

He did not come to conquer by force of armies and physical weapons but by love planted in the hearts of individuals.—W. W. MELTON.

> All hail the power of Jesus' name!
>     Let angels prostrate fall;
> Bring forth the royal diadem,
>     And crown Him Lord of all.
>
> Let every kindred, every tribe
>     On this terrestrial ball,
> To Him all majesty ascribe
>     And crown Him Lord of all.
>                 —EDWARD PERRONET.

The greatest triumph of Jesus over death was his coming to life again.—WILLIAM THOMAS ROUSE.

It seems strange to us that Jesus should suffer for He had no sin Himself, but His sufferings were occasioned by His relationship to others.—WILLIAM THOMAS ROUSE.

The ascension has not taken Him away from you, but it has carried you up to Him.—ANONYMOUS.

The death of Christ did not terminate but did germinate his work.—ANONYMOUS.

# CHRISTIANITY

Go ye into all the world and preach the gospel to every creature.—MARK 16:15.

I am not ashamed of the gospel of Jesus Christ, for it is the power of God unto salvation to every one that believeth; to the Jew first, and also to the Greek.—ROM. 1:16.

# CHRISTIANITY

Woe is unto me if I preach not the gospel.—I Cor. 9:16.

If any man preach any other gospel unto you than that ye have received, let him be accursed.—Gal. 1:9.

I saw another angel fly in the midst of heaven, having the everlasting gospel to preach unto them that dwell on the earth, and to every nation, and kindred, and tongue, and people.—Rev. 14:6.

See how these Christians love one another.—Florens Tertullian.

The Scriptures give four names to Christians—saints, for their holiness; believers, for their faith; brethren, for their love; disciples for their knowledge.—Andrew Fuller.

A Christian is the highest style of man.—Alexander Pope.

There is no leveler like Christianity, but it levels by lifting all who receive it to the lofty table-land of a true character and of undying hope both for this world and the next.—Jonathan Edwards.

He who shall introduce into public affairs the principles of primitive Christianity will revolutionize the world.—Benjamin Franklin.

I have known what the enjoyments and advantages of this life are, and what are the more refined pleasures which learning and intellectual power can bestow; and with all the experience that more than three-score years can give, I now, on the eve of my departure declare to you, that health is a great blessing; competence obtained by honorable industry is a great blessing; and a great blessing it is to have kind, faithful and loving friends and relatives; but that the greatest blessing, as it is the most ennobling of all privileges, is to be indeed a Christian.—Samuel Taylor Coleridge.

Christianity is not a theory or speculation, but a life; not a philosophy of life, but a living presence.—Samuel Taylor Coleridge..

# CHRISTIANITY

The only truly happy men I have ever known were Christians.—JOHN RANDOLPH.

My faith is, that though a great man, may, by a rare possibility, be an infidel, an intellect of the highest order must build on Christianity. A very clever architect may choose to show his power by building with insufficient materials, but the supreme architect must require the very best; because the perfection of the forms cannot be shown but in the perfection of the matter.—THOMAS DeQUINCY.

The distinction between Christianity and all other systems of religion consists largely in this, that in these other, men are found seeking after God, while Christianity is God seeking after men.—THOMAS ARNOLD.

It does not require great learning to be a Christian and to be convinced of the truth of the Bible. It requires only an honest heart and a willingness to obey God.—ERNEST WILLIAM BARNES.

The real security of Christianity is to be found in its benevolent morality; in its exquisite adaptation to the human heart; in the facility with which its scheme accommodates itself to the capacity of every human intellect; in the consolation which it bears to the house of mourning; in the light with which it brightens the great mystery of the grave.—THOMAS BABINGTON MACAULAY.

Talk about the question of the day! There is but one question and that is the Gospel. It can and will correct everything needing correction. All men at the head of great movements are Christian men. During the many years I was in the cabinet I was brought into association with sixty master minds, and all but five of them were Christians. My only hope for the world is in bringing the human mind into contact with Divine revelation.—WILLIAM EWART GLADSTONE.

Christianity is a battle—not a dream.—WENDELL PHILLIPS.

Christianity is the basis of republican government, its bond of cohesion, and its life-giving law. More than the Magna Charta itself the Gospels are the roots of English liberty. That Magna

# CHRISTIANITY

Charta, and the Petition of Rights, with our completing Declaration, was possible only because the Gospels had been before them.—Richard Salter Storrs.

The true social reformer is the faithful preacher of Christianity; and the only organization truly potent for the perfection of society is the Christian Church. I know of nothing which as a thought is more superficial, or which as a feeling is better entitled to be called hatred of men, than that which disregards the influence of the gospel in its efforts for social good, or attempts to break its hold on mankind by destroying their faith in its living power.—Julius H. Seelye.

The only significance of life consists in helping to establish the kingdom of God; and this can be done only by means of the acknowledgment and profession of the truth by each one of us.—Leo Tolstoi.

Is it not perfectly erroneous to speak of the failure of missions when they started out with a hundred and twenty despised Galileans, and when there are now at least 120,000,000 Protestants, and they have in their power almost all the wealth and almost all of the resources of the world?—Frederic W. Farrar.

A child of God should be a visible beatitude for joy and happiness, and a living doxology for gratitude and adoration.—Charles Haddon Spurgeon.

Christianity is the companion of liberty in all its conflicts—the cradle of its infancy, and the divine source of its claims.—Alexis De Tocqueville.

Christ built no church, wrote no book, left no money, and erected no monuments; yet show me ten square miles in the whole earth without Christianity, where the life of man and purity of women are respected and I will give up Christianity.—Henry Drummond.

A Christian life is not an imitation but a reproduction of the life of Christ.—Henry Van Dyke.

# CHRISTIANITY

The true Christian is the true citizen, lofty of purpose, resolute in endeavor, ready for a hero's deeds, but never looking down on his task because it is cast in the day of small things; scornful of baseness, awake to his own duties as well as to his rights, following the higher law with reverence, and in this world doing all that in his power lies, so that when death comes he may feel that mankind is in some degree better because he lived.—THEODORE ROOSEVELT.

Christianity has not failed. It is simply that nations have failed to try it. There would be no war in a God-directed world.—REAR ADMIRAL RICHARD E. BYRD.

Christians are supposed not merely to endure change, nor even to profit by it, but to cause it.—HARRY EMERSON FOSDICK.

Christianity will gain by every step that is taken in the knowledge of man.—JOHANN CASPAR SPURZHEIM.

Christianity is intensely practical. She has no trait more striking than her common sense.—CHARLES BUXTON.

The religion of Christ has made a Republic like ours possible; and the more we have of this religion the better the Republic.—H. M. FIELD.

It is not the business of Christianity to provide an organization for the world but to infuse the spirit of Christ into the organizations of the world.—DR. FRED FISHER.

The missionaries are right. The world needs more than policy. It needs healing and practical instruction and an appreciation of other people which is the essence of applied Christianity.—BROOKS HAYS.

The glory of Christianity is not in an empty tomb, but in a living Lord. It is not the tomb that is vital, but the One who occupied it and is alive forevermore. He is regnant and active in our world now. He indwells the heart of the believer. He is the inspiration of the world's greatest men and its holiest women. He goes before the obedient in the line of duty, even as He has promised. He walks with us in our sorrows until our hearts burn within us. He wants to be the comrade of the way. He would have us recognize Him. He comes to the eager and expectant heart. He invites such; He seeks all.—H. D. HOUSEHOLDER.

If the skeptical world is to be convinced of the beauty and reality of our Christian faith, then the harmonized individual believers also must be synchronized into a symphonic unity of love and purpose.—F. E. ROBINSON.

A Christian in this world is but gold in the ore; at death, the pure gold is smelted out and separated and the dross cast away and consumed.—JOHN FLAVEL.

Every other faith in India is decaying. Christianity alone is beginning to run its course.—SIR HERBERT EDWARDS.

It is a truth that stands out with startling distinctness on the pages of the New Testament that God has no sons who are not servants.—H. D. WARD.

There are many in the Church as well as out of it who need to learn that Christianity is neither a creed nor a ceremonial, but a life vitally connected with a loving Christ.—JOSIAH STRONG.

Heathenism was the seeking religion; Judaism, the hoping religion; Christianity is the reality of what heathenism sought and Judaism hoped for.—CHRISTOPH ERNST LUTHARDT.

The sword conquered once, but the Spirit conquers forever.—SHOLEM ASCH.

The measure of a Christian is not in the height of his grasp but in the depth of his love.—CLARENCE JORDAN.

Unless there's a rebirth of religious spirit in the hearts of its leaders and in people throughout the world, our civilization, despite tremendous victories, will slide into an abyss—perhaps for centuries.—DOROTHY THOMPSON.

The blood of Jesus is sacrifice; the sweat of Jesus is toil and labor; the tears of Jesus are love and compassion. They abide as eternal symbols of God's way of meeting the needs of a lost world.—W. A. CRISWELL.

# CHRISTIANITY

The world's great heart is aching,
   Aching fiercely in the night;
And God alone can heal it,
   And God alone give light;
And the ones to take that message—
   To bear the living Word
Are you and I, my Brothers,
   And the missions who have heard.
                              —ANONYMOUS.

However much the priestlings of science may prate against the
Bible, the high priests of science are in accord with Christianity.—
ANONYMOUS.

God calls His children:
         Saints because of their character,
         Disciples because they are learners,
         Believers because of their Faith,
         Brethren because of their relationship,
         Christians because of their birth in Christ.
                              —ANONYMOUS.


# CHRISTMAS

And she brought forth her first born son, and wrapped him
in swaddling clothes, and laid him in a manger; because there
was no room for them in the inn.

And there were in the same country shepherds abiding in the
field, keeping watch over their flock by night.

And, lo, the angel of the Lord came upon them, and the glory
of the Lord shone round about them; and they were sore afraid.

And the angel said unto them, Fear not: for, behold, I bring
you good tidings of great joy, which shall be to all people.

For unto you is born this day in the city of David a Saviour,
which is Christ the Lord. . . .

And suddenly there was with the angel a multitude of the
heavenly host praising God, and saying,

Glory to God in the highest, and on earth peace, good will
toward men.—LUKE 2:7-14.

# CHRISTMAS

Some say that ever 'gainst that season comes
Wherein our Saviour's birth is celebrated,
The bird of dawning singeth all night long;
And then, they say, no spirit dares stir abroad;
The nights are wholesome; then no planets strike,
No fairy takes, nor witch hath power to charm,
So hallow'd and so gracious is the time.
—WILLIAM SHAKESPEARE.

It is good to be children sometimes, and never better than at Christmas, when its mighty Founder was a child Himself.— CHARLES DICKENS.

The feet of the humblest may walk in the fields
Where the feet of the holiest have trod.
This, this is the marvel to mortals revealed,
When the silvery trumpets of Christmas have pealed,
That mankind are the children of God.
—PHILLIPS BROOKS.

Men always have hope of a better world when they see the miracle of Christmas. All the selfishness, bitterness and hatreds pause, and for a day surrender to the sweet charm of a little Divine Prince who cast His spell over the earth two thousand years ago,—a spell that has not been broken, a charm that has increased to become a spiritual dominion stretching around the earth and from pole to pole.

Thus we can always know that men could live with goodwill and understanding for each other, because one day in each year the little Divine Prince of Peace still compels them to do it.— CHARLES WELLS.

## THE CONQUERING CHRIST
The night the angels sang that song
Of "peace on earth, good will toward men,"
A veil fell from a woman's face,
And in its place,
A crown was given her to wear
Adorned with gems surpassing fair.

70

# CHRISTMAS

The same night, in its little crib,
A baby smiled in peaceful sleep
    Because a King had come to earth;
    And since His birth,
The babe is monarch in the home
Wherever His dear Name is known.

Lo! as they sang that wondrous song
Of "peace on earth, good will toward men,"
    A slave leaped forth into the light,
    And since that night
Captivity has been set free
Where rings that heav'n born melody.

O Eyes that cannot see the light!
O Hearts cast down with fear!
    The clouds of war will be swept by,
    And in the sky
The carrolling hosts will sing again
Of "peace on earth, good will toward men."
            —VIRGINIA ELY.

The joy of brightening other lives, bearing others' burdens, easing others' loads and supplanting empty hearts and lives with generous gifts becomes for us the magic of Christmas.—W. C. JONES.

Light of the world so clear and bright,
Enter our homes this Christmas night;
Re-light our souls so tenderly,
That we may grow to be like Thee.
            —ANONYMOUS.

# CHURCH

How amiable are thy tabernacles, O Lord of Hosts!
Blessed are they that dwell in thy house: . . .
I had rather be a doorkeeper in the house of my God,
    Than to dwell in the tents of wickedness.
            —PSALM 84:1, 4, 10.

# CHURCH

I will build my Church and the gates of hell shall not prevail against it.—MATT. 16:18.

Feed the Church of God which He hath purchased with His own blood.—ACTS 20:28.

Other foundations can no man lay than that is laid, which is Jesus Christ.—I COR. 3:11.

Christ . . . loved the church and gave himself for it; that he might sanctify and cleanse it with the washing of water by the word, that He might present it to Himself a glorious church, not having spot or wrinkle, or any such thing; but that it should be holy and without blemish.—EPH. 5: 25b-26-27.

> I love thy Church, O God!
>     Her walls before Thee stand,
> Dear as the apple of Thine eye,
>     And graven on Thy hand.
>         —TIMOTHY DWIGHT.

Persecution has not crushed the church; power has not beaten it back; time has not abated its forces; and what is most wonderful of all, the abuses of its friends have not shaken its stability.—HORACE BUSHNELL.

The Church may have seen its duty imperfectly, for it is made up of fallible things, but when all is said it has been the one power through nearly two thousand years which has stood for peace, for brotherhood and for the cause of the poor and distressed.—ERNEST F. SCOTT.

> God bless the church on the avenue that hears the city's
>     cry;
> The church that sows the Seed of the Word where the
>     masses of men go by;
> The church that makes, midst the city's roar, a place
>     for an Altar of Prayer,
> With a heart for the rich and a heart for the poor, and
>     rejoices in their burdens to share.
>
> The church that's true to the call of Christ who wept
>     o'er the city's need,

# CHURCH

And who sent His disciples to labor for Him where the
    forces of evil breed,
The church that gives and the church that lives, as seen
    by the Master's eye—
God bless the church on the avenue that answers the
    city's cry.—RALPH WALKER.

Any evangelism which does not magnify the church is
doomed to ultimate failure.—OLIVER DeWITT CUMMINGS.

While serving as director of the Federal Bureau of Investiga-
tion during the past twenty years, I have been profoundly impressed with the fact that the "Church-Going people" are the
most substantial group of citizens in the nation. Church attendance and crime appear to be like the ingredients of oil and
water—they do not mix.—J. EDGAR HOOVER.

The Church stands as a symbol of the finest aims and aspirations of the human heart. It has outlived persecution from without and open disloyalty from within. It has withstood bitter and
unrelenting attacks of atheists and cynics of every age. It has
outlived changing times of peace and war, prosperity and de-
pression, and many a fad and fancy.
A Church to me is the symbol of faith in the life eternal; it
typifies decency, kindliness and fair dealing; it offers comfort to
the sorrowing. With the golden rule it would make neighbors
of us all.—EDGAR A. GUEST.

God has no perfect individuals or institutions through which
to work. He has to get along with us just the way we are the best
He can.—W. O. CARVER.

The Church that compromises Truth today will compromise
Morals tomorrow.—H. D. BRUCE.

If we build on and around our churches, the greater respect
the world will have for them. Too many ministries that should be
reserved for our churches are farmed out to other organizations.
—W. R. WHITE.

The nations in pagan lands have gods of wood and stone, but
the unchurched in America are coming to have no gods at all.—
ANONYMOUS.

# CHURCH

Before I was born my church gave to my parents ideals of life and love that made my home a place of strength and beauty.

My church enriched my childhood with the romance and religion and the lessons of life that have woven into the texture of my soul. Sometimes I seem to have forgotten and then, when else I might surrender to foolish and futile ideals of life, the truths my church taught became radiant, insistent, and inescapable.

In the stress and storm of adolescence my church heard the surge of my soul and she guided my footsteps by lifting my eyes toward the stars.

When first my heart knew the strange awakenings of love my church taught me to chasten and spiritualize my affections; she sanctified my marriage and blessed my home.

When my heart was seamed with sorrow, and I thought the sun could never shine again, my church drew me to the friend of all the weary and whispered to me the hope of another morning, eternal and tearless.

When my steps have slipped and I have known the bitterness of sin, my church has believed in me and wooingly she has called me back to live within the heights of myself.

Now have come the children dearer to me than life itself and my Church is helping me to train them for all joyous and clean and Christly living.

My Church calls me to her heart. She asks my service and my loyalty. She has a right to ask it! I will help her to do for others what she has done for me. In this place in which I live, I will help her keep aflame and aloft the torch of a living faith.—ANONYMOUS.

Deep in my heart I know that the Church is of God; that in spite of human frailties she has brought blessings untold to all generations including my own; that she has made my community and my country a better place in which to live, to work, to establish a home, and to rear my children; that I would not want to live or die in a land where no church spire points its people heavenward.

I also know that the Church continues to live triumphantly, even when man and nations reject her by indifference or open hostility.

# CHURCH

In this knowledge I gladly give myself to my Church and offer her my loyal support by intelligent membership, regular attendance, generous giving, ardent prayer and devoted service.—ANONYMOUS.

My church is the place where the word of God is preached, the power of God is felt, the spirit of God is manifested, the love of God is revealed, and the unity of God is perceived.

It is the home of my soul, the altar of my devotion, the hearth of my faith and the center of my affections.

I have united with it in solemn covenant, pledging myself to attend its services, to pray for its members, to give to its support.

It claims the first place in my heart, the highest place in my mind, the principal place in my activities; and its unity, peace and progress concern my life in this world and in that which is to come.

I owe to it my zeal, my benevolence and my prayers. When I neglect its services, I injure its good name, I lessen its power, I discourage its members, and I chill my own soul.

I have solemnly promised, in the sight of God and men, to advance the interests of the church by my faithful attendance, by never neglecting its ordinances, by meeting with my fellow members, by watching over their welfare, by joining with them in prayer and praise and service; and that promise I this day renew before God, my Father, Christ, my Redeemer, and the Holy Spirit, my Comforter.—ANONYMOUS.

I go to church because I have an appointment with God. He set the date 1900 years ago when he said "Assemble yourselves." With this command ringing in my ear I do not need church bells. True, I meet Him in other places, but Sunday is by special appointment. I cannot afford to miss it.

I need my church because it helps me to have a sane perspective. It renews my faith in humanity. It keeps alive those spiritual perspectives which all too often are almost smothered under the week's load of grinding events.

By going to Church I am made to realize that I have the complete responsibility for making or breaking some individual. Wonderful books have been written on proper feeding, but no book ever written matches the Bible's teaching on how to become a decent human being. The Church takes for its text the Bible, and for its model, Jesus Christ.

I go to Church because there is beauty in any church service, and food for thought in every sermon. The hurry of existence leaves little enough of time for the finest thing, for contemplation, from which creative ideas arise. Going to Church is one of the vital necessities.—ANONYMOUS.


# CITIZENSHIP

Render therefore unto Caesar the things which be Caesar's; and unto God, the things which be God's.—LUKE 20:25.

When citizens become so truly Christian that they unhesitatingly vote, legislate and administer the government in the spirit of Christ the nations will become the kingdom of our Lord and His Christ. Every step taken in that direction is a step toward a Christian nation in fact as well as in name.—R. E. DUDLEY.

> Without a sign his sword the brave man draws;
> He asks no omen but his country's laws.
> —ALEXANDER POPE.

When a man assumes a public trust he should consider himself public property.—THOMAS JEFFERSON.

Whatever makes men good Christians makes them good citizens.—DANIEL WEBSTER.

I repeat—that all power is a trust; that we are accountable for its exercise; that from the people and for the people all springs, and all must exist.—BENJAMIN DISRAELI.

> No sound is breathed so potent to coerce
> And to conciliate, as their names who dare
> For that sweet motherland which gave them birth
> Nobly to do, nobly to die.
> —ALFRED TENNYSON.

# CITIZENSHIP

Manpower is the real wealth of a nation and it takes generations to grow it.—MME. CHIANG KAI-SHEK.

Before man made us citizens, great Nature made us men.—FREDERICK J. POWELL.

America began with hungry men who thought a free fast was better than a fettered feast. Yet something more than hunger came out of that preference. And the glory of America is not in its tall towers nor vast acres. The glory of America is the American citizen, free, sovereign and unafraid. We do well to thank God for that.—LYNN LANDRUM.

> God give us men. The time demands
> Strong minds, great hearts,
>    True faith and willing hands;
>   Men whom the lust of office does not kill;
>    Men whom the spoils of office cannot buy;
>   Men who possess opinions and a will;
>    Men who have honor; men who will not lie;
>   Men who can stand before a demagogue
>    And damn his treacherous flatteries without
>     winking;
>   Tall men, sun-crowned, who live above the fog
>    In public duty and in private thinking.
>              —JOHN G. HOLLAND.

There are things that are worth dying for—the honor of one's country, the sanctity of the home, the virtue of women and the safety of little children. But, if they are worth dying for, they are worth living for.—GEORGE W. TRUETT.

# COMPANIONSHIP

Entreat me not to leave thee, or to return from following after thee: for whither thou goest, I will go; and where thou lodgest, I will lodge: thy people shall be my people, and thy God my God:

# COMPANIONSHIP

Where thou diest, will I die, and there will I be buried: The Lord do so to me, and more also, if ought but death part thee and me.—RUTH 1:16-17.

Blessed is the man that walketh not in the counsel of the ungodly, nor standeth in the way of sinners, nor sitteth in the seat of the scornful.—PSALM 1:1.

It is meet that noble minds keep ever with their likes;
For who so firm that cannot be seduced.
                              —WILLIAM SHAKESPEARE.

Good company and good discourse are the very sinews of virtue.—IZAAK WALTON.

It is best to be with those in time we hope to be with in eternity.—THOMAS FULLER.

No man can be provident of his time who is not prudent in the choice of his company.—JEREMY TAYLOR.

If you wish to be held in esteem, you must associate only with those who are estimable.—JEAN DE LABRUYERE.

The most agreeable of companions is a simple, frank man, without any high pretensions to an oppressive greatness; one who loves life, and understands the use of it; obliging alike at all hours; above all, of golden temper, and steadfast as an anchor. For such an one we gladly exchange the greatest genius, the most brilliant wit, the most profound thinker.—GOTTHOLD E. LESSING.

You may depend upon it that he is a good man whose intimate friends are all good, and whose enemies are decidedly bad.—JOHANN KASPAR LAVATER.

Tell me with whom thou art found and I will tell thee who thou art.—JOHANN WOLFGANG VON GOETHE.

Be cautious with whom you associate, and never give your company or your confidence to those of whose good principles you are not sure.—SAMUEL TAYLOR COLERIDGE.

No man can possibly improve in any company for which he has not respect enough to be under some degree of restraint.—LORD CHESTERFIELD.

# COMPANIONSHIP

Evil companions are the devil's agents whom he sends abroad into the world to debauch virtue, and to advance his kingdom; and by these ambassadors he effects more than he could in his own person.—ANTHONY HORNECK.

No company is far preferable to bad, because we are more apt to catch the vices of others than their virtues, as disease is more contagious than health.—C. C. COLTON.

Draw your chair beside me here,
As in other times, my dear;
Do not talk or even smile—
Sit in silence for a while,
Sweet contentment over all,
As the shadows on us fall.
'Tis the best of all my life,
After each day's toil and strife,
In the time of night and dew—
Thus to sit alone with you.
—HENRIETTA HERON.

# COMPENSATION

They that seek the Lord shall not want any good thing.—PSALM 34:10.

Behold, the Lord God will come with a strong hand, and his arm shall rule for Him: behold, his reward is with him, and his work before him.—ISA. 40:10.

He that receiveth a prophet in the name of a prophet shall receive a prophet's reward; and he that receiveth a righteous man in the name of a righteous man shall receive a righteous man's reward.

Whosoever shall give to drink unto one of these little ones a cup of cold water only in the name of a disciple . . . shall in no wise lose his reward.—MATT. 10:41, 42 .

Every man shall receive his own reward according to his own labor.—I COR. 3:8.

# COMPENSATION

When the chief Shepherd shall appear, ye shall receive a crown of glory that fadeth not away.—I Pet. 5:4.

Behold, I come quickly, and my reward is with me.—Rev. 22:12.

He who wishes to secure the good of others has already secured his own.—Confucius.

He is well paid that is well satisfied.—William Shakespeare.

As there is no worldly gain without some loss, so there is no worldly loss without some gain. If thou hast lost thy wealth, thou hast lost some trouble with it. If thou art degraded from thy honor, thou art likewise freed from the stroke of envy. If sickness hath blurred thy beauty, it hath delivered thee from pride. Set the allowance against the loss and thou shalt find no loss great. He loses little or nothing who reserves himself.— Francis Quarles.

During a long life I have proved that not one kind word ever spoken, not one kind deed ever done, but sooner or later returns to bless the giver and becomes a chain, binding men with golden bands to the throne of God.—Anthony Ashley Cooper, Earl of Shaftesbury.

It is rare when injustice or slights, patiently borne, do not leave the heart at the close of the day filled with marvelous joy and peace.
Even if the sacrifices which are made to duty and virtue are painful to make, they are well repaid by the sweet recollection which they leave at the door of the heart.—Jean Jacques Rousseau.

> From toil he wins his spirits light,
> From busy day and peaceful night!
> Rich, from the very want of wealth,
> In heaven's best treasures, peace and health.
> —Thomas Gray.

> And when the stream
> Which overflowed the soul was passed away,

# COMPENSATION

A consciousness remained that it had left
Deposited upon the silent shore
Of memory images and precious thoughts
That shall not die, and cannot be destroyed.
        —WILLIAM WORDSWORTH.

I am drawing near to the close of my career; I am fast shuffling
off the stage. I have been perhaps the most voluminous author of
the day; and it is a comfort to me to think I have tried to un-
settle no man's faith, to corrupt no man's principle, and that I
have written nothing which on my deathbed I should wish
blotted.—SIR WALTER SCOTT.

Blessings ever wait on virtuous deeds;
And tho' a late, a sure reward succeeds.
        —WILLIAM CONGREVE.

The thorns which I have reap'd are of the tree
I planted; they have torn me, and I bleed.
I should have known what fruit would spring
      from such seed.
        —GEORGE GORDON, LORD BYRON.

The reward of a thing well done is to have done it.—RALPH
WALDO EMERSON.

He sendeth sun; he sendeth shower,
Alike they're needful to the flower;
And joys and tears alike are sent
To give the soul fit nourishment.
As comes to me or cloud or sun
Father, thy will, not mine be done.
        —SARAH FLOWER ADAMS.

Thine is the seed time:
God alone beholds the end of what is sown;
Beyond our vision weak and dim
The harvest time is hid with Him.
        —JOHN GREENLEAF WHITTIER.

# COMPENSATION

The tissues of the life to be
    We weave with colors, all our own;
And in the field of Destiny
    We reap as we have sown.
        —HENRY WADSWORTH LONGFELLOW.

Every quivering tongue of flame,
Seems to murmur some great name,
        Seems to say to me "Aspire!"
No endeavor is in vain;
        Its reward is in doing
        And the rapture of pursuing
Is the prize of vanquished gain.
        —HENRY WADSWORTH LONGFELLOW.

If what shone afar so grand
Turn to nothing in thy hand,
On again—the virtue lies
In the struggle, not the prize.
        —RICHARD MONCKTON MILNES, Lord Houghton.

The most solid comfort one can fall back upon is the thought that the business of one's life is to help in some small way to reduce the sum of ignorance, degradation and misery on the face of this beautiful earth.—GEORGE ELIOT.

The reward of one duty is the power to fulfill another.—GEORGE ELIOT.

Not in rewards, but in the strength to strive the blessing lies.—JOHN TOWNSEND TROWBRIDGE (PAUL CREYTON).

There is nothing the body suffers that the soul may not profit by.—GEORGE MEREDITH.

No man who continues to add something to the material, intellectual and moral well-being of the place in which he lives, is left long without proper reward.—BOOKER T. WASHINGTON.

Out of suffering have emerged the strongest souls; the most massive characters are seared with scars.—E. H. CHAPIN.

# COMPENSATION

He who sows, even with tears, the precious seed of faith, hope and love, shall doubtless come again with joy bringing his sheaves with him, because it is the very nature of that seed to yield a joyful harvest.—RICHARD CECIL.

Every duty brings its peculiar delight, every denial its appropriate compensation, every thought its recompense, every cross its crown; pay goes with performance as effect with cause; the wicked wrong their own souls; generosity greatens; virtue exalts; charity transfigures; and holiness is the essence of angelhood. God does not require us to live on credit; he pays us what we earn as we earn it, good or evil, according to our choice.—CHARLES MILMAY.

Send me to the hearts without a home,
To the lives without a love,
To the crowd without a compass,
To the ranks without a refuge.
Send me to the children whom none have blessed,
To the famished whom none have fed,
To the sick whom none have visited,
To the demoniacs whom none have claimed,
To the fallen whom none have lifted,
To the lepers whom none have touched,
To the bereaved whom none have comforted,
Then shall I have the birthright of the first born;
Then shall I have the blessing of the mighty God of Jacob.
—GEORGE MATHESON.

No father ever served with Jesus Christ but that reaped a rich reward in the lives of his children.—PERRY WEBB.

I ask no heaven till earth be Thine,
No glory crown while work of mine remaineth here.
When earth shall shine among the stars,
Her sins wiped out, her captives free,
Her voice a music unto Thee,
For crown, for more work give these to me.
Lord, here am I.
—ANONYMOUS.

# COMPENSATION

He that does good to another does also good to himself; not only in the consequence, but in the very act of doing it; for the conscience of well doing is an ample reward.—ANONYMOUS.

One little hour of watching with the Master,
   Eternal years to walk with Him in white;
One little hour to bravely meet disaster,
   Eternal years to reign with Him in light;
One little hour for weary toils and trials,
   Eternal years for calm and peaceful rest;
One little hour for patient self-denials;
   Eternal years for life, where life is blest.
                              —ANONYMOUS.

The day will come when Jesus will give the rewards, and He makes no mistakes, although some people may wonder how you came to merit such a reward as they had never heard of you before.—ANONYMOUS.

The world awards its prizes to men of firmness and self-reliance.—ANONYMOUS.


# CONCENTRATION

This one thing I do.—PHIL. 3:13.

Did you ever hear of a man who had striven all his life faithfully and singly toward a thing and in no measure obtained it?—HENRY DAVID THOREAU.

The man who seeks but one thing in life
      And but one,
May hope to achieve it before life is done;
But he who seeks all things, wherever he goes
Only reaps from the hopes which around him he sows
      A harvest of barren regrets.
                              —GEORGE MEREDITH.

Concentration is my motto—first honesty, then industry, then concentration.—ANDREW CARNEGIE.

84

# CONCENTRATION

It is better to say, "This one thing I do," than to say "These forty things I dabble in."—WASHINGTON GLADDEN.

Success in life is a matter not so much of talent or opportunity as of concentration and perseverance.—C. W. WENDTE.

All men who have accomplished great things have been men of one unwavering aim; men who have sacrificed all conflicting desires and ambitions to that one aim.—ORISON SWETT MARDEN.

He who would do some great thing in this short life must apply himself to the work with such a concentration of forces, as, to idle spectators, who live only to amuse themselves, looks like insanity.—ANONYMOUS.

# CONDUCT

Keep thy tongue from evil, and thy lips from speaking guile.—PSALM 34:13.

As ye would that men should do to you, do ye also to them likewise.—LUKE 6:31.

Evil communications corrupt good manners.—I COR. 15:33.

Whatsoever ye do in word or in deed, do all to the glory of God.—COL. 3:17.

There is a proper dignity and proportion to be observed in the performance of every act of life.—MARCUS AURELIUS.

A well bred man is always sociable and complacent.—MICHEL DE MONTAIGNE.

Nothing costs less than the compliments of civility.—MIGUEL DE CERVANTES.

Approved valor is made precious by natural courtesy.—SIR PHILIP SIDNEY.

Discretion of speech is more than eloquence; and to speak agreeably to him with whom we deal is more than to speak in good words or in good order.—FRANCIS BACON.

# CONDUCT

Whilst thou livest, keep a good tongue in thy head.—WILLIAM SHAKESPEARE.

As the sword of the best tempered metal is most flexible, so the truly generous are most pliant and courteous in their behavior to their inferiors.—THOMAS FULLER.

Every man is valued in this world as he shows by his conduct he wishes to be valued.—JEAN DE LA BRUYÈRE.

Discourtesy does not spring merely from one bad quality, but from several—foolish vanity, from ignorance of what is due to others, from indolence, from stupidity, from distraction of thought, from contempt of others, from jealousy.—JEAN DE LA BRUYÈRE.

Good manners is the art of making those people easy with whom we converse. Whoever makes the fewest people uneasy is the best bred.—JONATHAN SWIFT.

Inquisitive people are merely funnels of conversation. They do not take in anything for their own use but merely to pass it on to others.—RICHARD STEELE.

We can not always oblige, but we can always speak obligingly.—FRANCOIS VOLTAIRE.

A man has no more right to say an uncivil thing to another man than he has to knock him down.—SAMUEL JOHNSON.

What better school for manners than the company of virtuous women, where the mutual endeavor to please must insensibly polish the mind.—DAVID HUME.

There is a courtesy of the heart; it is allied to love. From it springs the purest courtesy in the outward behavior.—JOHANN WOLFGANG VON GOETHE.

> Give me the avowed, the erect, the manly foe,
> Bold I can meet—perhaps may turn his blow
> But of all plagues, good Heaven, thy wrath can send,
> Save, ah save me from the "candid" friend.
>                                   —GEORGE CANNING.

# CONDUCT

Politeness is good nature regulated by good sense.—SYDNEY SMITH.

In all the affairs of life, social as well as political, courtesies of a small and trivial character are the ones which strike deepest to the grateful and appreciating heart.—HENRY CLAY.

Even power itself hath not one-half the might of gentleness.—LEIGH HUNT.

True politeness requires humility, good sense and benevolence. To think more highly of ourselves than we ought to think destroys its quickening principle.—LYDIA HUNTLEY SIGOURNEY.

Politeness has been well defined as benevolence in small things.—THOMAS BABINGTON MACAULAY.

Fine manners need the support of fine manners in others.—RALPH WALDO EMERSON.

Life is not so short but that there is always room for courtesy.—RALPH WALDO EMERSON.

The distinguishing trait of people accustomed to good society is a calm, imperturable quiet which pervades all their actions and habits, from the greatest to the least. They eat in quiet, move in quiet, live in quiet, and lose even their money in quiet; while low persons cannot take up either a spoon or an affront without making an amazing noise about it.—EDWARD GEORGE BULWER-LYTTON.

Always behave as if nothing has happened, no matter what has happened.—ARNOLD BENNETT.

The greater a man is, the greater the courtesy.—ALFRED TENNYSON.

Manners are not idle, but the fruit of a loyal nature and of noble mind.—ALFRED TENNYSON.

A man can never be a true gentleman in manner until he is a true gentleman at heart.—CHARLES DICKENS.

The only correct actions are those which require no explanation and no apology.—BERTHOLD AUERBACH.

# CONDUCT

A man ought to carry himself in the world as an orange tree would if it could walk up and down in the garden, swinging perfume from every little corner it holds up to the air.—HENRY WARD BEECHER.

No man is a true gentleman who does not inspire the affection and devotion of his servants.—ANDREW CARNEGIE.

Good manners and good morals are sworn friends and fast allies.—HANS VON BARTELS.

If you never break a promise; if you always pay the money you owe exactly on the day it is due, nobody will know but that you are worth a billion. And you will be just as good a risk as a man worth a billion, for all that he could do would be to pay promptly on the due date.—HAMILTON FISH.

Good breeding is the result of much good sense, some good nature and a little self-denial for the sake of others.—LORD CHESTERFIELD.

True politeness is perfect ease and freedom. It simply consists in treating others just as you love to be treated.—LORD CHESTERFIELD.

A man's own good breeding is the best security against other people's ill manners.—LORD CHESTERFIELD.

A man's fortune is frequently decided by his first address. If pleasing, others at once conclude he has merit; but if ungraceful they decide against him.—LORD CHESTERFIELD.

Civility is the charm that attracts the love of all men; and too much is better than to show too little.—BISHOP THOMAS H. HORNE.

True chivalry is meeting life bravely and serving in a sensible way one's fellowmen.—ROSALIE MILLS APPLEBY.

Chivalry is no outward creed or strutting pose; it is unseen, intangible, a light within the life of men. No word can tell of it; it lies deep down within, and quickens into life when men discover it and, without ceasing, strive to carry the high commands into the outward action of their life.—EDWARD GILL.

# CONDUCT

Small kindnesses, small courtesies, small considerations, habitually practiced in our social intercourse, give greater charm to the character than the display of great talents and accomplishments.—M. A. KELLY.

Small courtesies sweeten life; the greater ennoble it.—C. N. BOVEE.

You might as well fall flat on your face as lean over too far backward.—JAMES THURBER .

Tact is the knack of making a point without making an enemy.—HOWARD W. NEWTON.

The attainment of proper self love must become the concern of religion because as long as human beings are enslaved to wrong attitudes toward themselves, they cannot help expressing wrong attitudes toward others.—JOSHUA LOTH LIEBMAN.

I am a little thing with a big meaning . . . I help everybody . . . I unlock doors, open hearts, do away with prejudices . . . I create friendship and good will . . . I inspire respect and confidence . . . Everybody loves me . . . I bore nobody . . . I violate no law . . . I cost nothing . . . Many have praised me, none have condemned me . . . I am pleasing to everyone . . . I am useful every moment of the day . . . I am Courtesy.—ANONYMOUS.

How sweet and gracious, even in common speech is the fine sense which men call Courtesy! Wholesome as air and genial as the light, welcome in every clime as breath of flowers, it transmutes aliens into trusting friends, and gives its owner passport around the globe.—ANONYMOUS.

Respect for human life, and tenderness towards every form of human suffering is one of the most marked features of the best culture.—ANONYMOUS.

A good deed is never lost; he who sows courtesy reaps friendship, and he who plants kindness gathers love.—ANONYMOUS.

Politeness is as natural to delicate natures as perfume is to flowers.—ANONYMOUS.

# CONFIDENCE

Trust the Lord, and serve him in truth with all your heart; for consider what great things He hath done for you.—I SAM. 12:24.

I know that my Redeemer liveth.—JOB 19:25.

For the Lord shall be thy confidence and shall keep thy feet from being taken.—PROV. 3:26.

This is the confidence that we have in him: that, if we ask anything according to His will, He heareth us. I JOHN 5:14.

A person under the firm persuasion that he can command resources virtually has them.—LIVY (TITUS LIVIUS).

Beware of despairing about yourself; you are commanded to put your trust in God, not in yourself.—SAINT AUGUSTINE.

>                     Our doubts are traitors
> And make us lose the good we oft might win
> By fearing to attempt.
>                     —WILLIAM SHAKESPEARE.

He that taketh all his own cares upon himself loads himself in vain with an uneasy burden. I will cast all my cares on God; he hath bidden me; they cannot burden Him.—BISHOP JOSEPH HALL.

The flower that follows the sun does so even on cloudy days. —ROBERT LEIGHTON.

Confidence in conversation has a greater share than wit.— FRANCOIS DE LA ROCHEFOUCAULD.

Look at that beautiful butterfly and learn from it to trust in God. One might wonder where it could live in tempestuous nights, in the whirlwind, or in the stormy day; but I have noticed it is safe and dry under the broad leaf while rivers have been flooded and the mountain oaks torn up from their roots.— JEREMY TAYLOR.

Trust in God does not supersede the employment of prudent means on our part. To expect God's protection while we do nothing is not to honor but to tempt Providence.—PASQUIER QUESNEL.

# CONFIDENCE

Society is built upon trust and trust upon confidence in one another's integrity.—ROBERT SOUTH.

The soul and spirit that animates and keeps up society is mutual trust.—ROBERT SOUTH.

Nothing will ever be attempted if all possible objections must be first overcome.—SAMUEL JOHNSON.

> Trust him little who praises all;
> him less who censures all;
> and him least who is indifferent to all.
> —JOHANN KASPAR LAVATER.

How calmly may we commit ourselves to the hands of Him who bears up the world.—JEAN PAUL RICHTER.

The human heart, at whatever age, opens only to the heart that opens in return.—MARIA EDGEWORTH.

The barriers are not yet erected which can say to aspiring genius: "Thus far and no further."—LUDWIG VAN BEETHOVEN.

> One there lives whose guardian eye
> Guides our earthly destiny;
> One there lives, who, Lord of all,
> Keeps His children lest they fall;
> Pass we, then, in love and praise,
> Trusting Him through all our days,
> Free from doubt and faithless sorrow—
> God provideth for the morrow.
> —REGINALD HEBER.

I know of no such unquestionable badge and ensign of a sovereign mind as that tenacity of purpose which through all changes of companions or parties, or fortunes, changes never, bates no jot of heart or hope, but wearies out opposition and arrives at its port.—RALPH WALDO EMERSON.

Self-trust is the essence of heroism.—RALPH WALDO EMERSON.

Trust men and they will be true to you; treat them greatly and they will show themselves great.—RALPH WALDO EMERSON.

# CONFIDENCE

Trust thyself; every breast vibrates to that iron string.—
RALPH WALDO EMERSON.

We must not calculate on the weather, or on fortune, but
upon God and ourselves. He may fail us in the gratification of
our wishes, but never in the encounter with our exigencies.—
WILLIAM G. SIMMS.

He who trusts men will make fewer mistakes than he who
distrusts them.—CAMILLO BENSO DI CAVOUR.

Self respect is the noblest garment with which a man may
clothe himself—the most elevating feeling with which the mind
can be inspired.—SAMUEL SMILES.

The spirit of self-help is the root of all genuine growth in
the individual; and, exhibited in the lives of many, it constitutes
the true source of national vigor and strength. Help from without is often enfeebling in its effects, but help from within in-
variably invigorates.—SAMUEL SMILES.

No great deed is done by falterers who ask for certainty.—
GEORGE ELIOT.

We trust as we love and where we love. If we love Christ much,
surely we shall trust Him much.—PHILLIPS BROOKS.

An undivided heart which worships God alone, and trusts
him as it should is raised above all anxiety for earthly wants.
—JAMES GEIKIE.

All social life, stability, progress, depend upon each man's
confidence in his neighbor, a reliance upon him to do his duty.—
A. LAWRENCE LOWELL.

Self-distrust is the cause of most of our failures. In the assurance of strength there is strength; and they are the weakest, however strong, who have no faith in themselves or their powers.—
C. N. BOVEE.

No external advantages can supply the place of self-reliance.—
R. W. CLARKE.

# CONFIDENCE

I have never committed the least matter to God that I have not had reason for infinite praise.—ANNA SHIPTON.

Trust God where you cannot trace Him. Do not try to penetrate the cloud He brings over you; rather look to the bow that is on it. The mystery is God's; the promise is yours.—J. R. MACDUFF.

To be trusted is a greater compliment than to be loved.—GEORGE MCDONALD.

He that does not respect confidence will never find happiness in his path.—MORITZ RITTER VON AUFFENBERG-KOMARO.

To think you can creates the force that can.—SAMUEL MARSDEN.

> I like the man who faces what he must
> With step triumphant and with heart of cheer.
> —ANONYMOUS.

Believe in yourself and you will turn more of yourself into practical use.—ANONYMOUS.


# CONSCIENCE

My righteousness I hold fast and will not let it go. My heart shall not reproach me so long as I live.—JOB 27:6.

The spirit of man is the candle of the Lord, searching all the inward parts of the heart.—PROV. 20:27.

Herein do I exercise myself to have always a conscience void of offence toward God and toward men.—ACTS 24:16.

There is no witness so terrible—no accuser so powerful as conscience.—SOPHOCLES.

He that is conscious of crime, however bold by nature, becomes a coward.—MENANDER.

# CONSCIENCE

A good conscience is the palace of Christ; the temple of the Holy Ghost; the paradise of delight, the standing Sabbath of the saints.—SAINT AUGUSTINE.

He will easily be content and at peace whose conscience is pure.—THOMAS Á KEMPIS.

> I feel within me a peace above all earthly dignities,
> A still and quiet conscience.
> —WILLIAM SHAKESPEARE.

I owe obedience of the conscience to no mortal man.—WILLIAM PENN.

Labor to keep alive in your heart that little spark of celestial fire—Conscience.—GEORGE WASHINGTON.

A conscience void of offence before God and man is an inheritance for eternity.—DANIEL WEBSTER.

> His gain is loss;
> For he that wrongs his friends
> Wrongs himself more,
> And ever has about him a silent court and jury
> And himself, the prisoner at the bar
> ever condemned.
> —ALFRED TENNYSON.

The truly honest man is not only without thought of legal, religious or social compulsion, when he discharges an equitable claim on him; but he is without thought of self compulsion. He does the right thing with a simple feeling of satisfaction in doing it, and is indeed impatient if anything prevents him from having the satisfaction of doing it.—HERBERT SPENCER.

There is always a voice saying the right thing to you somewhere, if you'll only listen for it.—THOMAS HUGHES.

A tender conscience is an inestimable blessing; that is, a conscience not only quick to discern what is evil but instantly to shun it, as the eyelid closes itself against the mote.—N. ADAMS.

The keenness and purity of one's conscience reveals the height of his ideals.—J. N. HUNT.

# CONSCIENCE

Conscience can be trusted as a guide for conduct only when it is guided by a perfect standard.—M. E. Dodd.

It is not difficult to get away into retirement, and there live upon your own conviction; nor is it difficult to mix with men and follow their convictions; but to enter into the world, and there live firmly and fearlessly according to your own conscience, that is Christian greatness.—Anonymous.

It is a beautiful idea that every man has within a Guardian Angel; and that is true, too, for Conscience is ever on the watch, ever ready to warn us of danger.—Anonymous.


# CONSECRATION

The very God of peace sanctify you wholly; and I pray God your whole spirit and soul and body be preserved blameless unto the coming of our Lord, Jesus Christ.—I Thes. 5:23.

He shall be a vessel unto honor, sanctified, and meet for the Master's use, and prepared unto every good work.—II Tim. 2:21.

Both he that sanctifieth and they who are sanctified are all of one: for which cause he is not ashamed to call them brethren. —Heb. 2:11.

Dare to look up to God and say, "Make use of me for the future as Thou wilt. I am of the same mind; I am one with Thee. I refuse nothing which seems good to Thee. Lead me whither Thou wilt. Clothe me in whatever dress Thou wilt."—Epictetus.

What's hallowed ground? 'Tis what gives birth
To sacred thoughts in souls of worth;
Peace, independence, truth go forth earth's compass round
And your priesthood shall make all earth hallowed ground.
                    —Thomas Campbell.

The soul alone, like a neglected harp,
    Grows out of tune and needs a hand divine.
Dwell Thou within it, tune and touch the chords
    Till every note and string shall answer Thine.
                    —Harriet Beecher Stowe.

# CONSECRATION

My body, soul and spirit thus redeemed,
Sanctified and healed I give, O Lord, to Thee,
A consecrated offering, Thine evermore to be.
That all my powers with all their might
In thy sole glory may unite.
                                        —HENRY WILSON.

Every cross is turned into a crown, every burden becomes a blessing, every sacrifice becomes sacred and sublime the moment that our Lord and Redeemer writes on it, "For My Sake."— THEODORE L. CUYLER.

The consecrated, one-talent man or woman has promise of a larger influence for good than any intellectual genius who has not met the Master.—SAMUEL M. ZWEMMER.

God will always reveal His will to one who is willing to do it.—HILYS JASPER.

Man alone is the supreme ruler in the realm of his own will. —HILYS JASPER.

I'm going by the upper road,
    For that still holds the sun;
I'm climbing through night's pastures
    Where the starry rivers run:
If you should think to seek me
    In my old dark abode,
You'll find this writing on the door:
    "He's on the Upper Road."
                                —ANONYMOUS.

You never "talked religion," friend;
    You never spoke of any creed;
You never queried of life's end,
    There seemed no need.
You never chided me for aught,
    Nor proudly claimed a higher place
In "principles" and yet you taught
    Of heavenly grace.

96

# CONSECRATION

You passed along life's workaday
　With God set first—your neighbor next
And all things selfish out away—
　You lived your "text."

—Anonymous.

O matchless honor, all unsought,
High Privilege, surpassing thought
That Thou shouldst call us, Lord, to be
Linked in work-fellowship with thee;
To carry out thy wondrous plan,
To bear thy messages to man:
"In trust," with Christ's own word of grace
To every soul of human race.

—Anonymous.

Christ lifted up in our heart will redeem our feelings, emotions and passions by the love, grace and understanding of the Son of God. Inharmony has no hold on us, passion no place in us, hatred nor misunderstanding no expression through us when Christ is lifted up in our heart.—Anonymous.

Laid on Thine altar, O my Lord, Divine,
　Accept my gift this day, for Jesus' sake;
I have no jewels to adorn thy shrine,
　No world-famed sacrifice to make;
And here I bring within my trembling hands
　This will of mine, a thing that seemeth small,
Yet Thou alone canst understand
　How when I yield Thee this, I yield Thee all.

—Anonymous.

# CONSOLATION

Fear not, for I am with thee; be not dismayed; for I am thy God; I will strengthen thee; yea, I will help thee; yea, I will uphold thee with the right hand of my righteousness.—Isa. 41:10.

97

# CONSOLATION

As one whom his mother comforteth, so will I comfort you.
—Isa. 66:13.

Blessed are ye when men shall revile you, and persecute you and shall say all manner of evil against you falsely, for my sake.

Rejoice and be exceeding glad, for great is your reward in heaven; for so persecuted they the prophets which were before you.—Matt. 5:11, 12.

Let not your heart be troubled. Ye believe in God; believe also in me.—John 14:1.

I reckon that the sufferings of this present time are not worthy to be compared with the glory which shall be revealed in us. —Rom. 8:18.

Blessed be God, even the Father of our Lord Jesus Christ, the Father of mercies, and the God of all comfort;

Who comforteth us in all our tribulation, that we may be able to comfort them which are in any trouble, by the comfort wherewith we ourselves are comforted.—II Cor. 1:3, 4.

Our remedies oft in ourselves doth lie, which we ascribe to heaven.—William Shakespeare.

> Sweet are the uses of adversity,
> Which, like the toad, ugly and venomous,
> Wears yet a precious jewel in his head;
> And this our life, exempt from public haunt
> Finds tongues in trees, books in the running brooks
> Sermons in stones and good in everything.
> —William Shakespeare.

Consolation indiscreetly pressed upon us when we are suffering under affliction, only serves to increase our pain and to render our grief more poignant.—Jean Jacques Rousseau.

God has commanded time to console the unhappy.—Joseph Joubfrt.

Many men owe the grandeur of their lives to their tremendous difficulties.—Charles Haddon Spurgeon.

# CONSOLATION

If all of life were sunshine,
  Our faces would be fain
To feel once more upon them
  The cooling splash of rain.
            —HENRY VAN DYKE.


All sunshine makes a desert.—WILLIAM DAWSON.


In times of uncertainty and confusion, let us not forget that this great nation was built by faith, toil and thrift.—TOM C. GOOCH.


The everlasting covenant and the everlasting consolations that flow from it are indeed everlasting arms.—H. T. WAGNER.


Life's disappointments are veiled Love's appointments.—C. A. FOX.

When we have exhausted our store of endurance,
When our strength has failed ere the day is half done,
When we reach the end of our hoarded resources
Our Father's full giving is only begun.

His love has no limit, His grace has no measure,
His power no boundary known unto men;
For out of His infinite riches in Jesus
He giveth, and giveth and giveth again.
            —ANNIE JOHNSON FLINT.


In these troublous days when the foundations of the world are shaken and nations are torn asunder with war and death, let us atune our souls to the call of the still small Voice to "be strong in the Lord and in the power of His might." We yet can trust in Him who created man in His own image; we can depend upon Him to lead us out of the darkness; we can "sail ahead, and leave the rest to God."—PAT M. NEFF.


God does not comfort us to make us comfortable but to make us comforters.—ALEXANDER NOWELL.

99

# CONSOLATION

The soft, sweet summer was warm and glowing;
Bright were the blossoms on every bough;
I trusted Him when the roses were blooming—
    I trust Him now.

—ANONYMOUS.

O Thou of little faith,
    God hath not failed thee yet!
When all looks dark and gloomy
    Thou dost so soon forget—

Forget that He has led thee,
    And gently cleared thy way;
On clouds has poured His sunshine,
    And turned thy night to day.

And if He's helped thee hitherto
    He will not fail thee now;
How it must wound His loving heart
    To see thy anxious brow!

Oh, doubt not any longer
    To Him commit thy way,
Who in the past thou trusted,
    And is "just the same today."

—ANONYMOUS.

# CONTENTMENT

The Lord heareth the murmurings which ye murmur against him.—EXO. 16:8.

I have learned in whatsoever state I am, therewith to be content.—PHIL. 4:11.

... Be content with such things as ye have. ...—HEB. 13:5.

# CONTENTMENT

'Tis better to be lowly born,
And range with humble livers in content,
Than to be perked up in a glistering grief,
And wear a golden sorrow.
—WILLIAM SHAKESPEARE.

Contentment with the divine will is the best remedy we can apply to misfortune.—SIR WILLIAM TEMPLE.

A contented mind is the greatest blessing a man can enjoy in this world; and if, in the present life, his happiness arises from the subduing of his desires, it will rise to the next from the gratification of them.—JOSEPH ADDISON.

No longer forward nor behind
I look in hope or fear;
But grateful, take the good I find
The best of now and here.
—JOHN GREENLEAF WHITTIER.

Never dwell on the morrow. Remember that it is God's, not thine. The heaviest part of sorrow often is to look forward to it. "The Lord will provide."—E. B. BUSY.

Without murmur, uncomplaining,
In His hand,
Leave whatever things thou canst not
Understand.
K. R. HAGENBACH.

It is right to be contented with what we have, never with what we are.—SIR J. MACKINTOSH.

# COURAGE

There shall not any man be able to stand before thee all the days of thy life: as I was with Moses so I will be with thee: I will not fail thee, nor forsake thee. Be strong and of good courage. —JOSH. 1:5, 6b.

# COURAGE

The Lord is with thee, thou mighty man of valor....Go in this thy might. . . . Have not I sent thee? . . . Surely I will be with thee.—JUDG. 6:12, 14, 16.

The Lord is my light and my salvation; whom shall I fear? The Lord is the strength of my life: of whom shall I be afraid? —PSALM 27:1.

For God hath not given us the spirit of fear; but of power, and of love and of a sound mind.—II TIM. 1:7.

Courage is the love of the morally beautiful more than life. —PLATO.

There is a wide difference between true courage and mere contempt of life.—CATO, THE ELDER.

No man can be brave who considers pain the greatest evil of life; or temperate, who regards pleasure as the highest good. —CICERO.

Courage consists not in hazarding without fear, but being resolutely minded in a just cause.—PLUTARCH.

The bravery founded on hope of recompense, fear of punishment, experience of success, on rage, or on ignorance of danger, is but common bravery, and does not deserve the name. True bravery proposes a just end; measures the dangers, and meets the result with calmness and unyielding decision.—LA NOUE.

A true knight is fuller of bravery in the midst than in the beginning of danger.—SIR PHILIP SIDNEY.

> Suspicion always haunts the guilty mind;
> The thief doth fear each bush an officer.
> —WILLIAM SHAKESPEARE.

When valor preys on reason it eats the sword it fights with. —WILLIAM SHAKESPEARE.

The better part of valor is discretion.—WILLIAM SHAKESPEARE.

# COURAGE

Let come what will, I mean to bear it out,
And either live with glorious victory
Or die with fame, renowned in chivalry:
He is not worthy of the honeycomb
That shuns the hive because the bees have stings.
—WILLIAM SHAKESPEARE.

I dare do all that may become a man;
Who dares do more is none.
—WILLIAM SHAKESPEARE.

Cowards die many times before their deaths;
The valiant never taste of death but once.
—WILLIAM SHAKESPEARE.

Wise men ne're sit and wail their loss
But cheerly seek how to redress their harms
What though the mast be now blown overboard,
The cable broke, the holding anchor lost,
And half our sailors swallow'd in the flood.
Yet lives our Pilot still; is't meet, that He
Should leave the helm, and, like a fearful lad
With tearful eyes, add water to the sea,
And give more strength to that which hath too much;
Whiles, in his moan, the ship splits on the rock
Which industry and courage might have saved.
—WILLIAM SHAKESPEARE.

True bravery is shown by performing without witness what one might be capable of doing before all the world.—FRANCOIS DE LA ROCHEFOUCAULD.

No man can answer for his courage who has never been in danger.—FRANCOIS DE LA ROCHEFOUCAULD.

The best hearts are ever the bravest.—LAURENCE STERNE.

Courage consists not in blindly overlooking danger, but in seeing and conquering it.—JEAN PAUL RICHTER.

A great deal of talent is lost in this world for want of a little courage.—SYDNEY SMITH.

# COURAGE

In spite of sorrow, loss and pain,
Our course be onward still;
We sow on Burma's barren plain;
We reap on Zion's hill.
—ADONIRAM JUDSON.

The courage we desire and prize is not the courage to die decently but to live manfully.—THOMAS CARLYLE.

All brave men love; for he only is brave who has affections to fight for, whether in the daily battle of life, or in physical contests.—NATHANIEL HAWTHORNE.

And having thus chosen our course, let us renew our trust in God and go forward without fear and with manly hearts.—ABRAHAM LINCOLN.

To sin by silence when they should protest makes cowards out of men.—ABRAHAM LINCOLN.

Bravery never goes out of fashion.—WILLIAM MAKEPEACE THACKERAY.

Why comes temptation, but for man to meet
And master, and make crouch beneath his feet.
—ROBERT BROWNING.

No coward soul is mine,
No trembler in the world's storm-troubled sphere;
I see Heaven's glories shine,
And Faith shines equal, arming me from fear.
—EMILY BRONTE.

They are slaves who dare not be
In the right with two or three.
—JAMES RUSSELL LOWELL.

If there be one thing upon earth that mankind love and admire better than another, it is a brave man—a man who dares look the devil in the face and tell him he is the devil.—JAMES A. GARFIELD.

Take courage. It is sweet to talk with God; we walk in the wilderness today and in the promised land tomorrow.—DWIGHT L. MOODY.

# COURAGE

Whether you be man or woman you will never do anything in this world without courage. It is the greatest quality of the mind next to honor.—JAMES L. ALLEN.

Keep your fears to yourself, but share your courage with others.—ROBERT LOUIS STEVENSON.

> Renew the courage that prevails,
> The steady faith that never fails,
> And makes us stand in every fight
> Firm as a fortress to defend the right.
> —HENRY VAN DYKE.

It is only through labor and painful effort, by grim energy and resolute courage that we move on to better things.—THEODORE ROOSEVELT.

Let me not pray to be sheltered from dangers, but to be fearless in facing them.—RABINDRANATH TAGORE.

Because a fellow has failed once or twice, or a dozen times, you don't want to set him down as a failure till he's dead or loses his courage—that's the same thing.—GEORGE HORACE LORIMER.

> De da'kest hour, dey allus say,
> Is jes' befo' de dawn,
> But it's moughty ha'd a-waitin'
> When de night goes frownin' on;
> An' it's moughty ha'd a-hopin'
> W'en de clouds is big and black,
> An' all de t'ings you's waited fo'
> Has failed, or gone to wrack—
> But jes' keep on a-joggin
> Wid a little bit o' song
> De mo'n is allus brightah
> W'en de night's bin long.
> —PAUL LAWRENCE DUNBAR.

The highest type of heroism is not the courage and nerve of the warrior, facing the foe, but the courage to face the daily issues of life, opposing wrong and upholding right.—ROSWELL C. LONG.

# COURAGE

Dare to do your duty always; this is the height of true valor.
—CHARLES SIMMONS.

Spiritual cowardice is not only weakness but wickedness.
—J. B. GAMBRELL.

Lines of least resistance make crooked rivers and crooked men.—WILLIAM H. DANFORTH.

> God has His best things for the few
> Who dare to stand the test;
> He has His second choice for those
> Who will not have His best.
>
> —ANONYMOUS.

No smile is so beautiful as the one that struggles through tears.—ANONYMOUS.

> Men may misjudge thy aim,
> Think they have cause to blame,
> Say thou art wrong;
> Keep on thy quiet way,
> Christ is the Judge, not they,
> Fear not; be strong.
>
> —ANONYMOUS.

> The clouds have a silver lining—don't forget;
> And though he's hidden, still the sun is shining;
> Courage! instead of tears and vain repining
> Just bide a wee and dinna fret.
>
> —ANONYMOUS.

# DEATH

The Lord gave, and the Lord hath taken away. Blessed be the name of the Lord.—JOB 1:21.

The memory of the Just is blessed.—PROV. 10:7.

Precious in the sight of the Lord is the death of his saints.
—PSALM 116:15.

# DEATH

I am the resurrection and the life; he that believeth in me, though he were dead, yet shall he live again. And whosoever liveth and believeth in me shall never die. Believest thou this? —John 11:25-26.

Blessed are the dead which die in the Lord from henceforth; yea, saith the Spirit, that they may rest from their labors, and their works do follow them.—Rev. 14:13.

We who would teach men to die, would at the same time teach them to live.—Michel de Montaigne.

> Be still prepared for death
> And death or life shall thereby be the sweeter.
> —William Shakespeare.

> Oh, what a sign it is of evil life
> When death's approach is seen so terrible.
> —William Shakespeare.

Let dissolution come when it will, it can do the Christian no harm, for it will be but a passage out of a prison into a palace; out of a sea of troubles into a haven of rest; out of a crowd of enemies into an innumerable company of true, loving and faithful friends; out of shame, reproach and contempt, into exceeding great and eternal glory.—John Bunyan.

Our piety must be weak and imperfect if it does not conquer the fear of death.—Francois de la Fenelon.

It is impossible that anything so natural, so necessary and so universal as death should ever have been designed by Providence as an evil to mankind.—Jonathan Swift.

To live in hearts we leave behind is not to die.—Thomas Campbell.

Is Death the last sleep?—No, it is the last and final awakening. —Sir Walter Scott.

> Oh, when a mother meets on high
> The babe she lost in infancy
> Hath she not then for pains and fears,
> The way of woe, the watchful night,
> For all her sorrow, all her tears,
> An over-payment of delight.
> —Robert Southey.

107

# DEATH

We understand death for the first time when he puts his hand upon one whom we love.—MME. DE STAEL.

One may live as a conqueror, a king, or a magistrate; but he must die a man. The bed of death brings every human being to his pure individuality, to the intense contemplation of that deepest and most solemn of all relations—the relation between the creature and his Creator.—DANIEL WEBSTER.

We sometimes congratulate ourselves at the moment of waking from a troubled dream; it may be so the moment after death. —NATHANIEL HAWTHORNE.

Of all the thoughts of God that are  
Borne inward into souls afar,  
    Along the Psalmist's music deep,  
Now tell me if there any is,  
For gift or grace, surpassing this—  
    "He giveth His beloved sleep!"  
        —ELIZABETH BARRETT BROWNING.

God calls our loved ones,  
    But we lose not wholly  
        What He hath given;  
They live on earth  
    In thought and deed  
        As truly as in His heaven.  
        —JOHN GREENLEAF WHITTIER.

Death's truer name  
Is "Onward," no discordance in the roll  
And march of that Eternal Harmony  
Whereto the world beats time.  
        —ALFRED TENNYSON.

When sinks the soul  
    Subdued by toil to slumber,  
    It's closing eye looks up  
To Thee in prayer.  
    Sweet the repose  
    Beneath Thy wings o'er shading  
    But sweeter still to wake  
And find Thee there.  
        —HARRIET BEECHER STOWE.

# DEATH

I cannot say, and I will not say
That he is dead. He is just away.

With a cheery smile, and a wave of the hand,
He has wandered into an unknown land

And left us dreaming how very fair
It needs must be, since he lingers there.

And you—oh, you, who the wildest yearn
For an old-time step, and the glad return,

Think of him faring on, as dear
In the love of There as the love of Here.

Think of him still as the same. I say,
He is not dead—he is just away.
                    —JAMES WHITCOMB RILEY.

Last Easter when my voice was lifted up
    To sing the praises of my Risen Lord,
I had not tasted sorrow's bitter cup;
    The music held for me no minor chord.
This Eastertide my stricken heart sends up
    The strains I lift in accents clear and strong,
For I have drained the dregs of sorrow's cup
    And learned the meaning of the Easter song.
I know the sweetness of the minor chord,
    The glory of the major full and clear;
I know the power of the Risen Lord—
    He lives, and they shall live whom I hold dear.
And though I cannot help the tears that flow,
    And though my heart is sad as heart can be,
I sing the Easter song because I know
    The blessed Easter message is for me.
                    —ANONYMOUS.

This world is the land of the dying; the next is the land of the living.—TRYON EDWARDS.

Death, to a good man, is but passing through a dark entry, out of one little dusky room of his Father's house into another that is fair and large, lightsome and glorious, and divinely entertaining.—MACDONALD CLARKE.

# DEATH

To the Christian death has redemptive significance. It is the portal through which we enter the presence of our Lord.—HILYS JASPER.

> The tomb is not an endless night—
> It is a thoroughfare, a way
> That closes in a soft twilight
> And opens in eternal day.
> —ANONYMOUS.

Death and Love are two wings which bear men from earth to Heaven.—ANONYMOUS.

> Not dead—no, no! but borne beyond the shadows
> Into the full, clear light;
> Forever done with mist and cloud and tempest,
> Where all is calm and bright.
> Not even sleeping—called to glad awakening
> In Heaven's endless day;
> Not still and moveless—stepped from earth's rough places
> To walk the King's Highway.
> Not silent—just passed out of earthly hearing
> To sing Heaven's sweet, new song;
> Not lonely—dearly loved and dearly loving,
> Amid the white-robed throng.
> But not forgetful—keeping fond remembrance
> Of dear ones, left awhile;
> And looking gladly to the bright reunion
> With hand clasp and with smile.
> Oh, no, not dead! but past all fear of dying
> And with all suffering o'er.
> Say not that I am dead when Jesus calls me
> To live forevermore.
> —ANONYMOUS.

# DILIGENCE

The king's business required haste.—I SAM. 21:8.

He becometh poor that dealeth with a slack hand; but the hand of the diligent maketh rich.—PROV. 10:4.

# DILIGENCE

Seest thou a man diligent in his business? He shall stand before kings.—Prov. 22:29.

In the morning when thou findest thyself unwilling to rise, consider with thyself presently, if it is to go about a man's work that I am stirred up. Or was I made for this, to lay me down, and make much of myself in a warm bed.—Marcus Aurelius.

Diligence is the mother of good fortune.—Miguel de Cervantes.

Few things are impossible to diligence and skill.—Samuel Johnson.

The leading rule for a man of every calling is diligence; never put off until tomorrow what you can do today.—Abraham Lincoln.

He who wakes to find himself famous hasn't been asleep. —Roger Babson.

> If you were busy being kind
> Before you knew it, you would find
> You'd soon forget to think 'twas true
> That someone was unkind to you.
>
> If you were busy being glad
> And cheering people who were sad,
> Although your heart might ache a bit
> You'd soon forget to notice it.
>
> If you were busy being true
> To what you know you ought to do,
> You'd be so busy you'd forget
> The blunders of the folks you've met.
> —Anonymous.

Every man is worth just as much as the things are worth about which he busies himself.—Anonymous.

# DREAMS

And Joseph remembered the dreams which he had dreamed.
—GEN. 42:9.

And it shall come to pass afterward, that I will pour out my
spirit upon all flesh; and your sons and your daughters shall
prophesy, your old men shall dream dreams, your young men
shall see visions.—JOEL 2:28.

Dream manfully and nobly and thy dreams shall be prophets.
—EDWARD GEORGE BULWER-LYTTON.

> I keep some portion of my early dream,
>   Broken bright, like moonbeams on a river;
> It lights my life, a far illusive gleam
>   Moves as I move, and leads me on forever.
>                    —JOHN TOWNSEND TROWBRIDGE.

> Great it is to believe the dream
> When we stand in youth by the starry stream;
> But a greater thing is to fight life through
> And say at the end, "The dream is true!"
>                    —EDWIN MARKHAM.

> I pray thee, spare me, Fate,
> The woeful, wearying weight
>     Of a heart that feels no pain
>     At the sob of the autumn rain,
> And takes no breath of glee
> From the organ-surge of the sea—
> Of a mind where memory broods
> Over songless solitude—
>     I shall be satisfied
>     If only dreams abide.
>                    —CLINTON SCOLLARD.

He whom a dream hath possessed treads the impalpable marches;
From the dust of the day's long road he leaps to a laughing star.
And the ruin of worlds that fall he views from eternal arches,
And rides God's battlefield in a flashing and golden car.
                    —SHAEMUS O'SHEEL.

112

# DREAMS

I slept, and dreamed that life was Beauty,
I woke and found that life was Duty.
Was thy dream then a shadowy lie?
Toil on, poor heart, unceasingly;
And thou shalt find thy dream to be
A truth and noonday light to thee.
—ELLEN STURGIS HOOPER.

The poor man is not he who is without a cent, but he who is without a dream.—HARRY KEMP.

One broken dream is not the end of dreaming;
One shattered hope is not the end of all—
Beyond the storm and tempests stars are gleaming—
Still build your castles, though your castles fall.
—ANONYMOUS.

# DUTY

Fear God and keep His commandments: for this is the whole duty of man.—ECC. 12:13.

He hath showed thee, O man, what is good: and what doth the Lord require of thee, but to do justly, and to love mercy, and to walk humbly with thy God?—MIC. 6:8.

He that knoweth to do good and doth it not, to him it is sin.
—JAS. 4:17.

How well in thee appears
The constant service of the antique world,
When service sweat for duty, are for meed!
Thou art not for the fashion of these times,
Where none will sweat but for promotion.
—WILLIAM SHAKESPEARE.

The consciousness of a duty performed gives us music at midnight.—GEORGE HERBERT.

Try to put well into practice what you already know; and in so doing, you will, in good time, discover the hidden things which you now inquire about. Practice what you know and it will help to make clear what you do not know.—HARMENSZOON VAN RIJN REMBRANDT.

> When I'm not thank'd at all, I'm thank'd enough—
> I've done my duty and I've done no more.
> —HENRY FIELDING.

The duty of man is plain and simple, and consists of but two points: his duty to God, which every man must feel; and his duty to his neighbor—to do as he would be done by.—THOMAS PAINE.

> The primal duties shine aloft, like stars;
> The charities that soothe and heal and bless
> Are scattered at the feet of men like flowers.
> —WILLIAM WORDSWORTH.

It is wonderful what strength of purpose and boldness and energy of will are aroused by the assurance that we are doing our duty.—SIR WALTER SCOTT.

Every human being has a work to carry on within, duties to perform abroad, influences to exert, which are peculiarly his, and which no conscience but his own can teach.—WILLIAM ELLERY CHANNING.

A sense of duty pursues us ever. It is omnipotent, like the Deity. If we take to ourselves the wings of the morning and dwell in the uttermost parts of the sea, duty performed or duty violated is still with us, for our happiness or our misery. If we say the darkness shall cover us, in the darkness as in the light our obligations are yet with us.—DANIEL WEBSTER.

There are not good things enough in life to indemnify us for the neglect of a single duty.—MME. SOYMONOFF SWETCHINE.

Let him who gropes painfully in darkness of uncertain light and prays vehemently that the dawn may ripen into the day, lay this precept well to heart: Do the duty which lieth nearest to thee, which thou knowest to be a duty. Thy second duty will already have become clearer.—THOMAS CARLYLE.

# DUTY

Our grand business is, not to see what lies dimly at a distance, but to do what lies closely at hand.—THOMAS CARLYLE.

There is nothing in the universe that I fear but that I shall not know my duty, or fail to do it.—MARY LYON.

Duty is the grandest of ideas, because it implies the idea of God, of the soul, of liberty, of responsibility, of immortality.—JEAN BAPTISTE HENRI LACORDAIRE.

> The sweetest lives are those to duty wed,
> Whose deeds, both great and small,
> Are close knit strands of an unbroken thread
> Where love ennobles all.
>
> The world may sound no trumpets, ring no bells;
> Thy love shall chant its own beatitudes
> After its own life-working. A child's kiss
> Set on thy sighing lips shall make thee glad;
> A poor man served by thee shall make thee rich;
> A sick man helped by thee shall make thee strong;
> Thou shalt be served thyself by every sense
> Of service which thou renderest.
> —ELIZABETH BARRETT BROWNING.

Duty is the sublimest word in the language; you can never do more than your duty; you should never wish to do less.—ROBERT E. LEE.

Let us have faith that right makes might; and in that faith let us to the end dare to do our duty as we understand it.—ABRAHAM LINCOLN.

Let men laugh, if they will, when you sacrifice desire to duty. You have time and eternity to rejoice in.—THEODORE PARKER.

Duty done is the soul's fireside.—ROBERT BROWNING.

Your daily duties are a part of your religious life just as much as your devotions.—HENRY WARD BEECHER.

Do right, and God's recompense to you will be the power of doing more right.—FREDERICK WILLIAM ROBERTSON.

# DUTY

Every duty that is bidden to wait comes back with seven fresh duties at its back.—CHARLES KINGSLEY.

Do today's duty; fight today's temptations; and do not weaken and distract yourself by looking forward to things which you cannot see, and could not understand if you saw them.—CHARLES KINGSLEY.

Thank God every morning when you get up that you have something to do that day which must be done, whether you like it or not. Being forced to work and forced to do your best will breed in you temperance and self control, diligence and strength of will, cheerfulness and content, and a hundred virtues which the idle never know.—CHARLES KINGSLEY.

Every duty which we omit, obscures some truth which we should have known.—JOHN RUSKIN.

Do the truth you know, and you shall learn the truth you need to know.—GEORGE McDONALD.

A duty dodged is like a debt unpaid; it is only deferred, and we must come back and settle the account at last.—JOSEPH FORT NEWTON.

This span of life was lent for lofty duties, not for selfishness; not to be whiled away in aimless dreams, but to improve ourselves and serve mankind.—AUBREY DE VERE.

Power to its last particle is duty.—ALEXANDER MacLAREN.

Happy is he who has learned to do this one thing: To do the plain duty of the moment quickly and cheerfully, whatever it may be.—ANONYMOUS.

We ought not to picture Duty to ourselves, or to others, as a stern taskmistress. She is rather a kind and sympathetic mother, ever ready to shelter us from the cares and anxieties of this world, and to guide us in the paths of peace.—ANONYMOUS.

# EDUCATION

Learn of Me.—MATT. 11:29.

Thou shalt love the Lord thy God . . . with all thy mind.—LUKE 10:27.

Study to show thyself approved unto God; a workman that needeth not to be ashamed.—II TIM. 2:15.

It is only the ignorant who despise education.—PUBLIUS SYRUS.

As the soil, however rich it may be, cannot be productive without culture, so the mind without cultivation can never produce good fruits.—SENECA.

Some books are to be tasted, others to be swallowed, and some few to be chewed and digested. . . . Reading maketh a full man, conference a ready man, and writing an exact man. . . . Histories make men wise, poets witty; the mathematics, subtle; natural philosophy, deep, moral, grave; logic and rhetoric, able to contend.—FRANCIS BACON.

My library was dukedom large enough.—WILLIAM SHAKESPEARE.

The common curse of mankind—folly and ignorance.—WILLIAM SHAKESPEARE.

What sculpture is to a block of marble, education is to the human soul. The philosopher, the saint, the hero, the wise and the good, or the great, very often lie hid and concealed in a plebeian, which a proper education might have disinterred and brought to light.—JOSEPH ADDISON.

Some people never learn anything because they understand everything too soon.—ALEXANDER POPE.

A little learning is a dangerous thing. . . .—ALEXANDER POPE.

> 'Tis education forms the common mind
> As the twig is bent the tree's inclined.
> —ALEXANDER POPE.

If a man empties his purse in his head, no man can take it away from him.—BENJAMIN FRANKLIN.

# EDUCATION

To me the meanest flower that blows can give
Thoughts that do often lie too deep for tears.
—WILLIAM WORDSWORTH.

Knowledge does not comprise all which is contained in the large term of education. The feelings are to be disciplined; the passions are to be restrained; true and worthy motives are to be inspired; a profound religious feeling is to be instilled, and pure morality inculcated under all circumstances. All this is comprised in education.—DANIEL WEBSTER.

The destiny of nations lies far more in the hands of women—mothers—than in the hands of those who possess power. We must cultivate women, who are educators of the human race, else a new generation cannot accomplish its task.—FRIEDRICH WILLIAM FROEBEL.

Education is a debt due from the present to the future generations.—GEORGE PEABODY.

The hearts of men are their books; events are their tutors; great actions are their eloquence.—THOMAS BABINGTON MACAULAY.

It would be better to abandon our over-rapid development of the intellect and to aim rather at training the heart and the affections.—VICTOR HUGO.

Neither piety, virtue, nor liberty can long flourish in a community where the education of youth is neglected.—THOMAS COOPER.

The Riches of a commonwealth
Are free, strong minds and hearts of health,
And more to her than gold or grain,
The cunning hand and cultured brain.
—JOHN GREENLEAF WHITTIER.

See some good picture—in nature, if possible, or on a canvas,—hear a page of the best music, or read a great poem every day. You will always find a free half hour for one or the other, and at the end of the year your mind will shine with such an accumulation of jewels as will astonish even yourself.—HENRY WADSWORTH LONGFELLOW.

# EDUCATION

The best education in the world is that got by struggling to get a living.—WENDELL PHILLIPS.

Let us not always say
"Spite of this flesh today
I strove, made head, gained ground upon the whole!"
As the bird wings and sings,
Let us cry, "All good things are ours,
Nor soul helps flesh more now, than flesh helps soul!"
—ROBERT BROWNING.

'Tis the taught already that profits by teaching.—ROBERT BROWNING.

Education is the knowledge of how to use the whole of one's self. Many men use but one or two faculties out of the score with which they are endowed. A man is educated who knows how to make a tool of every faculty—how to open it, how to keep it sharp, and how to apply it to all practical purposes.—HENRY WARD BEECHER.

The more you know, the more you can save yourself and that which belongs to you, and do more work with less effort.—CHARLES KINGSLEY.

It was in making education not only common to all, but in some sense compulsory on all, that the destiny of the free republic of America was practically settled.—JAMES RUSSELL LOWELL.

Education does not mean teaching people to know what they do not know; it means teaching them to behave as they do not behave.—JOHN RUSKIN.

Perhaps the most valuable result of all education is the ability to make yourself do the thing you have to do when it ought to be done, whether you like it or not; it is the first lesson which ought to be learned, and, however early a man's training begins, it is probably the last lesson he learns thoroughly.—THOMAS HUXLEY.

To be well informed, one must read quickly a great number of merely instructive books. To be cultivated, one must read

# EDUCATION

slowly and with a lingering appreciation the comparatively few books that have been written by men who lived, thought and felt with style.—THOMAS HUXLEY.

The distinctive characteristic of the college man should be that he is capable of intense, rapid, sustained thought.—CHARLES WILLIAM ELIOT.

Liberal education develops a sense of right, duty and honor; and more and more in the modern world, large business rests on rectitude and honor as well as on good judgment.—CHARLES WILLIAM ELIOT.

Knowledge and timber shouldn't be used until they are seasoned.—OLIVER WENDELL HOLMES.

Let us learn upon earth those things which can prepare us for heaven.—JEROME KLAPKA JEROME.

There are five tests of the evidences of education—correctness and precision in the use of the mother tongue; refined and gentle manners, the result of fixed habits of thought and action; sound standards of appreciation of beauty and of worth; and a character based on these standards; power and habit of reflection; efficiency or the power to do.—NICHOLAS MURRAY BUTLER.

The educated man is a man with certain spiritual qualities which make him calm in adversity, happy when alone, just in his dealings, rational and sane in the fullest meaning of that word in all the affairs of life.—RAMSAY MACDONALD.

Education is nothing if it is not the methodical creation of the habit of thinking.—ABBÉ ERNEST DIMNET.

Never regard study as a duty, but as the enviable opportunity to learn to know the liberating influence of beauty in the realm of the spirit for your own personal joy and to the profit of the community to which your later work belongs.—ALBERT EINSTEIN.

Every student must be a volunteer in the intellectual and spiritual struggle to preserve freedom for mankind.—FRANKLIN DELANO ROOSEVELT.

# EDUCATION

A democracy can only be strong if all the citizens are properly educated and careers are freely open to all the talented.—Dr. James Bryant Conant.

Education is not enough; it must be education in Christ.—J. W. ("Bill") Marshall.

All education should be directed toward the development of character. Sound character cannot be achieved if spiritual development is neglected. I do not like to think of turning out physical and mental giants who are spiritual pygmies.—Dr. Walter C. Coffey.

All education that is not God and Christ centered is the wrong kind of education. Education without the recognition of God makes men fools, and the more of such education they get, the greater fools they become.—W. S. Hottel.

The great end of education is to discipline rather than to furnish the mind; to train it to the use of its own powers, rather than fill it with the accumulation of others.—Tryon Edwards.

Truth incarnate is the only spiritual truth that makes an effective appeal. Hence every teacher must feel, "My most effective lesson is myslf."—A. H. McKinney.

The first thing education teaches you is to walk alone.—Trader Horn.

The greatest thing the disciples got from the teaching of Jesus was not a doctrine but an influence. To the last hour of their lives the big thing was that they had been with him.—John Marquis.

Learning makes a man fit company for himself as well as others.—Anonymous.

The price of mastery in any field is thorough preparation.—Anonymous.

Religious education should exalt and dignify the body and give a religious interpretation to the whole physical environment.—Anonymous.

# EDUCATION

Education is not learning; it is the exercise and development of the powers of the mind; and the two great methods by which this end may be accomplished are in the halls of learning, or in the conflicts of life.—ANONYMOUS.

# EXAMPLE

I have given you an example, that ye should do as I have done.—JOHN 13:15.

Now the God of patience and consolation grant you to be likeminded one toward another, according to Christ Jesus.—ROM. 15:5.

Be thou an example of the believer in word, in conversation, in love, in spirit, in faith, in purity.—I TIM. 4:12b.

Of all the commentaries on the Scriptures, Good examples are the best.—JOHN DONNE.

No man is so insignificant as to be sure his example can do no hurt.—EDWARD HYDE, LORD CLARENDON.

Be so that thy conduct can become law universal.—IMMANUEL KANT.

> From scheme and creed the light goes out,
>   The saintly fact survives:
> The blessed Master none can doubt
>   Revealed in Holy lives.
>           —JOHN GREENLEAF WHITTIER.

One example is worth a thousand arguments.—WILLIAM EWART GLADSTONE.

Train up a child in the way he should go, and walk there yourself, once in a while.—JOSH BILLINGS (*pseud. of* HENRY WHEELER SHAW).

If you want your neighbor to see what the Christ spirit will do for him, let him see what it has done for you.—HENRY WARD BEECHER.

# EXAMPLE

Nothing is so infectious as example.—CHARLES KINGSLEY.

Search thine own heart,—what paineth thee in others,
    In thyself may be;
All dust is frail, all flesh is weak;
Be thou the true man thou dost seek.
    —JAMES RUSSELL LOWELL.

Nobody will know what you mean by saying that "God is Love" unless you act it as well.—LAWRENCE PEARSALL JACKS.

The first great gift we can bestow on others is a good example.—FREDERIC MORELL.

Teach by your loves.—HORATIUS BOMAR.


# EXPERIENCE

I have learned by experience that the Lord hath blessed me for thy sake.—GEN. 30:27.

We glory in tribulation also: knowing that tribulation worketh patience; and patience, experience; and experience hope, and hope maketh not ashamed; because the love of God is shed abroad in our hearts by the Holy Ghost which is given unto us.—ROM. 5:3-5.

Experience is by industry achieved,
    And perfected by the swift course of time.
    —WILLIAM SHAKESPEARE.

Experience is a jewel, and it had need be so, for it is often purchased at an infinite rate.—WILLIAM SHAKESPEARE.

To wilful men, the injuries that they themselves procure
    Must be their school masters.
    —WILLIAM SHAKESPEARE.

For just experience tell, in every soil,
That those who think must govern those who toil.
    —OLIVER GOLDSMITH.

# EXPERIENCE

Where lives the man that has not tried
How mirth can into folly glide,
    And folly into sin!
        —Sir Walter Scott.

We are often prophets to others, only because we are our own historians.—Mme. Soymonoff Swetchine.

Experience is a safe light to walk by, and he is not a rash man who expects success in the future by the same means which secured it in the past.—Wendell Phillips.

We learn wisdom from failure much more than from success. We often discover what will do by finding out what will not do; and probably he who never made a mistake never made a discovery.—Samuel Smiles.

Experience joined with common sense
    To mortals is a providence.
        —Matthew Green.

It may serve as a comfort to us in all our calamities and afflictions that he who loses anything and gets wisdom by it is a gainer by the loss.—Roger L'Estrange.

Development is only possible through experience; and experience is an unbending teacher; she flogs her lessons home, but graduates of her school are thoroughly taught.—Anonymous.

Why ask for proof, when need for none is shown,
    Or limit Truth by Logic's stumbling art?
Love is real to all who Love have known—
    And Faith is no riddle to the trusting heart.
        —Anonymous.

This is one of the sad conditions of life, that experience is not transmissible. No man will learn from the suffering of another. He must suffer for himself.—Anonymous.

# FAITH

I went and washed and I received sight.—JOHN 9:11.

Faith is the substance of things hoped for; the evidence of things not seen.—HEB. 11:1.

Without faith it is impossible to please him.—HEB. 11.6.

Faith is to believe on the word of God, what we do not see, and its reward is to see and enjoy what we believe.—SAINT AUGUSTINE.

Love is the crowning grace in heaven; but faith is the conquering grace upon earth.—THOMAS WATSON.

Atheism is rather in the life than in the heart of a man.—FRANCIS BACON.

Faith is the root of all blessings. Believe, and you shall be saved; believe and you must needs be satisfied; believe, and you cannot but be comforted and happy.—JEREMY TAYLOR.

Epochs of faith are epochs of fruitfulness; but epochs of unbelief, however glittering, are barren of all permanent good.—JOHANN WOLFGANG VON GOETHE.

All the scholastic scaffolding falls, as a ruined edifice, before one single word—Faith.—NAPOLEON BONAPARTE.

There is one sure criterion of judgment as to religious faith in doctrinal matters: can you reduce it to practice? If not, have none of it.—HOSEA BALLOU.

> Forth from his dark and lonely hiding place
> (Portentous sight) the owlet Atheism,
> Sailing on obscene wings athwart the noon,
> Drops his blue-fringed lids, and holds them close,
> And hooting at the glorious sun in heaven
>     Cries out, "Where is it?"
>         —SAMUEL TAYLOR COLERIDGE.

All of my theology is reduced to this narrow compass: "Jesus Christ came into the world to save sinners."—ARCHIBALD ALEXANDER.

# FAITH

I prefer a firm religious faith to every other blessing. For it makes life a discipline of goodness; creates new hopes, when those of the world vanish; throws over the decay of life the most gorgeous of all lights; and awakens life even in death.—SIR HUMPHRY DAVY.

All I have seen teaches me to trust the Creator for all I have not seen.—RALPH WALDO EMERSON.

As the bird trims her to the gale
I trim myself to the storm of time;
I man the rudder, reef the sail,
Obey the voice at even obeyed at prime;
Lowly faithful, banish fear,
The port well worth the cruise is near
  And every wave is charmed.
    —RALPH WALDO EMERSON.

Christian faith is a grand cathedral, with divinely pictured windows. Standing without you see no glory, nor can imagine any. But standing within every ray of light reveals a harmony of unspeakable splendors.—NATHANIEL HAWTHORNE.

The beginning of anxiety is the end of faith; and the beginning of true faith is the end of anxiety.—GEORGE MÜLLER.

Strong Son of God, immortal Love,
  Whom we, that have not seen thy face,
  By faith, and faith alone, embrace,
Believing where we cannot prove . . .

Thou wilt not leave us in the dust:
  Thou madest man, he knows not why;
  He thinks he was not made to die;
And thou hast made him: thou are just . . .

We have but faith: we cannot know;
  For knowledge is of things we see;
  And yet we trust it comes from thee,
A beam in darkness: let it grow.
    —ALFRED TENNYSON.

# FAITH

The man who trusts men will make fewer mistakes than he who distrusts them.—CAMILLO BENSO DI CAVOUR.

Faith in order, which is the basis of science, cannot reasonably be separated from faith in an ordainer, which is the basis of religion.—ASA GRAY.

'Tis not the dying for a faith that's so hard; 'tis the living up to it that is difficult.—WILLIAM MAKEPEACE THACKERAY.

The only faith that wears well and holds its color in all weather is that which is woven of conviction and set with the sharp mordant of experience.—JAMES RUSSELL LOWELL.

Little faith will bring your soul to heaven; great faith will bring heaven to your soul.—CHARLES HADDON SPURGEON.

An undivided heart, which worships God alone, and trusts him as it should, is raised above all anxiety for earthly wants.—JAMES GEIKIE.

Faith is the daring of the soul to go farther than it can see.—WILLIAM NEWTON CLARKE.

He who has conquered doubt and fear has conquered failure.—JAMES ALLEN.

> I will not doubt though all my ships at sea
> Come drifting home with broken masts and sails;
> I will believe the Hand which never fails
> From seeming evil worketh good for me;
> And though I weep because those sails are tattered,
> Still will I cry, while my best hopes lie shattered—
> "I trust in Thee."
> —ELLA WHEELER WILCOX.

Faith is Reason grown courageous.—LAWRENCE PEARSALL JACKS.

It is cynicism and fear that freeze life; it is faith that thaws it out, releases it, sets it free.—HARRY EMERSON FOSDICK.

Dark as my path may seem to others, I carry a magic light in my heart. Faith, the spiritual strong searchlight illumines the

way, and although sinister doubts lurk in the shadow, I walk unafraid toward the Enchanted Wood where the foliage is always
green, where joy abides, where nightingales nest and sing, and
where life and death are one in the presence of the Lord.—
HELEN KELLER.

The only limit to our realization of tomorrow will be our
doubts of today.—FRANKLIN D. ROOSEVELT.

I have never committed the least matter to God that I have
not had reason for infinite praise.—ANNA SHIPTON.

Unbelief starves the soul; faith finds food in famine, and a
table in a wilderness. In the greatest danger, faith says, "I have
a great God." When outward strength is broken, faith rests on
the promises. In the midst of sorrow, faith draws the sting out of
every trouble, and takes out the bitterness from every affliction.—
RICHARD CECIL.

Christian faith is nothing else but the soul's venture. It ventures to Christ in opposition to all legal terms. It ventures on
Christ in opposition to our guiltiness. It ventures for Christ in
opposition to all difficulties and discouragements.—W. BRIDGES.

To worry about tomorrow is to fail of devotion to the tasks
of today, and so to spoil both days.—WILLIAM DEWITT HYDE.

The Stoic bears, the Epicurean seeks to enjoy, the Buddhist
and Hindo stand apart disillusioned; the Moslem submits, but
only the Christian exults!—E. STANLEY JONES.

In actual life every great enterprise begins with and takes its
first forward step in Faith.—AUGUST WILLIAM SCHLEGEL.

Faith can place a candle in the darkest night.—MARGARET
E. SANGSTER.

He who believes in goodness has the essence of all faith. He is
a man of "cheerful yesterdays and confident tomorrows."—J. F.
CLARK.

While Reason is puzzling herself about the mystery, Faith is
turning it into her daily bread and feeding on it thankfully in
her heart of hearts.—F. D. HUNTINGTON.

# FAITH

The errors of faith are better than the best thoughts of unbelief.—THOMAS RUSSELL.

Faith in an all-seeing personal God, elevates the soul, purifies the emotions, sustains human dignity, and lends poetry, nobility and holiness to the commonest state, condition and manner of life.—JUAN VALERA.

Worry is a kind of insult to the Lord. It's like throwing His promises and assurances back into His face and saying they're no good and you don't trust Him.—JOE FLETCHER.

Faith marches at the head of the army of progress. It is found beside the most refined life, the freest government, the profundest philosophy, the noblest poetry, the purest humanity.—T. T. MUNGER.

Desperate days are the stepping stones in the path of light. They seem to have been God's opportunity and Man's school of wisdom.—SELBY CHADWICK.

Browning speaks of "grasping the skirts of God," but no man ever grasped the skirts of God by knowledge alone. Knowledge may have raised his arm, but faith moved his fingers and closed them in deathless grip.—R. O. LAWTON.

Faith is not a sense, nor sight, nor reason, but taking God at his word.—A. B. EVANS.

There are no atheists in foxholes and rubber rafts.—JAMES WHITAKER.

There is not one great American in history who was born in a home of infidelity.—WILBUR M. SMITH.

Faith is the eye that sees Him, the hand that clings to Him, the receiving power that appropriates Him.—J. E. WOODBRIDGE.

Associate with men of faith. This tends to be reciprocal. Your faith will communicate itself to them, and their faith to you. Do your work in a "faith" atmosphere, and you will work at a maximum advantage. You impress others by your own faith, and they will have faith in you only in the degree that you have faith in yourself.—GRENVILLE KLEISER.

# FAITH

Faith is the setting of the entire self Godward.—Bishop Horace Mellard Dubose.

You may be deceived if you trust too much, but you will live in torment if you do not trust enough.—Frank N. Crane.

We master fear through faith—faith in the worthwhileness of life and the trustworthiness of God; faith in the meaning of our pain and our striving, and confidence that God will not cast us aside but will use each one of us as a piece of priceless mosaic in the design of His universe.—Joshua Loth Liebman.

I am trusting Jesus Christ and His righteousness for my salvation.—Hilys Jasper.

> Unanswered yet? Faith cannot be unanswered.
> Her feet are firmly planted on the Rock;
> Amid the wildest storms she stands undaunted
> Nor quails before the loudest thunder shock.
> She knows Omnipotence has heard her prayer,
> And cries, "It shall be done, sometime, somewhere."
> —Anonymous.

Faith is not reason's labor, but repose.—Anonymous.

> If you trust, you will not worry;
> If you worry, you do not trust.
> —Anonymous.

> The Shepherd does not ask of thee
> Faith in thy faith, but only faith in Him:
> And this he meant in saying "come to me".
> In light or darkness, seek to do His will,
> And leave the work of faith to Jesus still.
> —Anonymous.

The skepticism of the twentieth century is different from former types only in its mental shallowness, its insufferable conceit and its academic freshness.—Anonymous.

> Passive Faith but praises in the light,
> When sun doth shine.
> Active Faith will praise in darkest night—
> Which faith is thine?
> —Anonymous.

# FAITH

Isn't it strange how long a night can grow
    Ere morning and the dew?
Isn't it queer how black a cloud can blow
    Before the sun breaks through?
Faith is remembering ere break of day,
    Or ere the storm is done,
That out of somewhere speeding on their way
    Are the morning and the sun!
                    —ANONYMOUS.

Faith is a grasping of Almighty power;
    The hand of man laid on the arm of God;
The grand and blessed hour
In which the things impossible to me
Become the possible, O Lord, through thee.
                    —ANONYMOUS.

God is His own best evidence.—ANONYMOUS.

# FAME

All flesh is as grass, and all the glory of man as the flower of grass; the grass withereth and the flower thereof falleth away.—I PET. 1:24.

Fame is the perfume of heroic deeds.—SOCRATES.

    Only the actions of the just
    Smell sweet and blossom in the dust.
              —JAMES SHIRLEY.

I am not covetous for gold, but if it is a sin to covet honor I am the most offending soul alive. Those who despise fame seldom deserve it. We are apt to undervalue the purchase we cannot reach, to conceal our poverty the better. It is a spark that kindles upon the best fuel, and burns brightest in the bravest breast.—JEREMY COLLIER.

    Nor Fame I slight, nor for her favours call;
    She comes unlooked for if she comes at all.

# FAME

Unblemished let me live, or die unknown;
O grant an honest fame, or grant me none!
—ALEXANDER POPE.

What a heavy burden is a name that has too soon become famous.—FRANCOIS VOLTAIRE.

Who despises fame will soon renounce the virtues that deserve it.—DAVID MALLET.

If you would not be forgotten as soon as you are dead, either write things worth reading or do things worth writing.—BENJAMIN FRANKLIN.

Of all the possessions of this life, fame is the noblest. When the body has sunk into the dust, the great name will live.—FRIEDRICH SCHILLER.

Do good and leave behind you a monument of virtue that the storm of time can never destroy. Write your name in kindness, love and mercy on the hearts of thousands you come in contact with year after year; you will never be forgotten. No, your name, your deeds will be as legible on the hearts you leave behind as the stars on the bow of the evening. Good deeds will shine as the stars of heaven.—THOMAS CHALMERS.

He who would acquire fame must not show himself afraid of courage. The dread of censure is the death of genius.—WILLIAM G. SIMMS.

The surest pledge of a deathless name is the silent homage of thoughts unspoken.—HENRY WADSWORTH LONGFELLOW.

No true and permanent fame can be founded except in labors which promote the happiness of mankind.—CHARLES SUMNER.

It is better to live forever in the grateful memory of one true heart, than to float for a little hour on the highest crest of fame.—CHARLES C. ALBERTSON.

The truly illustrious are they who do not court the praise of the world, but perform the actions which deserve it.—GEORGE HENRY TILTON.

# FAME

Battles nor song can from oblivion save,
But Fame upon a white deed loves to build;
From out the cup of water Sidney gave,
Not one drop has been spilled.
—LIZETTE WOODWORTH REESE.

Fame means nothing to those who take an inward view of life, for they see that at best it is but the symbol of intrinsic worth.—ANONYMOUS.


# FIDELITY

Blessed are those servants whom the Lord, when He cometh, shall find watching.—LUKE 12:37.

Be thou faithful unto death, and I will give thee a crown of life.—REV. 2:10.

Faithfulness and truth are the most sacred excellences and endowments of the human mind.—CICERO.

Fidelity is the sister of justice.—HORACE.

It goes far toward making a man faithful to let him understand that you think him so.—SENECA.

This above all: to thine own self be true,
And it must follow, as the night the day,
Thou canst not then be false to any man.
—WILLIAM SHAKESPEARE.

O Heaven! were man but constant, he were perfect;
That one error fills him with faults.
—WILLIAM SHAKESPEARE.

Trust reposed in noble natures obliges them the more.—JOHN DRYDEN.

The way to fill a large sphere is to glorify a small one.—EDWARD BRAISLIN.

133

# FORBEARANCE

Therefore will the Lord wait, that He may be gracious unto you, and therefore will He be exalted, that He may have mercy upon you; for the Lord is a God of judgment; blessed are all they that wait for him.—Isa. 30:18.

Judge not, that ye be not judged. For with what judgment ye judge, ye shall be judged; and with what measure ye mete, it shall be measured to you again.—Matt. 7:1-2.

I . . . beseech you that ye walk worthy of the vocation wherewith ye are called, with all lowliness and meekness, with longsuffering, forbearing one another in love.—Eph. 4:1-2.

The servant of the Lord must not strive, but be gentle unto all men.—II Tim. 2:24.

The two powers which in my opinion constitute a wise man are those of bearing and forbearing.—Epictetus.

Use every man after his deserts, and who shall escape whipping.—William Shakespeare.

If thou woulds't be borne with, then bear with others.—Thomas Fuller.

It is a noble and great thing to cover the blemishes and excuse the failings of a friend; to draw a curtain before his stains, and to display his perfection; to bury his weaknesses in silence, but to proclaim his virtues on the house-top.—Robert South.

> The kindest and the happiest pair
> Will find occasion to forbear;
> Find something every day they live
> To pity, and perhaps, forgive.
> —William Cowper.

To bear is to conquer our fate.—Thomas Campbell.

Cultivate forbearance till your heart yields a fine crop of it. Pray for a short memory as to all unkindnesses.—Charles Haddon Spurgeon.

We anticipate a time when the love of truth shall have come up to our love of liberty, and men shall be cordially tolerant and earnest believers both at once.—Phillips Brooks.

# FORBEARANCE

To bear injuries, or annoying and vexatious events, meekly, patiently, prayerfully, and with self-control, is more than taking a city.—CHARLES SIMMONS.

If we say apathetically, "One notion is as good as another," we are not being tolerant; we are merely being lazy. Yet if we attempt to force our neighbor to conform to our convictions, we run the gravest of all risks—the risk of violating the rights of others.—JOSHUA LOTH LIEBMAN.

# FORGIVENESS

Forgive our debts as we forgive our debtors.—MATT. 6:12.

And when they were come to the place, which is called Calvary, there they crucified him. . . . Then said Jesus, Father, forgive them; for they know not what they do. . . .—LUKE 23:33, 34.

If we confess our sins, he is faithful and just to forgive us our sins and to cleanse us from all unrighteousness.—I JOHN 1:9.

It is the prince's part to pardon.—FRANCIS BACON.

> Who from crimes would pardoned be
> In mercy should set others free.
> —WILLIAM SHAKESPEARE.

He is below himself that is not above an injury.—FRANCES QUARLES.

He who cannot forgive others breaks the bridge over which he must pass himself.—GEORGE HERBERT.

We pardon in the degree that we love.—FRANCOIS DE LA ROCHEFOUCAULD.

They never pardon who commit the wrong.—JOHN DRYDEN.

The narrow soul knows not the Godlike quality of forgiving. —NICHOLAS ROWE.

Little vicious minds abound with anger and revenge, and are incapable of feeling the pleasure of forgiving their enemies.— LORD CHESTERFIELD.

# FORGIVENESS

It is easier for the generous to forgive than for the offender to ask forgiveness.—JAMES THOMSON.

Pass smoothly over the perverseness of those you have to do with, and go straight forward. It is abundantly sufficient that you have the testimony of a good conscience toward God.—JOHN WESLEY.

Only the brave know how to forgive; it is the most refined and generous pitch of virtue human nature can arrive at.—LAURENCE STERNE.

Humanity is never so beautiful as when praying for forgiveness, or else when forgiving another.—JEAN PAUL RICHTER.

The heart has always the pardoning power.—MME. SOYMONOFF SWETCHINE.

His heart was as great as the world, but there was no room in it to hold the memory of a wrong.—RALPH WALDO EMERSON.

> And if we do but watch the hour
> There never yet was human power
> Which could evade, if unforgiven,
> The patient search and vigil long
> Of him who treasures up a wrong.
> —GEORGE GORDON, LORD BYRON.

> Dear Lord, and Father of mankind,
> Forgive our foolish ways!
> Reclothe us in our rightful mind,
> In purer lives thy service find,
> In deeper reverence, praise.
> —JOHN GREENLEAF WHITTIER.

> My heart was heavy, for its trust had been
> Abused, its kindness answered with foul wrong;
> So, turning gloomily from my fellowmen
> One summer Sabbath day I strolled among
> The green mounds of the village burial place,
> Where, pondering how all human love and hate
> Find one sad level, and how, soon or late,
> Wronged and wrongdoer, each with meekened face

# FORGIVENESS

And cold hands folded over a still heart,
  Pass the green threshold of our common grave,—
Awed for myself, and pitying my race, depart,
  Our common sorrow, like a mighty wave
Swept all my pride away, and trembling, I forgave.
                    —JOHN GREENLEAF WHITTIER.

We win by tenderness; we conquer by forgiveness.—FREDERICK WILLIAM ROBERTSON.

We hand folks over to God's mercy and show none ourselves.—GEORGE ELIOT.

God forgives—forgives not capriciously, but with wise, definite, Divine pre-arrangement; forgives universally, on the ground of an atonement and on the condition of repentance and faith.—RICHARD SALTER STORRS.

Someone asked Luther: "Do you feel that you have been forgiven?" He answered: "No, but I'm as sure as there's a God in heaven. For feelings come and feelings go, and feelings are deceiving; my warrant is the Word of God,—naught else is worth believing. Though all my heart should feel condemned for want of some sweet token, there is One greater than my heart whose Word cannot be broken. I'll trust in God's unchanging Word till soul and body sever; for though all things shall pass away, His Word shall stand forever!—W. M. CZAMANSKE.

There is a noble forgetfulness—that which does not remember injuries.—CHARLES SIMMONS.

He who forgives ends the quarrel.—AFRICAN PROVERB.

The best way to get even is to forget.—ANONYMOUS.

The habit of judging and condemning others is usually a great deal more serious blemish than are the things we so glibly point out as flaws or faults.—ANONYMOUS.

# FRIENDSHIP

A man that hath friends must show himself friendly.—Prov. 18:24.

Greater love hath no man than this, that a man lay down his life for his friends.—John 15:13.

> Those friends thou hast, and their adoption tried,
> Grapple them to thy soul with hoops of steel.
> > —William Shakespeare.

Nature teaches beasts to know their friends.—William Shakespeare.

A friend should bear his friend's infirmities.—William Shakespeare.

Nothing is more dangerous than a friend without discretion; even a prudent enemy is preferable.—Jean de LaFontaine.

A friendship that makes the least noise is very often the most useful; for which reason I prefer a prudent friend to a zealous one.—Joseph Addison.

> On the choice of friends
> Our good or evil name depends.
> > —John Gay.

> A generous friendship no cold medium knows,
> Burns with one love, with one resentment glows.
> > —Alexander Pope.

Real friendship is a slow growth and never thrives unless engrafted upon a stock of known and reciprocal merit.—Lord Chesterfield.

> Small service is true service while it lasts.
> Of humblest friends, bright creatures! scorn not one;
> The daisy, by the shadow that it casts,
> Protects the lingering dewdrop from the sun.
> > —William Wordsworth.

Friendship is Love without his wings.—George Gordon, Lord Byron.

# FRIENDSHIP

The man who has a thousand friends
　　Has not a friend to spare;
But he who has an enemy
　　Will meet him everywhere.
　　　　　—RALPH WALDO EMERSON.

God evidently does not intend us all to be rich, or powerful or great, but He does intend us all to be friends.—RALPH WALDO EMERSON.

We force no doors in friendship, but like the Christ in Revelation, we stand reverently at the door without, to knock. And only if the door be opened from within, may we be welcome in to sup with our friend and he with us.

The glory of Friendship is not the outstretched hand, nor the kindly smile, nor the joy of companionship; it is the spiritual inspiration that comes to one when he discovers that someone else believes in him and is willing to trust him with his friendship.

My friends have come unsought. The great God gave them to me.—RALPH WALDO EMERSON.

O Friend, my bosom said,
Through thee alone the sky is arched,
　　Through thee alone the rose is red;
All things through thee take nobler form,
　　All look beyond the earth,
The mill-round of our fate appears
　　A sun-oath in thy worth.
Me, too, thy nobleness has taught,
　　To master my despair;
The fountains of my hidden life
　　Are through thy friendship fair.
　　　　　—RALPH WALDO EMERSON.

Our chief want in life is somebody who shall make us do what we can; this is the service of a friend.—RALPH WALDO EMERSON.

O how good it feels!
The hand of an old friend.
　　　　　—HENRY WADSWORTH LONGFELLOW.

# FRIENDSHIP

If you would win a man to your cause, first convince him that you are his true friend. Therein is a drop of honey that catches his heart, which, say what he will, is the greatest high-road to his reason, and which when once gained, you will find but little trouble in convincing his judgment of the justice of your cause, if, indeed, that cause be really a just one. On the contrary, assume to dictate to his judgment, or to command his action, or to make him as one to be shunned or despised, and he will retreat within himself, close all the avenues to his head and heart; and though your cause be naked truth itself, transformed to the heaviest lance, harder than steel and sharper than steel can be made, and though you throw it with more than Herculean force and precision, you shall be no more able to pierce him than to penetrate the hard shell of a tortoise with a rye straw.—Abraham Lincoln.

Think of the importance of friendship in the education of man. It will make a man honest; it will make him a hero; it will make him a saint. It is the state of the just dealing with the just; the magnanimous with the magnanimous; the sincere with the sincere; man with man.—Henry David Thoreau.

Animals are such agreeable friends. They ask no questions; they pass no criticisms.—George Eliot.

The friend of my adversity I shall always cherish most. I can better trust those who helped to relieve the gloom of my dark hours than those who are so ready to enjoy with me the sunshine of my prosperity.—Ulysses S. Grant.

Blessed are they who have the gift of making friends, for it is one of God's best gifts. It involves many things, but above all, the power of going out of one's self, and appreciating whatever is noble and loving in another.—Thomas Hughes.

Fame is the scentless sunflower with gaudy crown of gold;
But friendship is the breathing rose, with sweets in every fold.
                                        —Oliver Wendell Holmes.

Lead the life that will make you kindly and friendly to every-one about you, and you will be surprised what a happy life you will live.—Charles M. Schwab.

# FRIENDSHIP

Friendship is the great opportunity to demonstrate our capacity for lofty and ennobling relationships without the motive of selfishness.—ROSALIE MILLS APPLEBY.

Those are our best friends in whose presence we are able to be our best selves.—CHARLES W. KOHLER.

A friend of man was he, and thus, he was a friend of God.—WILSON MACDONALD.

No man can be happy without a friend, nor sure of him till he's unhappy.—OLD SCOTCH PROVERB.

A faithful friend is a strong defense.—ANONYMOUS.

No distance of place or lapse of time can lessen the friendship of those who are thoroughly persuaded of each other's worth.—ANONYMOUS.

A friend is a present you give yourself.—ANONYMOUS.

Before us is a future all unknown, a path untrod;
Beside us a friend well loved and known—
That friend is God.
                              —ANONYMOUS.

They who have loved together have been drawn close; they who have struggled together are forever linked; but they who have suffered together have known the most sacred bond of all.—ANONYMOUS.

Insomuch as any one pushes you nearer to God, he or she is your friend.—ANONYMOUS.

The strength and sweetness of friendship depend on sincerity tempered by sympathy.—ANONYMOUS.

# GENEROSITY

Whoso stoppeth his ears to the cry of the poor, he also shall cry himself, but shall not be heard.—PROV. 21:13.

Freely ye have received; freely give.—MATT. 10:8.

# GENEROSITY

God loveth a cheerful giver.—II COR. 9:7.

O, beware of jealousy; my Lord,
It is the green-ey'd monster which doth mock
The meat it feeds on.
—WILLIAM SHAKESPEARE.

Condemn the fault and not the actor of it.—WILLIAM
SHAKESPEARE.

Oftimes excusing of a fault doth make the fault the worse by
the excuse.—WILLIAM SHAKESPEARE.

Revenge, at first thought sweet,
Bitter, ere long back on itself recoils.
—JOHN MILTON.

Never elated when one man's oppressed;
Never dejected while another's blessed.
—ALEXANDER POPE.

Of all virtues Magnanimity is the rarest; there are a hundred
persons of merit for one who willingly acknowledges it in another.—WILLIAM HAZLITT.

We should be as generous with a man as we are with a picture
which we are always willing to give the benefit of the best light.
—RALPH WALDO EMERSON.

When a man does a noble act, date him from that. Forget his
faults. Let his noble act be the standpoint from which you regard him.—HENRY WHITNEY BELLOWS.

Men might be better if we better deemed of them. The worst
way to improve the world is to condemn it.—PHILIP JAMES BAILEY.

Every man should keep a fair-sized cemetery in which to bury
the faults of his nobles.—JOHN RUSKIN.

O, God! that men would see a little clearer
Or judge less harshly where they cannot see;
O God! that men would draw a little nearer
To one another. They'd be nearer Thee,
And understood.
—THOMAS BRACKEN.

# GENEROSITY

He who is not liberal with what he has, does but deceive himself when he thinks he would be liberal if he had more.—W. S. TULNER.

People are commonly so much occupied in pointing out faults in those ahead of them as to forget that some, astern, may at the same instant be descanting on theirs in like manner.—GEORGE DILLWYN..

> There is so much good in the worst of us,
> And so much bad in the best of us,
> That it hardly behooves any of us
> To talk about the rest of us.
> —ANONYMOUS.

Charity is a virtue of the heart; not of the hands.—ANONYMOUS.

When thou wishest to delight thyself, think of the virtue of those who live with thee.—ANONYMOUS.


# GRACE

Where sin abounded, grace did much more abound.—ROM. 5:20.

My grace is sufficient for thee; my strength is made perfect in weakness.—II COR. 12:9.

By grace are ye saved, through faith—and that not of yourselves—It is the gift of God, not of works, lest any man should boast.—EPH. 2:8-9.

God resisteth the proud, but giveth grace to the humble.—JAS. 4:6.

The word "grace," in an ungracious mouth, is profane.—WILLIAM SHAKESPEARE.

The Christian graces are like perfumes, and the more they are pressed, the sweeter they smell; like stars that shine brightest

GRACE

in the dark; like trees, which, the more they are shaken, the
deeper root they take, and the more fruit they bear.—FRANCIS
BEAUMONT.

I have never known the time when I have felt for a moment
free from a sense of unworthiness, or free from a consciousness of
imperfection and of a sinful nature, but since I have come to
understand that I am accepted of God on the ground of Christ's
righteousness and not my own, and therefore my standing is in
Him and His righteousness and not my own, I have ceased even to
question the fact of my present salvation.—GEORGE C. STEBBINS.

Grace is but glory begun, and glory is but grace perfected.—
JONATHAN EDWARDS.

> Amazing grace! how sweet the sound,
>   That saved a wretch like me;
> I once was lost, but now I'm found;
>   Was blind, but now I see.
> 'Twas grace that taught my heart to fear,
>   And grace my fear relieved;
> How precious did that grace appear
>   The hour I first believed.
> Through many dangers, toils and snares
>   I have already come,
> 'Tis grace that brought me safe thus far,
>   And grace will lead me home.
>                         —JOHN NEWTON.

God appoints our graces to be nurses to other men's weaknesses.—HENRY WARD BEECHER.

The growth of grace is like the polishing of metals. There is
first an opaque surface; by and by you see a spark darting out,
then a strong light; till at length it sends back a perfect image
of the sun that shines upon it.—EDWARD PAYSON.

> His grace is great enough to meet the great things—
>   The crashing waves that overwhelm the soul,
> The roaring winds that leave us stunned and breathless,
>   The sudden storms beyond our life's control.

# GRACE

His grace is great enough to meet the small things—
   The little pin-prick troubles that annoy,
The insect worries, buzzing and persistent,
   The squeaking wheels that grate upon our joy.
                 **—ANNIE JOHNSON FLINT.**

As dew never falls on a stormy night, so the dews of His grace
never come to the restless soul.—A. B. STIMPSON.

# GRATITUDE

O come, let us sing unto the Lord: let us make a joyful noise
to the rock of our salvation. Let us come before his presence with
thanksgiving, and make a joyful noise unto him with psalms.
—PSALM 95:1-2.

Enter into his gates with thanksgiving, and into his courts
with praise; be thankful unto him, and bless his name. For the
Lord is good; his mercy is everlasting; and his truth endureth to
all generations.—PSALM 100:4, 5.

O give thanks unto the Lord, for He is good.—PSALM 107:1.

Every good and perfect gift is from above and cometh down
from the Father of lights with whom is no variableness, neither
shadow of turning.—JAS. 1:17.

The worship most acceptable to God comes from a thankful
and cheerful heart.—PLUTARCH.

      How sharper than a serpent's tooth it is
        To have a thankless child!
           **—WILLIAM SHAKESPEARE.**

Or any ill escaped, or good attained,
   Let us remember still,
Heaven chalked the way that brought us thither.
           **—WILLIAM SHAKESPEARE.**

God has two dwellings; one in heaven, and the other in meek
and thankful hearts.—IZAAK WALTON.

# GRATITUDE

Swinish gluttony
Ne'er looks to heav'n amidst his gorgeous feast,
But with besotted base ingratitude
Crams, and blasphemes his feeder.
—JOHN MILTON.

Many favors which God giveth us ravel out for want of hem-
ming, through our own unthankfulness; for though prayer pur-
chaseth blessings, giving praise doth keep the quiet possession of
them.—THOMAS FULLER.

Gratitude is the fruit of great cultivation;
You do not find it among gross people.
—SAMUEL JOHNSON.

May silent thanks at least to God be given with a full heart;
Our thoughts are heard in heaven.
—WILLIAM WORDSWORTH.

Pride slays thanksgiving, but an humble mind is the soil out
of which thanks naturally grow. A proud man is seldom a grateful man, but he never thinks he gets as much as he deserves.
—HENRY WARD BEECHER.

Thank God every morning when you get up that you have
something to do that day which must be done, whether you like
it or not. Being forced to work, and forced to do your best, will
breed in you temperance and self control, diligence and strength
of will, cheerfulness and content, and a hundred virtues which
the idle never know.—CHARLES KINGSLEY.

Is not that the truest gratitude which strives to widen the
horizon of human happiness which has gladdened us?—BISHOP
HENRY CODMAN POTTER.

If a man carries his cross beautifully and makes it radiant
with glory of a meek and gentle spirit, the time will come when
the things that now disturb will be the events for which he will
most of all give gratitude to God.—ANONYMOUS.

Ingratitude is a mask of selfishness.—ANONYMOUS.

Cultivate the thankful spirit—it will be to thee a perpetual
feast. There is, or ought to be, with us no such things as small

mercies. A really thankful heart will extract motive for gratitude from everything, making the most even of scanty blessings.—ANONYMOUS.

## GREATNESS

Thine, O Lord, is the greatness and the power, and the glory, and the victory, and the majesty: for all that is in the heaven and in the earth is thine; thine is the kingdom, O Lord, and thou art exalted as head above all.—I CHRON. 29:11.

Whoever will be chief among you, let him be your servant. —MATT. 20:26.

Great is the man who does not lose his child's heart.—MENCIUS.

Some are born great, some achieve greatness, and some have greatness thrust upon them.—WILLIAM SHAKESPEARE.

> O, it is excellent
> To have a giant's strength, but it is tyrannous
> To use it like a giant.
> —WILLIAM SHAKESPEARE.

Little minds are too much wounded by little things; great minds see all and are not even hurt.—FRANCOIS DE LA ROCHE-FOUCAULD.

> Unbounded courage and compassion join'd
> Tempering each other in the victor's mind,
> Alternately proclaim him good and great,
> And make the hero and the man complete.
> —JOSEPH ADDISON.

Some must be great. Great offices will have great talents. And God gives to every man the virtue, temper, understanding, taste that lifts him into life and lets him fall just in the niche he was ordained to fall.—WILLIAM COWPER.

The most kingly line in history runs back to but a single successful soldier.—SIR WALTER SCOTT.

> Greatness and goodness are not means, but ends!
> Hath he not always treasures, always friends,

# GREATNESS

The good great man? Three treasures—love and light,
And calm thoughts, regular as infants' breath;
And three firm friends, more sure than day and night—
Himself, his Maker, and the angel Death.
—SAMUEL TAYLOR COLERIDGE.

He who ascends to mountaintops shall find
    The loftiest peaks most wrapt in clouds and snow;
He who surpasses or subdues mankind
    Must look down on the hate of those below.
—GEORGE GORDON, LORD BYRON.

The world knows nothing of its greatest men.—SIR HENRY TAYLOR.

Great men are they who see that spiritual is stronger than any material force; that thoughts rule the world.—RALPH WALDO EMERSON.

Human strength and human greatness
    Spring not from life's sunny side;
Heroes must be more than driftwood
    Floating on a waveless tide.
—HENRY WADSWORTH LONGFELLOW.

Greatness likes not so much in being strong but in the right use of strength.—HENRY WARD BEECHER.

He only is advancing in life whose heart is getting softer, whose blood warmer, whose brain quicker, and whose spirit is entering into living peace. And the men who have this life in them are the true Lords and kings of the earth.—JOHN RUSKIN.

Moral supremacy is the only one that leaves monuments and not ruins behind.—JAMES RUSSELL LOWELL.

No man has come to true greatness who has not felt in some degree that his life belongs to the race.—PHILLIPS BROOKS.

Greatness consists not in holding some high office; Greatness really consists in doing some great deed with little means; in the accomplishment of vast purposes from the private ranks of life.
—RUSSELL H. CONWELL.

# GREATNESS

There are some deeds so grand that their mighty doers stand ennobled, in a moment, more than kings.—NEWTON BAKER.

It is great to be great, but it is greater to be human.—WILL ROGERS.

No saint, no hero, no discoverer, no prophet, no leader ever did his work cheaply and easily, comfortably and painlessly, and no people was ever great which did not pass through the valley of the shadow of death on its way to greatness.—WALTER LIPP-MANN.

Great occasions do not make heroes of cowards; they simply unveil them to the eyes of men. Silent and imperceptible, as we wake or sleep, we grow strong or we grow weak, and at last some crisis shows us what we have become.—CANON WESCOTT.

It is not wealth or ancestry, but honorable conduct and noble disposition that make men great.—ANONYMOUS.

If you would attain greatness, think no little thoughts.—ANONYMOUS.

# HABIT

Train up a child in the way he should go: and when he is old, he will not depart from it.—PROV. 22:6.

Whatever you would make habitual, practice it; and if you would not make a thing habitual, do not practice it, but habituate yourself to something else.—EPICTETUS.

Powerful indeed is the empire of habit.—PUBLIUS SYRUS.

A man should not allow himself to hate even his enemies; because if you indulge this passion on some occasion, it will rise of itself in others. If you hate your enemies, you will contract such a vicious habit of mind as by degrees will break out upon those who are your friends, or those who are indifferent to you. —PLUTARCH.

# HABIT

Cleanness of body was ever deemed to proceed from a due reverence to God.—FRANCIS BACON.

> Neither a borrower nor a lender be;
> For loan oft loses both itself and friend,
> And borrowing dulls the edge of husbandry.
> This above all: to thine own self be true,
> And it must follow as the night the day,
> Thou canst not then be false to any man.
> —WILLIAM SHAKESPEARE.

How use doth breed a habit in a man.—WILLIAM SHAKESPEARE.

A man is first startled by sin; then it becomes pleasing, then easy, then delightful, then frequent, then habitual, then confirmed. The man is impenitent, then obstinate, and then he is damned.—JEREMY TAYLOR.

The chains of habit are too weak to be felt until they are too strong to be broken.—SAMUEL JOHNSON.

Cleanliness is indeed next to godliness.—JOHN WESLEY.

Habit second nature? Habit is ten times nature!—ARTHUR WELLESLEY, DUKE OF WELLINGTON.

It's a good safe rule to sojourn in every place as if you meant to spend your life there, never omitting an opportunity of doing a kindness, speaking a true word, or making a friend.—JOHN RUSKIN.

Seize the very first possible opportunity to act on every resolution you make, and on every emotional prompting you may experience in the direction of the habits you aspire to gain. —WILLIAM JAMES.

The cure of crime is not the electric chair, but the high chair. —J. EDGAR HOOVER.

In company, guard your tongue; in solitude, your heart. Our words need watching; but so also do our thoughts and imaginations which grow active when alone.—ANONYMOUS.

Habit, if not resisted, soon becomes a necessity.—ANONYMOUS.

# HABIT

It is a good thing to admire. By continually looking upwards our minds will themselves grow upwards. And as a man, by indulging in habits of scorn and contempt for others, is sure to descend to the level of what he despises, so the opposite habit of admiration and enthusiastic reverence for excellence impart in ourselves a portion of the qualities we admire.—ANONYMOUS.

# HARMONY

Abraham said unto Lot: Let there be no strife, I pray thee, between me and thee, for we be brethren.—GEN. 13:8.

As much as lieth in you, live peaceably with all men.—ROM. 12:18.

Keep the unity of the Spirit in the bond of peace.—EPH. 4:3.

There is a kind of sympathy in souls that fits them for each other; and we may be assured when we see two persons in the warmth of a mutual affection, that there are certain qualities in both their minds which bear a resemblance to one another.—RICHARD STEELE.

There are souls that are created for one another in the eternities, hearts that are predestined each to each, from the absolute necessities of their nature; and when this man and this woman come face to face, their hearts throb and are one.—ANNA E. DICKINSON.

Only a life built into God's plans can succeed. Half of our discouragements are due to the fact that we are not in tune with the infinite harmony of the Great Power. We should be helpers in building the city of God—a city that will endure when all earthly cities crumble to dust.—BISHOP HEBREBT E. WELCH.

People who are in perfect harmony may be highly entertained by each other's company, even though few words be spoken. And it is such companionship, or friendship, that awakens the best in human nature, that is cherished with the most tender memories for the longest time.—ANONYMOUS.

# HARMONY

Love is the radiant point for all virtues, and to live in accordance with it is to obey all moral laws. But to be benevolent for fear of criticism, to be virtuous for fear of consequence, honest for fear of magistrate, or respectable for fear of society, is not morality but cowardice.—ANONYMOUS.

# HEALTH

O Lord, my God, I cried unto thee, and thou has healed me. —PSALM 30:2.

The law of the Spirit of life in Christ Jesus hath made me free from the law of sin and death.—ROM. 8:2.

I wish above all things that thou mayest prosper and be in health, even as thy soul prospereth.—III JOHN 2.

I have only one counsel for you—be Master.—NAPOLEON BONAPARTE.

There is no kind of an achievement equal to perfect health. —THOMAS CARLYLE.

To man propose this test: Thy body at its best.
How far can that project thy soul on its lone way?
—ROBERT BROWNING.

With rare exceptions the great prizes of life fall to those of stalwart robust physique. Nature demands that man be ever at the top of his condition. He who violates her laws must pay the penalty though he sit upon a throne. Many a man pays for his success with a slice of his constitution.—JULIA WARD HOWE.

Go out doors and get rid of nerves.—FRANK N. CRANE.

A sound body is a fine witness to a good character.—HILYS JASPER.

To insure good health: eat lightly, breathe deeply; live moderately, cultivate cheerfulness, and maintain an interest in life. —WILLIAM LOUDEN.

Optimism itself is half physical; pessimism and low vitality go together.—ORISON SWETT MARDEN.

# HEALTH

A sound body implies a mind free from fear and anger, from negation and weakness.—ANONYMOUS.

# HEAVEN

There the wicked cease from troubling; and there the weary be at rest.—JOB 3:17.

There is a river, the streams whereof shall make glad the city of God.—PSALM 46:4.

The streets of the city shall be filled with boys and girls playing in the streets thereof.—ZECH. 8:5.

Not every one that shall say unto me, Lord, Lord, shall enter into the kingdom of heaven, but he that doeth the will of my Father which is in heaven.—MATT. 7:21.

In my Father's house are many mansions: if it were not so, I would have told you. I go to prepare a place for you. And if I go and prepare a place for you, I will come again, and receive you unto myself; That where I am, there ye may be also.—JOHN 14:2-3.

We know that if our earthly house of this tabernacle were dissolved we have a building of God, a house not made with hands, eternal in the heavens.—II COR. 5:1.

Ye have in heaven a better and an enduring substance.—HEB. 10:34.

Blessed be the God and Father of our Lord Jesus Christ, which according to his abundant mercy hath begotten us again unto a lively hope by the resurrection of Jesus Christ from the dead, to an inheritance incorruptible and undefiled, and that fadeth not away, reserved in heaven for you, who are kept by the power of God through faith unto salvation, ready to be revealed in the last time.—I PET. 1:3-5.

We, according to his promise, look for a new heaven and a new earth, wherein dwelleth righteousness.—I PET. 3:13.

# HEAVEN

There shall be no night there.—REV. 22:5.

The love of heaven makes one heavenly.—WILLIAM SHAKE-SPEARE.

Heaven, the treasury of everlasting joy.—WILLIAM SHAKE-SPEARE.

'Tis expectation makes a blessing dear;
Heaven were not heaven if we knew what it were.
—SIR JOHN SUCKLING.

Earth has no sorrow that heaven cannot heal.—THOMAS MOORE.

My gems are falling away; but it is because God is making up his jewels.—CHARLES WOLFE.

There is a land where everlasting suns shed everlasting brightness; where the soul drinks from the living streams of love that roll by God's high throne! Myriads of glorious ones bring their accepted offerings there. Oh! how blest to look from this dark prison to that shrine, to inhale one breath of Paradise divine, and enter into that eternal rest which unites the sons of God. —SIR JOHN BOWRING.

It cannot be that the earth is man's only abiding place. It cannot be that our life is a mere bubble cast up by eternity to float a moment on its waves and then sink into nothingness. Else why is it that the glorious aspirations which leap like angels from the temple of our heart are forever wandering unsatisfied? Why is it that all the stars that hold their festival around the midnight throne are set above the grasp of our limited faculties, forever mocking us with their unapproachable glory? And, finally, why is it that bright forms of human beauty presented to our view are taken from us, leaving the thousand streams of our affections to flow back in Alpine torrents upon our hearts? There is a realm where the rainbow never fades; where the stars will be spread out before us like islands that slumber in the ocean, and where the beautiful beings which now pass before us like shadows will stay in our presence forever.—GEORGE D. PRENTICE.

# HEAVEN

There are two unalterable prerequisites to man's being happy in the world to come. His sins must be pardoned and his nature must be changed. He must have a title to heaven and a fitness for heaven. These two ideas underlie the whole of Christ's work, and without the title to, and the fitness for, no man can enter the kingdom of God.—SIR JOHN ROBERT SEELEY.

> If God hath made this world so fair
> Where sin and death abound,
> How beautiful beyond compare
> Will paradise be found.
> —JAMES MONTGOMERY.

If there be a paradise for virtue, there must be a hell for crimes.—BERNARD CHANDELLOR CLAUSEN.

The greatest joy that will come to the heart of the saints in heaven will be not to behold the mansions, but the Master. —HILYS JASPER.

Character is not changed by passing into eternity except in degrees. The wilfully wicked on earth will continue so in the other world.—ANONYMOUS.

# HELPFULNESS

I will lift up mine eyes unto the hills, from whence cometh my help.—PSALM 121:1.

Bear ye one another's burdens and so fulfill the law of Christ. —GAL. 6:2.

To him that knoweth to do good and doeth it not, to him it is sin.—JAS. 4:17.

Blessed are the happiness makers; blessed are they that remove friction, that make the courses of life smooth and the converse of men gentle.—HENRY WARD BEECHER.

# HELPFULNESS

God taught mankind on that first Christmas day
What 'twas to be a man; to give, not take;
To serve, not rule; to nourish, not devour;
To help, not crush; if need, to die, not live.
                              —CHARLES KINGSLEY.

Do the work that's nearest, tho' it's dull at whiles,
Helping when we meet them, lame dogs over stiles.
                              —AFRICAN PROVERB.


# HOME

And the officers shall speak unto the people saying: What man is there that hath built a new house and hath not dedicated it?—DEUT. 20:5.

As for me and my house, we will serve the Lord.—JOSH. 24:15.

The first bond of security is the marriage tie; the next, our children, then the whole family of our house, and all things in common.—CICERO.

The voice of parents is the voice of gods, for to their children they are heaven's lieutenants.—WILLIAM SHAKESPEARE.

You take my house when you take the prop that sustains my house.—WILLIAM SHAKESPEARE.

One good mother is worth a hundred school-masters. In the home she is a lode-stone to all hearts and a lode-star to all eyes. —GEORGE HERBERT.

The first sure symptom of a mind at health, is rest of heart, and pleasure found at home.—EDWARD YOUNG.

The poorest man in his cottage may bid defiance to all the force of the Crown. It may be frail; its roof may shake; the wind may blow through it; the storms may enter, the rains may enter,— but the King of England cannot enter; all his forces dare not cross the threshold of the ruined tenement!—WILLIAM PITT, EARL OF CHATHAM.

# HOME

Domestic happiness! Thou only bliss
Of Paradise that has survived the fall.
—WILLIAM COWPER.

Our home joys are the most delightful earth affords, and the joy of parents in their children is the most holy joy of humanity. It makes their hearts pure and good, it lifts men up to their Father in heaven.—JOHANN HEINRICH PESTALOZZI.

He is happiest, be he king or peasant, who finds peace in his home.—JOHANN WOLFGANG VON GOETHE.

'Tis sweet to hear the watch-dog's honest bark
Bay deep mouth'd welcome as we draw near home;
'Tis sweet to know there is an eye will mark
Our coming, and look brighter when we come.
—GEORGE GORDON, LORD BYRON.

The ties of family and of country were never intended to circumscribe the soul. If allowed to become exclusive, engrossing, clannish, so as to shut out the general claims of the human race, the highest end of Providence is frustrated, and home, instead of being the nursery, becomes the grave of the heart.—WILLIAM ELLERY CHANNING.

The strength of a nation, especially of a republican nation, is in the intelligent and well-ordered homes of the people.—LYDIA HUNTLEY SIGOURNEY.

The happy family is but an earlier heaven.—SIR JOHN BOWRING.

A house without a roof would scarcely be a more different home than a family unsheltered by God's friendship and the sense of being always rested in His providential care and guidance.—HORACE BUSHNELL.

A babe in the house is a well-spring of pleasure.—MARTIN FARQUHAR TUPPER.

We never know the love of the parent till we become parents ourselves. When we first bend over the cradle of our own child, God throws back the temple door, and reveals to us the sacredness and mystery of the father's and mother's love to ourselves.

And in later years, when they have gone from us, there is always a certain sorrow, that we cannot tell them we have found it out. One of the deepest experiences of a noble nature in reference to the loved ones that have passed beyond this world is the thought of what he might have been to them if he had known, while they were living, what he has learned since they died.—HENRY WARD BEECHER.

Woman is the salvation or the destruction of the family. She carries its destiny in the folds of her mantle.—HENRI FREDERIC AMIEL.

All happy families resemble one another, every unhappy family is unhappy in its own way.—LEO TOLSTOI.

The woman who creates and sustains a home, and under whose hands children grow up to be strong and pure men and women is a creator second only to God.—HELEN HUNT JACKSON.

Home is a mighty test of character. What you are at home you are everywhere, whether you demonstrate it or not.—THOMAS DEWITT TALMADGE.

When home is ruled according to God's word, angels might be asked to stay with us, and they would not find themselves out of their element.—CHARLES HADDON SPURGEON.

The Crown of the Home is Godliness;
The Beauty of the Home is Order;
The Glory of the Home is Hospitality;
The Blessing of the Home is Contentment.
—HENRY VAN DYKE.

As are families, so is society. If well ordered, well instructed, and well governed, they are the springs from which go forth the stream of national greatness and prosperity—of civil order and public happiness.—WILLIAM ROSCOE THAYER.

America's future will be determined by the home and the school. The child becomes largely what it is taught, hence we must watch what we teach it, and how we live before it.—JANE ADDAMS.

# HOME

So long as there are homes to which men turn
  At close of day;
So long as there are homes where children are,
  Where women stay—
If love and loyalty and faith be found
  Across those sills—
A stricken nation can recover from
  Its gravest ills.

—GRACE NOLL CROWELL.

It is often a long way home, but it is better than a short cut to a mere lodging house.—LESLIE D. WEATHERHEAD.

The hand that rocks the cradle
Is the hand that rules the world.

—WILLIAM ROSS WALLACE.

We need to think of the home as the cradle into which the future is born, and the family as the nursery in which the new social order is being reared. The family is a covenant with posterity.—SIDNEY GOLDSTEIN.

The Christian home with its glowing atmosphere of refinement, joy and harmony is the most cogent force in the building of a community character and the most powerful corrective of low standards of morality.—ISABEL B. CALEB.

No church, nation, or civilization raises higher than the spirit of religious reverence and worship that prevails in the home life of its people. The home that is not genuinely Christian is not a true home. It is God's first institution of human society and is the ultimate basis of society. It is the citadel of both church and state which so nobly serves our social order.—ARTHUR A. HICKS.

The suspicious parent makes an artful child.—THOMAS C. HALLIBURTON.

We need not power nor splendor,
  Wide hall nor lordly dome;
The good, the true, the tender—
  These form the wealth of home.

—ANONYMOUS.

# HOME

The duties of home are discipline for the ministries of heaven.—ANONYMOUS.

Happy are the families where the government of parents is the reign of affection, and the obedience of the children is the submission of love.—ANONYMOUS.

What is home?
A world of strife shut out—a world of love shut in.
The only spot on earth where the faults and failings
    of fallen humanity are hidden under the mantle
    of charity.
The father's kingdom, the children's paradise, the
    mother's world.
Where you are treated the best and grumble the most.
—ANONYMOUS.

# HONOR

Before honor is humility.—PROV. 18:12.

In honor preferring one another.—ROM. 12:10.

Honor all men . . . honor the king.—I PET. 2:17.

What is left when honor is lost?—PUBLIUS SYRUS.

I am not covetous for gold,
But if it is a sin to covet honor,
I am the most offending soul alive.
—WILLIAM SHAKESPEARE.

'Tis the mind that makes the body rich:
And as the sun breaks through the darkest clouds
So honor peereth in the meanest habit.
—WILLIAM SHAKESPEARE.

Be noble minded; Our own heart and not other men's opinion of us forms our true honor.—FRIEDRICH SCHILLER.

I am not bound to win, but I am bound to be true. I am not bound to succeed, but I am bound to live up to what light I have.

# HONOR

I must stand with anybody that stands right; stand with him while he is right and part with him when he goes wrong.—ABRAHAM LINCOLN.

Honor is a harder master than law.—SAMUEL L. CLEMENS (MARK TWAIN).

No amount of ability is of the slightest avail without honor. —ANDREW CARNEGIE.

Honor lies in honest toil.—GROVER CLEVELAND.

Nothing more completely baffles one who is full of trick and duplicity than straightforward and simple integrity in another. —C. C. COLTON.

> It is a vain attempt
> To blind the ambitious and unjust by treaties
> These they elude a thousand ways.
> —ANONYMOUS.


# HOPE

I will hope continually, and will yet praise thee more and more.—PSALM 71:14.

Blessed is the man that trusteth in the Lord, and whose hope the Lord is.—JER. 17:7.

Now the God of hope fill you with all joy and peace in believing, that ye may abound in hope, through the power of the Holy Ghost.—ROM. 15:13.

Christ in you, the hope of glory.—COL. 1:27.

Our Lord Jesus Christ himself, and God, even our Father, which hath loved us and hath given us everlasting consolation and good hope through grace.—II THES. 2:16.

Lay hold of the hope set before us; which hope we have as an anchor of the soul, both sure and steadfast.—HEB. 6:18b-19.

# HOPE

O welcome, pure-ey'd Faith, white-handed Hope,
Thou hovering angel, girt with golden wings!
—JOHN MILTON.

Yet I argue not
Against Thy hand or will, nor bate a jot
Of heart or hope, but still bear up and steer
Right onward.
—JOHN MILTON.

Hope, of all ills that men endure
The only cheap and universal cure.
—ABRAHAM COWLEY.

Hope springs eternal in the human breast:
Man never is, but always to be blest;
The soul, unease and confined from home,
Rests and expatiates in the life to come.
—ALEXANDER POPE.

Hope, like the gleaming taper's light
Adorns and cheers our way;
And still, as darker grows the night
Emits a brighter ray.
—OLIVER GOLDSMITH.

Cease every joy to glimmer on my mind,
But leave, Oh leave the light of Hope behind!
—THOMAS CAMPBELL.

Every gift of noble origin
Is breathed upon by Hope's perpetual breath.
—WILLIAM WORDSWORTH.

The rose is fairest when 'tis budding new,
    And hope is brightest when it dawns from fears;
The rose is sweetest wash'd with morning dew,
    And love is loveliest when embalm'd in tears.
—SIR WALTER SCOTT.

He is the best physician who is the most ingenious inspirer
of hope.—SAMUEL TAYLOR COLERIDGE.

# HOPE

Hope, child, tomorrow and tomorrow still,
  And every morrow hope; trust while you live.
Hope, each time the dawn doth heaven fill,
  Be there to ask as God is there to give.
                 —VICTOR HUGO.

'Tis always morning somewhere.—HENRY WADSWORTH LONG-
FELLOW.

      Open the door of your hearts, my lads,
        To the angel of Love and Truth,
      When the world is full of unnumbered joys
        In the beautiful dawn of youth.
      Casting aside all things that mar,
        Saying to Wrong, "Depart!"
      To the voices of Hope that are calling you
      Open the door of your heart.
            —EDWARD EVERETT HALE.

      Sad soul, take comfort nor forget
      The sunrise never failed us yet.
            —CELIA THAXTER.

      Build a little fence of trust
        Around today;
      Fill the space with loving work
        And therein stay;
      Look not between the shelt'ring bars
        Upon tomorrow,
      But take whatever comes to thee
        Of joy or sorrow.
            —MARY F. BUTTS.

Ne'er was the sky so deep a blue
But that the sun came breaking through;
There never was a night so dark
But wakened to the singing lark;
Nor was there a lane so long
It had no turn for the weary throng;
Nor heart so sad that sometime after
There came no sound or lilting laughter;

# HOPE

And death's not the end 'neath the cold black sod—
'Tis the inn by the road on the way to God.
—CHARLES DUDLEY WARNER.

It is almost always when things are all blocked up and impossible that a happening comes. If you are sure you are looking and ready, that is all you need. God is turning the world around all the time.—MRS. A. D. T. WHITNEY.

When the Psalmist wrote: "Hope thou in God," he gave the world the only ground for hope that exists.—LESLIE D. WEATHERHEAD.


# HOSPITALITY

Oh, that I had in the wilderness a lodging place for wayfaring men.—JER. 9:2.

I was a stranger and ye took me in.—MATT. 25:35.

Be not forgetful to entertain strangers, for thereby some have entertained angels unawares.—HEB. 13:2.

> Our path is clean with sweeping,
>    The gate is opened wide,
> Who knows who may be passing,
>    This way at eventide.
>
> We lit our heart's bright candle;
>    Its beams shine far and clear
> To tell one who may need it
>    That rest and love are here.
>
> We baked the bread of friendship
>    For one may dine thereof;
> And poured in crystal goblets
>    The rare sweet wine of love.
>
> And though we may not know it—
>    We heard it from the wise—
> That often, very often,
>    Come Stars in strangers' guise.
>                    —RACHEL DAY.

# HOSPITALITY

There are those, who, like the seers of old,
   Can see the helpers God has sent,
And how life's rugged mountain side
   Is white with many an angel tent.
               —ANONYMOUS.

Come in the evening, come in the morning,
Come when expected, come without warning;
Thousands of welcomes, you'll find here before you,
And the oftener you come, the more we'll adore you.
               —ANONYMOUS.

# HUMILITY

Pride goeth before destruction and a haughty spirit before a fall.—PROV. 16:18.

The meek also shall increase their joy in the Lord, and the poor among men shall rejoice in the Holy One of Israel.—ISA. 29:19.

Blessed are the meek, for they shall inherit the earth.—MATT. 5:5.

Whosoever, therefore, shall humble himself as this little child, the same is greatest in the kingdom of heaven.—MATT. 18:4.

God resisteth the proud but giveth grace to the humble.—JAS. 4:6.

Humble yourselves therefore under the mighty hand of God, that he may exalt you in due time: casting all your care upon him: for he careth for you.—I PET. 5:6-7.

The eagle suffers little birds to sing.—WILLIAM SHAKESPEARE.

Who builds a church to God, and not to fame,
Will never mark the marble with his name.
               —ALEXANDER POPE.

Thy modesty's a candle to thy merit.—HENRY FIELDING.

# HUMILITY

Beware of too sublime a sense of your own consequence.—
WILLIAM COWPER.

> Soft is the music that would charm forever;
> The flower of sweetest smell is shy and lowly.
> —WILLIAM WORDSWORTH.

Give unto me, made lowly wise,
The spirit of self-sacrifice;
The confidence of reason give;
And in the light of Truth thy Bondman, let me live!
> —WILLIAM WORDSWORTH.

> And the Devil did grin, for his darling sin
> Is pride that apes humility.
> —SAMUEL TAYLOR COLERIDGE.

> Humility, that low, sweet root
> From which all heavenly virtues shoot.
> —THOMAS MOORE.

How like a mounting devil in the heart
Rules the unrein'd ambition! Let it once
But play the monarch, and its haughty brow
Flows with a beauty that bewilders thought
And unthrones peace forever. Putting on
The very pomp of Lucifer, it turns the heart to ashes.
> —NATHANIEL PARKER WILLIS.

> True Humility
> The highest virtue, mother of them all.
> —ALFRED TENNYSON.

My God, give me neither poverty nor riches, but whatsoever
it may be thy will to give, give me, with it, a heart that knows
humbly to acquiesce in what is thy will.—J. E. L. GOTTHOLD.

Humility is perfect quietness of heart. It is to have no trouble.
It is never to be fretted or irritated or sore or disappointed. It is
to expect nothing, to wonder at nothing that is done to me. It is
to be at rest when nobody praises me and when I am blamed or
despised. It is to have a blessed home in the Lord, where I can
go in and shut the door and kneel to my Father in secret, and

am at peace as in the deep sea of calmness when all around and above is trouble.—ANDREW MURRAY.

Meekness cannot well be counterfeited. It is not insensibility, or unmanliness, or servility; it does not cringe or whine. It is benevolence imitating Christ in patience, forbearance and quietness. It feels keenly, but not malignantly; it abounds in good will and bears all things.—W. S. PLUMER.

The truly godly are instinctively humble. There is no humility so deep and real as that which the knowledge of grace produces. —ANDREW MILLER.

People who parade their virtues seldom lead the procession. —ANONYMOUS.

> The parish priest of Austerlitz
>   Climbed up in a high church steeple,
> To be near to God that he might hand
>   God's words unto the people.
> And in the sermon script he daily wrote
>   What he thought was sent from heaven,
> And he dropped it down on the people's heads,
>   Two times one day in seven.
> In his time God said: "Come down and die."
>   And he cried from out his steeple:
> "Where art thou, Lord?" and the Lord replied:
>   "Down here among the people."
>                         —ANONYMOUS.

> Said de ole hoot owl to de whip-poor-will:
>   "You won't sing nothin', and you won't keep still;
> Looks like you'd notice that it would be
>   Polite to let folks listen to me.
> Said de whip-poor-will to de old hoot owl:
>   "You sleep all day and at night you prowl;
> You show your ignorance all complete
>   Interruptin' de music I make so sweet."
> So dat's de way wid man and bird:
>   Each thinks his voice should sure be heard,
> And de most ob us ain't got no more skill
>   Den de ole hoot owl, or de whip-poor-will.
>                         —ANONYMOUS.

# IDEALS

Lift ye up a banner upon the high mountain, . . . ISA. 13:2.

Set thee up waymarks, . . . set thine heart toward the highway,
. . . —JER. 31:21.

This one thing I do, forgetting those things which are behind, and reaching forth unto those things which are before, I
press toward the mark for the prize of the high calling of God in
Christ Jesus.—PHIL. 3:13, 14.

If ye then be risen with Christ, seek those things which are
above, . . .—COL. 3:1.

Fearless minds climb soonest unto crowns.—WILLIAM SHAKE-
SPEARE.

Too low they build who build beneath the stars.—EDWARD
YOUNG.

Still strive to be a man before your mother.—WILLIAM COWPER.

Let us raise a standard to which the wise and honest can
repair; the event is in the hand of God.—GEORGE WASHINGTON.

Happy those who here on earth have dreamt of a higher
vision! They will the sooner be able to endure the glories of the
world to come.—NOVALIS (*pseud. of* FRIEDRICH GEORG VON HAR-
DENBERG).

There is no man, no woman, so small but that they cannot
make their life great by high endeavor.—THOMAS CARLYLE.

Make the most of yourself, for that is all there is of you.
—RALPH WALDO EMERSON.

> Build on, and make thy castles high and fair,
> Rising and reaching upward to the skies;
> Listen to voices in the upper air,
> Nor lose thy simple faith in mysteries.
> —HENRY WADSWORTH LONGFELLOW.

> I held it truth, with him who sings
> To one clear harp in divers tones,
> That men may rise on stepping-stones
> Of their dead selves to higher things.
> —ALFRED TENNYSON.

# IDEALS

Man can never come to his ideal standard; it is the nature of the immortal spirit to raise that standard higher and higher, as it goes from strength to strength, still upward and onward. Accordingly, the wisest and greatest men are ever the most modest. —MARGARET FULLER.

Lofty designs must close in like effects.—ROBERT BROWNING.

Better to have failed in a high aim, as I
Than vulgarly in the low aim succeed.
—ROBERT BROWNING.

Whatever I have tried to do in this life, I have tried with all my heart to do well; whatever I have devoted myself to, I have devoted myself to completely; in great aims and in small, I have always been thoroughly in earnest.—CHARLES DICKENS.

Let each man think himself an act of God,
His mind a thought, his life a breath of God;
And let each try, by great thoughts and good deeds,
To show the most of Heaven he hath in him.
—PHILIP JAMES BAILEY.

All dust is frail; all flesh is weak;
Be thou the true man thou dost seek.
—JAMES RUSSELL LOWELL.

The wisest man could ask no more of Fate
Than to be simple, modest, manly, true,
Safe from the Many—honored by the Few.
—JAMES RUSSELL LOWELL.

O sacred hunger of ambitious minds!—HERBERT SPENCER.

The ideal life is in our blood and never will be still. We feel the things to be beating beneath the things we are.—PHILLIPS BROOKS.

Build thee more stately mansions, O my soul,
As the swift seasons roll!
Leave the low-vaulted past!
Let each new temple, nobler than the last,
Shut thee from heaven with a dome most vast,

# IDEALS

Till thou at length art free
Leaving thine outgrown shell by Life's unresting sea!
—OLIVER WENDELL HOLMES.

I do not prize the word "cheap." It is not a word of inspiration. It is the badge of poverty, the signal of distress. Cheap merchandise means cheap men and cheap men mean a cheap country.—WILLIAM McKINLEY.

Into your hands will be placed the exact results of your own thoughts; you will receive that which you earn; no more, no less. Whatever your present environment may be, you will fail, remain, or rise with your thoughts, your vision, your ideal. You will become as small as your controlling desire; as great as your dominant aspiration.—JAMES L. ALLEN.

Four things a man must learn to do
If he would make his record true:
To think, without confusion, clearly;
To act, from honest motives, purely;
To love his fellow man sincerely,
To trust in God and heaven securely.
—HENRY VAN DYKE.

The hunger and thirst of immortality is upon the human soul, filling it with aspirations and desires for higher and better things than the world can give. We can never be fully satisfied but in God.—TRYON EDWARDS.

Providence has nothing good or high in store for one who does not resolutely aim at something high or good.—T. T. MUNGER.

High aims and lofty purposes are the wings of the soul aiding it to mount to heaven. In God's word we have a perfect standard both of duty and character, that by the influence of both, appealing to the best principles of our nature, we may be roused to the noblest and best efforts.—SAMUEL SPRING.

A goal, to be worthy of us, must be far above our faltering feet. Life is no one day's journey. There will be a tomorrow and our goal must fit that, too.—HAROLD DYE.

# IDEALS

Our ideals are our possibilities.—ANONYMOUS.

We are noble today as our ideals, and tomorrow it may be we shall transcend these. We are as great as our idea of God, and just as little.—ANONYMOUS.

Life that is aimless is both restless and forceless. On the walls of society how many a trumpet hangs, as we saw in the case of young Raimund Lull, useless, voiceless, rusty! it has no lustre and gives forth no music.—ANONYMOUS.

Be your best. The worst disappointment you can experience is disappointment in yourself.—ANONYMOUS.

# IMMORTALITY

And it came to pass on the seventh day, that the child died. . . .
But when David saw that his servants whispered, David perceived that the child was dead. . . .
Then David arose from the earth, and washed, and anointed himself, and changed his apparel, and came into the house of the Lord, and worshipped. . . .
And he said . . . I shall go to him, but he shall not return to me.—II SAM. 12: Portions of verses 18, 19, 20, 22, 23.

If a man die, shall he live again? . . . I know that my redeemer liveth, and that he shall stand at a latter day upon the earth. . . . And though after my skin worms destroy this body, yet in my flesh shall I see God.—JOB 14:14; 19:25-26.

I shall be satisfied when I awake in thy likeness.—PSALM 17:15.

The spirit shall return to God who gave it.—ECC. 12:7.

I am the Resurrection and the Life. He that believeth in me, though he were dead, yet shall he live again.—JOHN 11:25.

He that raised up Christ from the dead shall also quicken your mortal bodies by His spirit that dwelleth in you.—ROM. 8:11.

# IMMORTALITY

Behold, I shew you a mystery: We shall not all sleep, but we shall all be changed,

In a moment, in the twinkling of an eye, at the last trump: for the trumpet shall sound, and the dead shall be raised incorruptible, and we shall be changed.

For this corruptible must put on incorruption, and this mortal must put on immortality.

So when this corruptible shall have put on incorruption, and this mortal shall have put on immortality, then shall be brought to pass the saying that is written, Death is swallowed up in victory.

O death, where is thy sting? O grave, where is thy victory?

The sting of death is sin; and the strength of sin is the law,

But thanks be to God, which giveth us the victory through our Lord Jesus Christ.—I Cor. 15:51-57.

There is in the minds of men a certain presage, as it were, of a future existence, and this takes the deepest root, and is most discoverable in the greatest geniuses and most exalted souls. —Cicero.

Whatever that be which thinks, which understands, which wills, which acts, it is something celestial and divine, and on that account must be eternal.—Cicero.

The mind is never right but when it is at peace within itself. The soul is in heaven even while it is in the flesh, if it be purged of its natural corruption and taken up with divine thoughts and contemplation.—Seneca.

All that lives must die
Passing through nature to eternity.
—William Shakespeare.

To look upon the soul as going on from strength to strength, to consider that it is to shine forever with new accessions of glory, and brighten to all eternity; that it will be still adding virtue to virtue, and knowledge to knowledge—carries in it something wonderfully agreeable to that ambition which is natural to the mind of men.—Joseph Addison.

# IMMORTALITY

The stars shall fade away, the sun himself grow dim with age, and nature sink in years, but thou, My Soul, shall flourish in immortal youth, unhurt amid the war of elements, the wreck of matter and the crash of worlds.—JOSEPH ADDISON.

Why will any man be so impertinently officious as to tell me all prospects of a future state is only fancy and delusion? Is there any merit in being the messenger of ill news? If it is a dream, let me enjoy it, since it makes me both happier and a better man.
—JOSEPH ADDISON.

> Whence this pleasing hope, this fond desire,
>     This longing for immortality?
> 'Tis the divinity that stirs within us;
> 'Tis heaven itself that points out an hereafter,
>     And intimates eternity to man.
>                         —JOSEPH ADDISON.

Disbelief in futurity loosens in a great measure the ties of morality, and may be for that reason pernicious to the peace of civil society.—DAVID HUME.

Had I no other proof of the immortality of the soul than the oppression of the just and the triumph of the wicked in this world, this alone would prevent my having the least doubt of it. So shocking a dischord amidst a general harmony of things would make me naturally look for a cause; I should say to myself, we do not cease to exist with this life; everything resumes its order after death.—JEAN JACQUES ROUSSEAU.

The thought of eternity consoles for the shortness of life.
—CHRÉTIEN GUILLAUME DE MALESHERBES.

I am fully convinced that the soul is indestructible, and that its activities will continue through eternity. It is like the sun, which, to our eyes, seems to set in night; but it has really gone to diffuse its light elsewhere.—JOHANN WOLFGANG VON GOETHE.

When death comes to me it will find me busy, unless I am asleep. If I thought I was going to die tomorrow, I should nevertheless plant a tree today.—STEPHEN GIRARD.

# IMMORTALITY

Either we have an immortal soul or we have not. If we have not, we are beasts; the first and wisest of beasts it may be; but still beasts. We only differ in degree, and not in kind; just as the elephant differs from the slug. But by the concession of the materialists, we are not the same kind as beasts; and this also we say from our own consciousness. Therefore, methinks, it must be the possession of a soul within us that makes the difference.—SAMUEL TAYLOR COLERIDGE.

Our restlessness in this world seems to indicate that we are intended for a better. We have all of us a longing after happiness; and surely the Creator will gratify all the natural desires he has implanted in us.—ROBERT SOUTHEY.

Divine wisdom, intending to detain us some time on earth, has done well to cover with a veil the prospect of the life to come; for if our sight could clearly distinguish the opposite bank, who would remain on this tempestuous coast of time?—MME. DE STAËL.

I feel my immortality o'ersweep all pains, all tears, all time, all fears, and like the eternal thunder of the deep, peal to my ears this truth: "Thou livest forever."—GEORGE GORDON, LORD BYRON.

Everything here, but the soul of man, is a passing shadow. The only enduring substance is within. When shall we awake to the sublime greatness, the perils, the accountableness, and the glorious destinies of the immortal soul!—WILLIAM ELLERY CHANNING.

What no eyes have seen, what no ears have heard—that is the eternal happiness which I expect when I have laid aside my human body.—KARL F. P. VON MARTIUS.

My mind can take no hold in the present world nor rest in it a moment, but my whole nature rushes onward with irresistible force toward a future and better state of being.—IMMANUEL HERMANN VON FICHTE.

Winter is on my head, but eternal spring is in my heart. The nearer I approach the end the plainer I hear around me the immortal symphonies of the worlds which invite me.—VICTOR HUGO.

# IMMORTALITY

When I go down to the grave I can say, like so many others, I have finished my work; but I cannot say I have finished my life. My day's work will begin the next morning. My tomb is not a blind alley. It is a thoroughfare. It closes in the twilight to open in the dawn.—VICTOR HUGO.

All great natures delight in stability; all great men find eternity affirmed in the very promise of their faculties.—RALPH WALDO EMERSON.

I have always thought that faith in immortality is proof of the sanity of a man's nature.—RALPH WALDO EMERSON.

We are born for a higher destiny than that of earth. There is a realm where the rainbow never fades, where the stars will be spread before us like islands that slumber on the ocean, and where the beings that now pass over before us like shadows will stay in our presence forever.—EDWARD GEORGE BULWER-LYTTON.

> There is no death! What seems so is transition;
>     This life of mortal breath
> Is but a suburb of the life elysian,
>     Whose portal we call Death.
>                     —HENRY W. LONGFELLOW.

> Life is ever Lord of Death
>     And Love can never lose its own.
>         —JOHN GREENLEAF WHITTIER.

To those who fully admit the immortality of the human soul, the destruction of our world will not appear so dreadful.—CHARLES DARWIN.

> My own dim life should teach me this,
>     That Life shall live forevermore.
>         —ALFRED TENNYSON.

Life is the soul's nursery—its training place for the destinies of eternity.—WILLIAM MAKEPEACE THACKERAY.

It is simple dogmatism that would deny immortality; on scientific grounds, at any rate, we have not the knowledge to take up such an attitude.—SIR JAMES YOUNG SIMPSON.

# IMMORTALITY

It is a far, far better thing that I do, than I have ever done; it is a far, far better rest that I go to than I have ever known. —CHARLES DICKENS.

The human soul is like a bird that is born in a cage. Nothing can deprive it of its natural longings, or obliterate the mysterious remembrance of its heritage.—EPES SARGENT.

A voice within us speaks that startling word, "Nay, thou shalt never die!" Celestial voices hymn it to our souls; according harps, by angel fingers touched, do sound forth still the song of our great immortality.—JAMES DWIGHT DANA.

I know only scientifically determined truth, but I am going to believe what I wish to believe, what I cannot help but believe —I expect to meet this dear child in another world.—LOUIS PASTEUR, at the bedside of his dying daughter.

Life is a narrow vale between the cold and barren peaks of two eternities. We strive in vain to look beyond the heights. We cry aloud—and the only murmur is the echo of our wailing cry. From the voiceless lips of the un-replying Dead there comes no word. But in the night of Death, Hope sees a star, and listening Love can hear the rustling of a wing.

> Is there beyond the silent night
> An endless day?
> The tongueless secret locked in fate
> We do not know—
> We hope and wait.
> —ROBERT G. INGERSOL, an avowed infidel,
> in an address delivered at the funeral of
> his brother.

The future is lighted for us with the radiant colors of hope. Strife and sorrow shall disappear. Peace and love shall reign supreme. The dream of poets, the lesson of priests and prophet, the inspiration of the great musician is confirmed in the light of modern knowledge.—JOHN FISKE.

In the presence of so many mysteries which have been unveiled, in the presence of so many yet unsolved, the scientific student cannot be dogmatic and deny the possibility of a future state . . . of the things that are unseen science knows nothing, and at present has no means of knowing anything.—Sir William Osler.

It is a great thing to know that if the eternal doors swing open the other way for you, you have a Friend on the other side waiting to receive you.—Dr. Howard Kelly.

The God about whose business I have tried to be busy will not forget to look after mine in any other world to which I may go.—William Rainey Harper.

When one strips himself of all convictions about the future he stops living altogether.—Harry Emerson Fosdick.

That which is boundless in you abides in a mansion in the sky whose door is the morning mist and whose windows are the songs and silences of the night.—Kahlil Gibran.

It is scarcely possible that a misleading instinct would be implanted in all men in all ages.—O. P. Eaches.

The saddest of all failures is that of a soul, with its capabilities and possibilities, failing of life everlasting, and entering on that night of death upon which no morning ever dawns.— Herrick Johnson.

> Beyond this vale of tears,
>     There is a life above,
> Unmeasured by the flight of years;
>     And all that life is love.
>         —James Montgomery.

There is fulfillment of the Easter promise
    Not only in Eternity,
But here and now to lonely, saddened hearts
    Who know their smaller Calvarys.

In better moments of desire and selfless longing
    We pray "Let self be crucified and slain"—
The answer forms a cross, and, prayer forgotten,
    We bear our irksome load with cries of pain.

# IMMORTALITY

But crosses need not end with crucifixion;
  The path leads onward, tinged with gloom,
And those who pray for self-renunciation
  Must follow Christ into the silent tomb.

Yet fetters cannot hold a life surrendered;
  There comes an Easter morning to the soul,
When we arise, all scars and wounds transcending,
  To find the living Christ has made us whole!
                              —ZULA EVELYN COON.

Thoughtful people cannot escape feeling that they were created for an everlasting purpose. They have wants and needs this present world cannot satisfy. They are familiar with thirsts for the unseen, infinite, and eternal. They know aspirations, ambitions and dreams that can never be realized in this mundane sphere. Time is too short for the accomplishment of the soul. —W. H. ROGERS.

Of course, I do not want to go—this is a mighty interesting world, and I'm having a mighty good time in it. But I am no more afraid of going than of going through the door of this study. For I know that I shall then have a spiritual body to do with as I please, and I won't have to worry about the aches and pains of this poor physical body.—OZORA S. DAVIS.

# INFLUENCE

None of us liveth unto himself, and no man dieth unto himself.—ROM. 14:7.

If meat make my brother to stumble, I will eat no flesh while the world standeth.—I COR. 8:13.

He being dead, yet speaketh.—HEB. 11:4.

Their works do follow them.—REV. 14:13b.

The very history of large and public souls inspires a man with generous thoughts.—SENECA.

# INFLUENCE

Wrongs do not leave off where they begin, but still beget new mischief in their course.—SAMUEL DANIEL.

It is certain that either wise hearing or ignorant speech is caught; therefore, let men take heed of their company.—WILLIAM SHAKESPEARE.

> Example is living law whose sway
> Men more than all the written laws obey.
> > —ALEXANDER POPE.

None preaches better than the ant, and she says nothing.—BENJAMIN FRANKLIN.

So act that your principle of action might safely be made the law for the whole world.—IMMANUEL KANT.

We are all of us more or less echoes, repeating involuntarily the virtues, the defects, the movements and the character of those among whom we live.—JOSEPH JOUBERT.

We reform others unconsciously when we walk uprightly. —MME. SOYMONOFF SWETCHINE.

One example is worth a thousand arguments.—THOMAS CARLYLE.

> Were a star quenched on high
> > For ages would its light
> Still traveling downward from the sky
> > Shine on our mortal sight.
> So when a great man dies,
> > For years beyond our ken
> The light he leaves behind him lies
> > Upon the paths of men.
> > > —HENRY WADSWORTH LONGFELLOW.

I am a part of all whom I have met.—ALFRED TENNYSON.

> Those who live as models for the mass
> Are singly of more value than they all.
> > —ROBERT BROWNING.

> Be noble! and the nobleness that lies in other men,
> > sleeping but never dead, will rise in majesty
> > to meet thine own.
> > > —JAMES RUSSELL LOWELL.

# INFLUENCE

No life can be pure in its purpose and strong in its strife and all life not be purer and stronger thereby.—OWEN MEREDITH.

The only way in which one human can properly attempt to influence another is to encourage him to think for himself, instead of endeavoring to instill ready-made opinions into his head. —SIR LESLIE STEPHEN.

No man or woman of the humblest sort can really be strong, gentle, pure and good without somebody being helped and comforted by the very existence of that goodness.—PHILLIPS BROOKS.

> The glory of love is brighter
>   When the glory of self is dim;
> And they have most compelled me
>   Who most have pointed to Him;
> They have held me, stirred me, swayed me—
>   I have hung on their every word
> Till I fain would rise and follow
>   Not them, not them, but their Lord.
>                         RUBY T. WEYBURN.

The imitative faculty is very strong in human makeup, and it has its valuable points and its very weak points. It must be watched or it will make monkeys of us all.—J. B. GAMBRELL.

The depth of one's conviction measures the breadth of his influence.—J. N. HUNT.

A godly life is the strongest argument you can offer to the skeptic.—M. M. BALLOU.

Example is more forcible than precept. People look at me six days a week to see what I mean on the seventh.—RICHARD CECIL.

> They are not dead who live in lives they leave behind;
> In those whom they have blessed, they live a life again,
>   And shall live, through the years,
> Eternal life, and grow each day more beautiful
>   As time declares their good,
> Forgets the rest, and proves their immortality.
>                         —HUGH ROBERT ORR.

# INFLUENCE

It is the law of influence that we become like those whom we habitually admire. Men are the mosaics of other men.—ANONYMOUS.

> This I learned from the shadow of a tree,
> Which to and fro did sway against a wall:
> Our shadow-selves, our influence, may fall
> Where we can never be.
> —ANONYMOUS.

The best way for a man to train up a child in the way he should go is to travel that way himself.—ANONYMOUS.

# JOY

They that sow in tears shall reap in joy.—PSALM 126:6.

The kingdom of God is not meat and drink, but righteousness, peace and joy.—ROM. 14:17.

Rejoice in the Lord alway; and again I say, rejoice.—PHIL. 4:4.

> Silence is the perfectest herald of joy:
> I were but little happy if I could say how much.
> —WILLIAM SHAKESPEARE.

> How fading are the joys we dote upon!
> Like apparitions seen and gone;
> But those which soonest take their flight
> Are the most exquisite and strong;
> Like angels' visits, short and bright
> Mortality's too weak to bear them long.
> —JOHN NORRIS.

False happiness renders men stern and proud, and that happiness is never communicated. True happiness renders them kind and sensible, and that happiness is always shared.—CHARLES LOUIS MONTESQUIEU.

> But pleasures are like poppies spread—
> You seize the flower, its bloom is shed;
> Or, like the snowfall in the river—
> A moment white, then melts forever.
> —ROBERT BURNS.

# JOY

And often, glad no more,
We wear a face of joy because
We have been glad of yore.
—WILLIAM WORDSWORTH

Happiness is not perfected until it is shared.—JANE PORTER.

All who joy would win must share it;
Happiness was born a twin.
—GEORGE GORDON, LORD BYRON.

Desire joy and thank God for it. Renounce it, if need be, for others' sake. That's joy beyond joy.—ROBERT BROWNING.

You were made for enjoyment, and the world was filled with things which you will enjoy, unless you are too proud to be pleased with them, or too grasping to care for what you cannot turn to other account than mere delight.—JOHN RUSKIN.

It is a comely fashion to be glad;
Joy is the grace we say to God.
—JEAN INGELOW.

Joy is distinctly a Christian word and a Christian thing. It is the reverse of happiness. Happiness is the result of what happens of an agreeable sort. Joy has its springs deep down inside. And that spring never runs dry, no matter what happens. Only Jesus gives that joy. He had joy, singing its music within, even under the shadow of the cross. It is an unknown word and thing except as He has sway within.—SAMUEL DICKEY GORDON.

It is not in life's chances but in its choices that happiness comes to the heart of the individual.—ROSWELL C. LONG.

A pleasure shared is a pleasure doubled.—JOHN KIERAN.

It takes so little to make us glad;
Just a cheering clasp of a friendly hand,
Just a word from one who can understand,
And we finish the task we long had planned,
And we lose the doubt and the fear we had—
So little it takes to make us glad.
—ANONYMOUS.

# JOY

When life seems just a dreary grind,
    And things seem fated to annoy,
Say something nice to someone else
    And watch the world light up with joy.
                        —ANONYMOUS.


# JUSTICE

I will defend this city to save it for mine own sake, and for
my servant David's sake.—II KINGS 19:34.

A false balance is abomination to the Lord: but a just weight
is his delight.—PROV. 11:1.

Thus saith the Lord: Execute ye judgment and righteousness,
and deliver the spoils out of the hand of the oppressor; and do
no violence to the stranger, the fatherless, nor the widow, neither
shed innocent blood in this place.—JER. 22:3.

Render therefore to all their dues, tribute to whom tribute
is due; custom to whom custom; reverence to whom reverence;
honor to whom honor.—ROM. 13:7.

Justice consists in doing no injury to men; decency in giving
them no offence.—CICERO.

Justice is the constant desire and effort to render to every
man his due.—JUSTINIAN I.

                    Be just and fear not;
        Let all the ends thou aimest at be thy country's
        Thy God's and Truth's.
                        —WILLIAM SHAKESPEARE.

What stronger breastplate than a heart untainted:
Thrice is he armed that hath his quarrel just,
And he but naked, though locked up in steel,
Whose conscience with injustice is corrupted.
                        —WILLIAM SHAKESPEARE.

Use every man after his desert and who should escape whipping?—WILLIAM SHAKESPEARE.

# JUSTICE

If thou desire rest unto thy soul, be just.—He that doeth no injury, fears not to suffer injury; the unjust mind is always in labor; it either practices the evil it hath projected; or projects to avoid the evil it hath deserved.—Francis Quarles.

To be perfectly just is an attribute of the divine nature; to be so to the utmost of our abilities is the glory of man.—Joseph Addison.

Justice discards party, friendship and kindred, and is therefore represented as blind.—Joseph Addison.

Justice is as strictly due between neighbor nations, as between neighbor citizens. A highwayman is as much a robber when he plunders in a gang as when single; and a nation that makes an unjust war is only a great gang of robbers.—Benjamin Franklin.

An honest man nearly always thinks justly.—Jean Jacques Rousseau.

Whenever separation is made between liberty and justice, neither is safe.—Edmund Burke.

How can a people be free that has not learned to be just? —Emmanuel Joseph Sieyés.

Truth is Justice's handmaid; freedom is its child, peace is its companion; safety walks in its steps; victory follows in its train; it is the brightest emanation from the gospel; it is an attribute of God.—Sydney Smith.

Who is only just is cruel.—Who on earth could live were all judged justly.—George Gordon, Lord Byron.

Justice is truth in action.—Benjamin Disraeli.

Justice is the great and simple principle which is the secret of success in all government, as essential to the training of an infant as to the control of a mighty nation.—William G. Simms.

Justice delayed is justice denied.—William Ewart Gladstone.

When Infinite Wisdom established the rule of the right and honesty, He saw to it that justice should be always in the highest expediency.—Wendell Phillips.

# JUSTICE

God's justice is a bed where we
  Our anxious hearts may lay
And, weary with ourselves, may sleep
  Our discontent away.
For right is right, since God is God;
  And right the day must win;
To doubt would be disloyalty,
  To falter would be sin.
            —Frederick William Faber.

Justice without wisdom is impossible.—James Anthony Froude.

We get back our mete as we measure,
  We cannot do wrong and feel right,
Nor can we give pain and feel pleasure,
  For justice avenges each slight.

The air for the wing of the sparrow,
  The bush for the robin and wren,
But always the path that is narrow
  And straight for the children of men.
            —Alice Cary.

Making life as honest as possible, and calmly doing our duty in the present as the hour and the act require, and not too curiously considering the future beyond us; standing ever erect, believing that God is just, we may make our passage through this life no dishonor to the power that placeth us there.—Anonymous.


# KINDNESS

Be kindly affectioned one to another with brotherly love; in honor preferring one another.—Rom. 12:10.

Be ye kind one to another, tenderhearted, forgiving one another, even as God for Christ's sake hath forgiven you.—Eph. 4:32.

More hearts pine away in secret anguish for unkindness from those who should be their comforters than for any other calamity in life.—Edward Young.

# KINDNESS

So perish all, whose breast ne'er learn'd to glow
For others' good, or melt at others woe.
                    —ALEXANDER POPE.

I would not enter on my list of friends
(Though graced with polished manners and fine sense
Yet wanting sensibility) the man
Who needlessly sets foot upon a worm.
                    —WILLIAM COWPER.

As unkindness has no remedy at law, let its avoidance be with you a point of honor.—HOSEA BALLOU.

Oh, many a shaft at random sent
Finds mark the archer little meant!
And many a word at random spoken
May soothe, or wound, a heart that's broken.
                    —SIR WALTER SCOTT.

Kindness has converted more sinners than zeal, eloquence or learning.—FREDERICK WILLIAM FABER.

No civilization is complete which does not include the dumb and defenseless of God's creatures within the sphere of charity and mercy.—VICTORIA, QUEEN OF ENGLAND.

There is nothing so kingly as kindness.—ALICE CARY.

A timely kindness is a double good.—GEORGE DILLWYN.

If the sum of our unspoken admiration, love, approval and encouragement could find expression, nine-tenths of the world's woes would be healed as if by magic.—MARGERY WILSON.

This day in honor I have toiled;
My shining crest is still unsoiled;
But on the mile I leave behind
Is one who says that I was kind.
                    —ANONYMOUS.

The ministry of kindness is a ministry which may be achieved by all men, rich and poor, learned and illiterate. Brilliance of mind and capacity for deep thinking have rendered great service to humanity, but by themselves they are impotent to dry a tear or mend a broken heart.—ANONYMOUS.

# KINDNESS

Kind hearts are the gardens;
Kind thoughts are the roots;
Kind words are the flowers;
Kind deeds are the fruits.
—ANONYMOUS.

Every moment is the right one to be kind.—ANONYMOUS.

Swift kindnesses are best; a long delayed kindness takes the kindness all away.—ANONYMOUS.

A kind deed often does more good than a large gift.—ANONYMOUS.

Opportunities of doing a kindness are often lost from mere want of thought.—ANONYMOUS.

# KNOWLEDGE

My people perish for lack of knowledge.—Hos. 4:6.

Who is a wise man and endued with knowledge among you? Let him show out of a good conversation his works with meekness and wisdom.—JAS. 3:13.

If you have knowledge, let others light their candles by it.—THOMAS FULLER.

An investment in knowledge always pays the best interest.—BENJAMIN FRANKLIN.

Knowledge is the only fountain both of the love and the principles of human liberty.—DANIEL WEBSTER.

Knowledge increases one's responsibility.—VICTOR HUGO.

To be conscious that you are ignorant is a great step to knowledge.—BENJAMIN DISRAELI.

Knowledge and timber shouldn't be much used until they are seasoned.—OLIVER WENDELL HOLMES.

# KNOWLEDGE

Knowledge is essential to conquest; only according to our ignorance are we helpless. Thought creates character. Character can dominate conditions.—ANNIE BESANT.

The world does not want to know what we are guessing or hoping. It wants to know what we know.—T. ROLAND PHILLIPS.

The larger the island of knowledge, the longer the shoreline of wonder.—RALPH W. SOCKMAN.

The love of God blooms in the lilac, murmurs in the brook, shines in the dawn, sings in the bird. The love of God is the truest key of knowledge.—ANONYMOUS.


# LIBERTY

If ye continue in my word, then are ye my disciples indeed; And ye shall know the truth, and the truth shall make you free.—JOHN 8:31,32.

And the chief captain answered: With a great sum obtained I this freedom. And Paul said: But I was born free.—ACTS 22:28.

Where the spirit of the Lord is, there is liberty.—II COR. 3:17b.

Stand fast, therefore, in the liberty wherewith Christ hath made us free, and be not entangled again with the yoke of bondage.—GAL. 5:1.

No man is free who cannot command himself.—PYTHAGORAS.

No man is free who is not master of himself.—EPICTETUS.

The human race is in the best condition when it has the greatest degree of liberty.—DANTE ALIGHIERI.

Do you wish to be free? Then above all things love God, love your neighbor, love one another, love the common weal; then you will have true liberty.—GIROMALA SAVONAROLA.

License they mean when they cry Liberty!
For who loves that must first be wise and good.
                                        —JOHN MILTON.

# LIBERTY

Stone walls do not a prison make,
   Nor iron bars a cage;
Minds innocent and quiet take
   That for an hermitage;
If I have freedom in my love
   And in my soul am free,
Angels alone, that soar above,
   Enjoy such liberty.
            —RICHARD LOVELACE.

Reason and virtue alone can bestow liberty.—ANTHONY
ASHLEY COOPER, EARL OF SHAFTESBURY.

Men must be governed by God or they will be ruled by
tyrants.—WILLIAM PENN.

An hour of virtuous liberty is worth a whole eternity of
bondage.—JOSEPH ADDISON.

Whatever day makes man a slave
Takes half his worth away.
            —ALEXANDER POPE.

A Bible and a newspaper in every home, a good school in
every district all studied and appreciated as they merit—are the
principal support of virtue, morality and civil liberty.—BENJAMIN
FRANKLIN.

They that can give up essential liberty to obtain a little
temporary safety deserve neither liberty nor safety.—BENJAMIN
FRANKLIN.

A country cannot subsist well without liberty, nor liberty
without virtue.—JEAN JACQUES ROUSSEAU.

O thus be it ever when freemen shall stand
   Between their lov'd home and the war's desolation!
Blest with vict'ry and peace may the heav'n rescued land
   Praise the Pow'r that hath made and preserved us a nation!
      Then conquer we must when our Cause it is just,
         And this be our motto—"In God is our trust."
And the Star-Spangled banner in triumph shall wave
O'er the land of the free and the home of the brave.
            —FRANCIS SCOTT KEY.

# LIBERTY

Thy spirit, Independence, let me share,
  Lord of the lion heart and eagle eye;
Thy steps I follow with my bosom bare,
  Nor heed the storm that howls along the sky.
                              —TOBIAS SMOLLETT.

People never give up their liberties but under some delusion.—EDMUND BURKE.

What is liberty without wisdom and without virtue? Such
liberty is the greatest of all possible evils, for it is a vice and folly
and madness, without tuition and restraint.—EDMUND BURKE.

Freedom has a thousand charms to show
That slaves, howe'er contented, never know.
                              —WILLIAM COWPER.

He is the freeman whom the truth makes free,
And all are slaves beside.
                              —WILLIAM COWPER.

Is life so dear or peace so sweet as to be purchased at the price
of chains and slavery? Forbid it, Almighty God! I know not
what course others may take, but as for me, give me liberty or
give me death.—PATRICK HENRY.

The God who gave us life gave us liberty at the same time.—
THOMAS JEFFERSON.

Freedom of religion, freedom of the press, and freedom of
persons under the protection of the habeas corpus, these are
principles that have guided our steps through an age of revolution
and reformation.—THOMAS JEFFERSON.

Eternal vigilance is the price of liberty.—THOMAS JEFFERSON.

Freedom is so beautiful a word that even if it did not exist
one would have to believe in it.—JOHANN WOLFGANG VON GOETHE.

How does the meadow-flower its bloom unfold?
Because the lovely little flower is free
Down to its root, and in that freedom, bold.
                              —WILLIAM WORDSWORTH.

# LIBERTY

Blandishments will not fascinate us, nor will threats of a "halter" intimidate. For under God we are determined that wheresoever, whensoever, or howsoever we shall be called to make our exit, we will die free men.—JOSIAH QUINCY.

We hold these truths to be self-evident—that all men are created equal; that they are endowed by their Creator with certain unalienable rights, that among these are Life, Liberty and the Pursuit of Happiness. That to secure these rights, governments are instituted among men, deriving their just powers from the consent of the governed.—THE DECLARATION OF INDEPENDENCE.

> Hereditary bondsmen! know ye not
> Who would be free, themselves must strike the blow?
> —GEORGE GORDON, LORD BYRON.

The spirit of liberty is not a jealousy of our own particular rights, but a respect for the rights of others, and an unwillingness that any one, whether high or low, should be wronged or trampled under foot.—WILLIAM ELLERY CHANNING.

God grants liberty only to those who love it and are always ready to guard and defend it. Let our object be our country. And, by the blessing of God, may that country itself become a vast and splendid monument, not of oppression and terror, but of wisdom, of peace and of liberty, upon which the world may gaze with admiration forever.—DANIEL WEBSTER.

Many politicians lay it down as a self-evident proposition, that no people ought to be free until they are fit to use their freedom. The maxim is worthy of the fool in the old story who resolved not to go into the water till he had learned to swim.—THOMAS BABINGTON MACAULEY.

Personal liberty is the paramount essential to human dignity and human happiness.—EDWARD GEORGE BULWER-LYTTON.

Christianity is the companion of liberty, in all its conflicts, the cradle of its infancy, and the divine source of its claims.—ALEXIS DE TOCQUEVILLE.

# LIBERTY

It is rather for us to be here dedicated to the great task remaining before us—that from these honored dead we take increased devotion to that cause for which they gave the last full measure of devotion—that we here highly resolve that these dead shall not have died in vain—that this nation, under God, shall have a new birth of freedom—and that government of the people, by the people and for the people shall not perish from the earth.—ABRAHAM LINCOLN.

In giving freedom to the slave we assure freedom to the free—honorable alike in what we give and what we preserve.—ABRAHAM LINCOLN.

The only freedom worth possessing is that which gives enlargement to a people's energy, intellect and virtue.—THEODORE PARKER.

It is impossible to enslave mentally or socially a Bible reading people. The principles of the Bible are the ground-work of human freedom.—HORACE GREELEY.

There is no liberty to men in whom ignorance predominates over knowledge.—HENRY WARD BEECHER.

In the beauty of the lilies Christ was born across the sea,
With a glory in His bosom that transfigures you and me;
As He died to make men holy, let us die to make men free,
    While God goes marching on.
                                    —JULIA WARD HOWE.

There are two freedoms—the false, where a man is free to do what he likes; the true, where a man is free to do what he ought.—CHARLES KINGSLEY.

Liberty is to be subserved, whatever occurs.—WALT WHITMAN.

There must be no tampering with the delicate machinery by which religious liberty and equality are secured, and no fostering of any spirits which would tend to destroy that machinery.—JAMES, CARDINAL GIBBONS.

Liberty has restraints but no frontiers.—DAVID LLOYD GEORGE.

# LIBERTY

Liberty is not merely a privilege to be conferred; it is a habit to be acquired.—DAVID LLOYD GEORGE.

The spirit of man grows in freedom; it withers in chains.—BERNARD M. BARUCH.

In the moral battle that engulfs the world, we must make firm our faith that the voluntary association of informed, free men is stronger than any police-whipped multitude.—THOMAS E. DEWEY.

When Freedom, from her mountain-height,
   Unfurled her standard to the air,
She tore the azure robe of night,
   And set the stars of glory there; . . .

Flag of the free heart's hope and home,
   By angel hands to valor given;
Thy stars have lit the welkin dome,
   And all thy hues were born in heaven.
Forever float that standard sheet!
   Where breathes the foe but falls before us,
With Freedom's soil beneath our feet,
   And Freedom's banner streaming o'er us?
                    —JOSEPH RODMAN DRAKE.

True freedom consists of the observance of law. Adam was as free in paradise as in the wilds to which he was banished for his transgression.—W. L. THORNTON.

There is a vast difference between toleration and liberty. Toleration is a concession; liberty is a right; toleration is a matter of expediency; liberty is a matter of principle; toleration is a grant of man; liberty is a gift of God.—GEORGE W. TRUETT.

If we define freedom we limit it, and if we limit it, we destroy it altogether.—EDITH NOURSE ROGERS.

Now more than ever we must keep in the forefront of our minds the fact that whenever we take away the liberties of those whom we hate, we are opening the way to loss of liberty for those whom we love.—WENDELL WILKIE.

# LIBERTY

Religious liberty is spiritual democracy.—GEORGE E. STEWART, JR.

The greatest glory of a free-born people is to transmit that freedom to their children.—W. HAVARD.

Void of freedom that would virtue be.—ALFONZE DE LAMERTINE.

No soul forced to live alone is free. We can be free souls only in interaction between souls. There cannot be free souls without free enterprise and there can be no free enterprise without free souls.—WALT N. JOHNSON.

To have freedom is only to have that which is absolutely necessary to enable us to be what we ought to be, and to possess what we ought to possess.—I. RAHEL.

Liberty will not descend to a people; a people must raise themselves to liberty. It is a blessing that must be earned before it can be enjoyed.—ANONYMOUS.

There is no liberty in wrong-doing. It chains and fetters its victims as surely as effect and cause.—ANONYMOUS.

There will be no freedom without democracy, no democracy without God, no help from God unless we make Him the focus of our loyalty and the Source of our strength to whom we will give, "The last full measure of our devotion."—ANONYMOUS.


# LIFE

In Him was life; and the Life was the Light of men.—JOHN 1:4.

I am come that they might have life, and that they might have it more abundantly.—JOHN 10:10b.

I am the way, the truth and the life: no man cometh unto the Father, but by me.—JOHN 14:6.

The gift of God is eternal life.—ROM. 6:23.

# LIFE

It is impossible to live pleasurably without living prudently and honorably and justly; or to live prudently and honorably and justly without living pleasurably.—Epicurus.

My Soul, sit thou a patient looker-on;
Judge not the play before the play is done.
Her plot hath many changes, every day,
Speaks a new scene; the last act crowns the play.
        —Frances Quarles.

I cannot tell what you and other men
Think of this life; but for my single self
I had as lief not be as live to be
In awe of such a thing as I myself.
        —William Shakespeare.

The time of life is short; to spend that shortness basely,
    'Twere too long.        —William Shakespeare.

The web of our life is of a mingled yarn, good and ill together; our virtues would be proud if our faults whipped them not; and our crimes would despair if they were not cherished by our virtues.—William Shakespeare.

The truest end of life is to know the life that never ends.—William Penn.

Though we seem grieved at the shortness of life in general, we are wishing every period of it at an end. The minor longs to be at age, then to be a man of business, then to make up an estate, then to arrive at honors, then to retire.—Joseph Addison.

He lives twice who can at once employ
The present well and e'en the past enjoy.
        —Alexander Pope.

The certainty that life cannot be long, and the probability that it will be shorter than nature allows, ought to waken every man to the active prosecution of whatever he is desirous to perform. It is true that no diligence can ensure success; death may intercept the swiftest career; but he who is cut off in the execution of an honest undertaking, has at least the honor of falling in his rank, and has fought the battle though he missed the victory.—Samuel Johnson.

# LIFE

So quickly, sometimes, has the wheel of life turned round, that many a man has lived to enjoy the benefit of that charity which his own piety projected.—LAURENCE STERNE.

Take care of your life; and the Lord will take care of your death.—GEORGE WHITEFIELD.

To turn all that we possess into the channels of universal life becomes the business of our lives.—JOHN WOOLMAN.

> He that holds fast the golden mean
> And lives contentedly between
>    The little and the great,
> Feels not the wants that pinch the poor,
> Nor plagues that haunt the rich man's door
>         —WILLIAM COWPER.

Act well at the moment, and you have performed a good action to all eternity.—JOHANN KASPAR LAVATER.

> Life! We've been long together
> Through pleasant and through cloudy weather;
> 'Tis hard to part when friends are dear,—
> Perhaps 'twill cost a sigh, a tear;
> Then steal away, give little warning,
>    Choose thine own time;
> Say not "Good night", but in some brighter clime
> Bid me "Good morning."
>         —ANITA LETITIA BARBAULD.

Life is the childhood of our immortality.—JOHANN WOLFGANG VON GOETHE.

Nine requisites for contented living:
> Health enough to make work a pleasure;
> Wealth enough to support your needs;
> Strength to battle with difficulties and overcome them;
> Grace enough to confess your sins and forsake them;
> Patience enough to toil until some good is accomplished;
> Charity enough to see some good in your neighbor;
> Love enough to move you to be useful and helpful to others;

# LIFE

Faith enough to make real the things of God;
Hope enough to remove all anxious fears concerning the
future.—JOHANN WOLFGANG VON GOETHE    .

Life, like the dome of many-colored glass,
Stains the white-radiance of eternity.
—PERCY BYSSHE SHELLEY.

So live that when thy summons comes to join
The innumerable caravan which moves
To that mysterious realm where each shall take
His chamber in the silent halls of death,
Thou goest not, like the quarry-slave at night,
Scourged to his dungeon, but sustained and soothed
By an unfaltering trust, approach thy grave
Like one that wraps the drapery of his couch
About him, and lies down to pleasant dreams.
—WILLIAM CULLEN BRYANT.

Perfect conformity to the will of God is the sole sovereign and
complete liberty.—JEAN HENRI MERLE D'AUBIGNÉ.

There is no heroic poem in the world but is at bottom . . .
the life of a man; there is no life of a man, faithfully recorded
but is a heroic poem.—THOMAS CARLYLE.

One life; a little gleam of time between two eternities; No
second chance for us forevermore.—THOMAS CARLYLE.

Thy life is no idle dream, but a solemn reality; it is thine own,
and it is all thou hast to front eternity with.—THOMAS CARLYLE.

Life is not a May-game, but a battle and a march, a warfare
with principalities and powers. No idle promenade through
fragrant orange groves and green flowery spaces, waited on by
coral muses and the rosy hours; it is a stern pilgrimage through
the rough burning, sandy solitudes through regions and thick-
ribbed ice.—THOMAS CARLYLE.

Life, if properly viewed in any aspect, is great, but mainly
great when viewed in its relation to the world to come.—ALBERT
BARNES.

# LIFE

Life is hardly respectable if it has no generous task, no duties or affections that constitute a necessity of existence. Every man's task is his life-preserver.—RALPH WALDO EMERSON.

Live truly and thy life shall be a great and noble creed.—RALPH WALDO EMERSON.

We find in life exactly what we put into it.—RALPH WALDO EMERSON.

I count life just the stuff to try the soul's strength on.—ROBERT BROWNING.

Life develops from within.—ELIZABETH BARRETT BROWNING.

How good is man's life, the mere living! How fit to employ
All the heart and the soul and the senses forever in joy!
—ROBERT BROWNING.

I have lived,
And seen God's hand thro a life time,
And all was for best.
—ROBERT BROWNING.

We live in deeds, not years; in thought, not breath;
In feelings, not in figures on a dial.
We should count time by heart-throbs. He most lives
Who thinks most, feels the noblest, acts the best.
Life's but a means unto an end; that end
Beginning, mean, and end of all things—God.
—PHILIP JAMES BAILEY.

But life is sweet, though all that makes it sweet
Lessens like sound of friend's departing feet:
And Death is beautiful as feet of friend
Coming with welcome at journey's end.
—JAMES RUSSELL LOWELL.

Life is fruitful in the ratio in which it is laid out in noble action or patient perseverance.—HENRY PARRY LIDDON.

Little self-denials, little honesties, little passing words of sympathy, little nameless acts of kindness, little silent victories over favorite temptations—these are the silent threads of gold which, when woven together, gleam out so brightly in the pattern of life that God approves.—FREDERIC W. FARRAR.

# LIFE

There is not one life which the Life-giver ever loses out of His sight; not one which sins so that He casts it away; not one which is not so near to Him that whatever touches it touches Him with sorrow or with joy.—PHILLIPS BROOKS.

> Be such a man, and live such a life,
> That if every man were such as you,
> And every life a life like yours,
> This earth would be God's Paradise.
> —PHILLIPS BROOKS.

Our todays make our tomorrows, and our present lives determine the bridge on which we must enter the next life.—MINOT J. SAVAGE.

The great use of life is to spend it for something that will outlast it.—WILLIAM JAMES.

The poorest way to face life is to face it with a sneer.—THEODORE ROOSEVELT.

We shall prosper as we learn to do the common things of life in an uncommon way. Let down your buckets where you are.—BOOKER T. WASHINGTON.

The life of every man is a diary in which he means to write one story and writes another; and his humblest hour is when he compares the volume as it is with what he hoped to make it.—JAMES M. BARRIE.

> When the one great Scorer comes
> To write against your name
> He'll write not that you won or lost,
> But how you played the game.
> —SIR HENRY J. NEWBOLT.

Live virtuously, my Lord, and you cannot die too soon, nor live too long.—LADY MARY ANNETTE RUSSELL ("ELIZABETH").

Doing what can't be done is the glory of living.—GENERAL SAMUEL C. ARMSTRONG.

What men need today in this time of trouble is not a way out so much as a way of high and manly living within.—WILMONT LEWIS.

# LIFE

Your daily life is your example and your religion.—KAHLIL GIBRAN.

It may be true that I have much less to live on than I had a year ago, but it is certainly true that I have just as much to live for. The real values of life are unshaken and solid. A financial crisis can rob us of all that we have, but it cannot affect what we are.—CLAIBORNE JOHNSON.

Every life should add to the sum total of the world's sweetness and light.—T. J. HOSNER.

We must make up for the threatened brevity of life by heightening the intensity of life.—JOSHUA LOTH LIEBMAN.

How small a portion of our life it is that we really enjoy! In youth we are looking forward to things that are to come; in old age we are looking backward to things that are gone past; in manhood, although we appear indeed to be more occupied in things that are present, yet even that is too often absorbed in vague determination to be vastly happy on some future day when we have time.—C. C. COLTON.

No man is living at his best who is not living at his best spiritually.—W. MARSHALL CRAIG.

All we can do is to make the best of each day.—EDDIE CANTOR.

The ultimate test of life is the living of it from day to day. —TAUTOMU FUKUYAMA.

> 'Tis not the whole of life to live,
> Nor all of death to die.
> —JAMES MONTGOMERY.

Live blameless; God is near. (Inscribed over the door of the House of Linnaeus, Sweden).

> Life is like a journey taken on a train,
> With two fellow travelers at each window pane:
> I may sit beside you all the journey through
> Or I may sit elsewhere, never knowing you;
> But should fate mark me to sit by your side,
> Let's be pleasant travelers, 'tis so short a ride.
> —ANONYMOUS.

# LIFE

Life is a journey, not a home; a road, not a city of habitation; and the enjoyments and blessings we have are but little inns on the roadside of life, where we may be refreshed for a moment, that we may with new strength press on to the end—to the rest that remaineth for the people of God.—ANONYMOUS.

This is what Christianity is for—to teach men the art of Life. And its whole curriculum lies in one word, "Learn of me."—ANONYMOUS.

> With every rising of the Sun
> Think of your life as just begun.
> —ANONYMOUS.

Life is sweet because of the friends we have made
And the things which in common we share;
We want to live on, not because of ourselves
But because of the ones who would care.
It's living and doing for somebody else—
On that, all of life's splendor depends,
And the joy of it all, when we count it all up,
Is found in the making of friends.
> —ANONYMOUS.

Much as we deplore our condition in life, nothing would make us more satisfied with it than the changing of places for a few days with our neighbors.—ANONYMOUS.

The converted Hottentot in Africa is nearer to the center of life than the most cultured pagan in America.—ANONYMOUS.

To complain that life has no joys while there is a single creature whom we can relieve by our bounty, assist by our counsels, or enliven by our presence, is to lament the loss of that which we possess, and is just as rational as to die of thirst with the cup in our hands.—ANONYMOUS.

# LIGHT

God said: Let there be light.—GEN. 1:3.

The Lord is my light and my salvation.—PSALM 27:1.

The path of the just is as a shining light that shineth more and more unto the perfect day.—PROV. 4:18.

The Lord shall be thine everlasting light.—ISA. 60:20.

Let your light so shine before men that they may see your good works and glorify your father which is in heaven.—MATT. 5:16.

In Him was life; and the life was the light of men.—JOHN 1:4.

I am the light of the world; he that followeth me shall not walk in darkness, but shall have the light of life.—JOHN 8:12.

Christ shall give thee light.—EPH. 5:14.

God is light and in Him is no darkness at all.—I JOHN 1:5.

The first creation of God, in the works of the days, was the light of sense; the last was the light of reason; and his Sabbath work, ever since, is the illumination of the Spirit.—FRANCIS BACON.

Hail, Holy Light, offspring of heaven.—JOHN MILTON.

The eye's light is a noble gift of heaven! All beings live from light; each fair created thing, the very planets, turn with a joyful transport to the light.—FRIEDRICH SCHILLER.

We should render thanks to God for having produced this temporal light, which is the smile of heaven and the joy of the world, spreading it like a cloth of gold over the face of the air and earth, and lighting it as a torch by which we may behold His works.—ARMAND PIERRE CAUSSIN.

Walk boldly and wisely in the light thou hast; there is a hand above will help thee on.—PHILIP JAMES BAILEY.

Light is the symbol of truth.—JAMES RUSSELL LOWELL.

> Light! Nature's resplendent robe;
> Without whose vesting beauty
> All were wrapt in gloom.
> —FRANCIS THOMPSON.

# LIGHT

In Christ man finds the way, the truth, the life. In science he finds the means to walk in the way, to realize the truth, and to enrich the life.—Bishop G. Bromley Oxnam.

Moral light is the radiation of the diviner glory.—Thomas Dick.

The light that shines the farthest shines brightest at home. —Bruce E. Baxter.

> If I stoop
> Into the dark, tremendous sea of cloud,
> It is but for a time: I press God's lamp
> Close to my breast; its splendor, soon or late,
> Will pierce the gloom: I shall emerge one day.
> —Robert Browning.

The light of nature, the light of science, the light of reason, are but as darkness, compared with the divine light which shines only from the Word of God.—J. K. Lord.

There is not darkness enough in all the world to put out the light of one little candle.—Epitaph found on a baby's monument in an old cemetery.


# LITTLE THINGS

He made the stars also.—Gen. 1:16b.

Who hath despised the day of small things.—Zech. 4:10.

Because thou hast been faithful in a very little, have thou authority over ten cities.—Luke 19:17.

Trifles make perfection, but perfection is no trifle.—Michel-angelo.

Little things console us because little things affect us.—Blaise Pascal.

> Think naught a trifle, though it small appear.
> Small sands make the mountain,
> Moments make the year, and trifles, life.
> —Edward Young.

# LITTLE THINGS

Great merit, or great failings, will make you respected or despised; but trifles, little attentions, mere nothings, either done or neglected, will make you either liked or disliked in the general run of the world.—LORD CHESTERFIELD.

There is nothing too little for so little a creature as man. It is by studying little things that we attain the great art of having as little misery and as much happiness as possible.—SAMUEL JOHNSON.

Trifles discover a character more than actions of importance. In regard to the former, a person is off his guard, and thinks it not material to use disguise.—WILLIAM SHENSTONE.

Those who place their affections at first on trifles for amusement, will find these become at last their most serious concerns. —OLIVER GOLDSMITH.

There is nothing insignificant.—SAMUEL TAYLOR COLERIDGE.

Life is made up, not of great sacrifices or duties, but of little things, in which smiles and kindness and small obligations, given habitually, are what win and preserve the heart and secure comfort.—SIR HUMPHRY DAVY.

He that has "a spirit of detail" will do better in life than many who figured beyond him in the university. Such an one is minute and particular. He adjusts trifles; and these trifles compose most of the business and happiness of life. Great events happen seldom, and affect few; trifles happen every moment to everybody; and though one occurrence of them adds little to the happiness or misery of life, yet the sum total of their continual repetition is of the highest consequence.—DANIEL WEBSTER.

The creation of a thousand forests is in one acorn.—RALPH WALDO EMERSON.

Most persons would succeed in small things if they were not troubled with great ambitions.—HENRY WADSWORTH LONGFELLOW.

All common things, each day's events,
That with the hour begin and end,

# LITTLE THINGS

Our pleasures and our discontents
Are rounds by which we may ascend.
—HENRY WADSWORTH LONGFELLOW.

Nothing is too little which relates to man's salvation, nor is there anything too little in which either to please God or to serve Satan.—EDWARD BOUVERIE PUSEY.

There is a care for trifles which proceeds from love of conscience, and is most holy; and a care for trifles which comes of idleness and frivolity, which is most base.—JOHN RUSKIN.

In Life's small things be resolute and great
To keep thy muscle trained; know'st thou when Fate
Thy measure takes, or when she'll say to thee,
"I find thee worthy; do this deed for me!"
—JAMES RUSSELL LOWELL.

The power of little things to give instruction and happiness should be the first lesson in life, and it should be inculcated deeply.—RUSSELL H. CONWELL.

The greatest things ever done on earth have been done by little and little—little agents, little persons, little things—by every one doing his own work, filling his own sphere, holding his own post and saying, "Lord, what wilt thou have me to do?"—THOMAS ANSTEY GUTHRIE.

In the great matters men show themselves as they wish to be seen; in small matters, as they are.—GAMALIEL BRADFORD.

He who waits to do a great deal of good at once will never do anything.—CHARLES SIMMONS.

Sometimes when I consider what tremendous consequences come from little things, a chance word, a tap on the shoulder, or a penny dropped on a news stand—I am tempted to think . . . there are no little things.—BRUCE BARTON.

There are no trifles in the moral universe of God. Speak but one true word today and it shall go ringing on through the ages.
—W. M. PUSHON.

If I can not do great things, I can do small things in a great way.—J. F. CLARKE.

# LITTLE THINGS

It is easier to risk one's life on the battlefield than to perform customary humble, humdrum duties, which, however, are just as necessary to winning the war.—MME. CHIANG KAI-SHEK.

The million little things that drop into our hands, the small opportunities each day brings, He leaves us free to use or abuse and goes unchanging along His silent way.—HELEN KELLER.

> O, what a little thing can turn
> A heavy heart from sighs to song!
> A smile can make the world less stern,
> A word can cause the soul to burn
> With glow of heaven, all night long.
> —ANONYMOUS.

Who doeth small things well will prove to higher trusts most true.—ANONYMOUS

# LOVE

He brought me to a banqueting house, and his banner over me was Love.—SONG OF SOL. 2:4.

I say unto you; Love your enemies.—MATT. 5:44.

God so loved the world that He gave His only begotten son, that whosoever believeth in Him should not perish but have everlasting life.—JOHN 3:16.

Though I speak with the tongues of men and of angels, and have not love, I am become as sounding brass, or a tinkling cymbal.

And though I have the gift of prophecy, and understand all mysteries, and all knowledge; and though I have all faith, so that I could remove mountains, and have not love, I am nothing.

Though I bestow all my goods to feed the poor, and though I give my body to be burned, and have not love, it profiteth me nothing.

Love suffereth long, and is kind: love envieth not; love vaunteth not itself, is not puffed up, doth not behave itself unseemly, seeketh not her own, is not easily provoked, thinketh no evil; rejoiceth not in iniquity, but rejoiceth in the truth; beareth all things, believeth all things, hopeth all things, endureth all things.

Love never faileth: but whether there be prophecies, they shall fail; whether there be tongues, they shall cease; whether there be knowledge, it shall vanish away.

For we know in part, and we prophesy in part,

But when that which is perfect is come, then that which is in part shall be done away.

When I was a child, I spake as a child, I understood as a child, I thought as a child: but when I became a man, I put away childish things.

For now we see through a glass, darkly; but then face to face: now I know in part; but then shall I know even as also I am known.

And now abideth faith, hope, love, these three; but the greatest of these is love.—I COR. 13.

All the law is fulfilled in one word, even this: Thou shalt love thy neighbor as thyself.—GAL. 5:14.

He that loveth not, knoweth not God, for God is Love.— I JOHN 4:8.

Perfect love casteth out fear.—I JOHN 4:18.

All loves should be simply stepping stones to God.—PLATO.

Love is the crowning grace of humanity, the holiest right of the soul, the golden link which binds us to duty and truth, the redeeming principle that chiefly reconciles the heart of life, and is prophetic of eternal good.—PLUTARCH.

Love is the image of God, and not a lifeless image, but the living essense of the divine nature which beams full of goodness. —MARTIN LUTHER.

As every lord giveth a certain livery to his servants, love is the very livery of Christ. Our Savior who is the Lord above all lords, would have his servants known by their badge, which is love. —BISHOP HUGH LATIMER.

Love sought is good, but given unsought is better.—WILLIAM SHAKESPEARE.

# LOVE

When Love speaks, the voice of all the gods
Makes heaven drowsy with the harmony.
—WILLIAM SHAKESPEARE.

Let me not to the marriage of true minds
Admit impediments. Love is not love
Which alters when it alteration finds,
Or bends with the remover to remove.
O, no! it is an ever-fixéd mark
That looks on tempests and is never shaken;
It is the star to every wand'ring bark,
Whose worth's unknown although his height be taken.
Love's not Time's fool, though rosy lips and cheeks
Within his bending sickle's compass come;
Love alters not with his brief hours and weeks,
But bears it out even to the edge of doom.
  If this be error and upon me proved,
  I never writ, nor no man ever loved.
—WILLIAM SHAKESPEARE.

The golden key
That opes the palace of eternity.
—JOHN MILTON.

Thy fatal shafts unerring move,
I bow before thine altar, Love.
—TOBIAS SMOLLETT.

Human things must be known to be loved; but Divine things
must be loved to be known.—BLAISE PASCAL.

The pains of love be sweeter far
Than all other pleasures are.
—JOHN DRYDEN.

Force may subdue, but love gains, and he who forgives first
wins the laurel.—WILLIAM PENN.

We are shaped and fashioned by what we love.—JOHANN
WOLFGANG VON GOETHE.

Mightier far
Than strength of nerve and sinew, or the sway

# LOVE

Of magic potent over sun and star
    Is love.

                        —WILLIAM WORDSWORTH.

There is a comfort and a strength in love;
'Twill make a thing endurable, which else
Would overset the brain, or break the heart.

                        —WILLIAM WORDSWORTH.

The rose is sweetest wash'd with morning dew,
    And Love is loveliest when embalm'd in tears.

                        —SIR WALTER SCOTT.

In peace, Love tunes the shepherd's reed;
In war, he mounts the warrior's steed;
In halls, in gay attire is seen;
In hamlets, dances on the green.
Love rules the court, the camp, the grove,
And man below and saints above;
For love is heaven and heaven is love.

                        —SIR WALTER SCOTT.

True Love's the gift which God has given
To man alone beneath the heaven:
    It is not fantasy's hot fire,
        Whose wishes soon as granted fly;
    It liveth not in fierce desire,
        With dead desire it doth not die;
It is the secret sympathy
The silver link, the silken tie,
Which heart to heart and mind to mind
In body and in soul can bind.

                        —SIR WALTER SCOTT.

In many ways doth the full heart reveal
The presence of the love it would conceal.

                        —SAMUEL TAYLOR COLERIDGE.

Love is indestructible;
Its holy flame forever burneth;
From heaven it came, to heaven returneth.

                        —ROBERT SOUTHEY.

# LOVE

Where there is room in the heart there is always room in the house.—SIR THOMAS MOORE.

> The heart that has truly loved never forgets,
>   But as truly loves on to the close;
> As the sunflower turns on her god when he sets
> The same look which she turn'd when he rose.
> —THOMAS MOORE.

Our affections are our life. We live by them. They supply our warmth.—WILLIAM ELLERY CHANNING.

Love is never lost. If not reciprocated it will flow back and soften and purify the heart.—WASHINGTON IRVING.

Instead of allowing yourself to be so unhappy, just let your love grow as God wants it to grow; seek goodness in others, love more persons more; love them more impersonally, more unselfishly, without thought of return. The return, never fear, will take care of itself.—HENRY DRUMMOND.

Without distinction, without calculation, without procrastination, Love. Lavish it upon the poor, where it is very easy; especially upon the rich, who often need it most; most of all, upon our equals, where it is very difficult, and for whom perhaps we each do least of all.—HENRY DRUMMOND.

Love is ever the beginning of Knowledge as fire is of light. —THOMAS CARLYLE.

Life is the flower of which love is the honey.—VICTOR HUGO.

The greatest happiness of life is the conviction that we are loved—loved for ourselves, or rather, loved in spite of ourselves. —VICTOR HUGO.

It seems to me that the coming of love is like the coming of spring—the date is not to be reckoned by the calendar. It may be slow and gradual; it may be quick and sudden. But in the morning, when we wake and recognize a change in the world without, verdure on the trees, blossoms on the sward, warmth in the sunshine, music in the air, we say spring has come.—EDWARD GEORGE BULWER-LYTTON.

# LOVE

It is a beautiful necessity of our nature to love something.
—Douglas William Jerrold.

If there is anything that keeps the mind open to angel visits,
and repels the ministry of evil, it is pure human love.—Nathaniel
Parker Willis.

Talk not of wasted affection; affection never was wasted;
If it enrich not the heart of another, its waters returning
Back to their springs, like the rain, shall fill them full
of refreshment. —Henry Wadsworth Longfellow.

Oh, how skilful grows the hand
That obeyeth love's command;
It is the heart, and not the brain
That to the highest doth attain,
And he who follows love's behest
Far exceedeth all the rest.
—Henry Wadsworth Longfellow.

When we climb to Heaven, 'tis on the rounds of love to men.
—John Greenleaf Whittier.

O Brother Man, fold to thy heart thy brother;
Where pity dwells, the love of God is there;
To worship rightfully is to love each other,
Each smile a psalm, each kindly deed a prayer.
—John Greenleaf Whittier.

God, from a beautiful necessity, is Love.—Martin Farquhar
Tupper.

How do I love thee? Let me count the ways.
I love thee to the depth and breadth and height
My soul can reach, when feeling out of sight
For ends of Being and ideal Grace.
I love thee to the level of everyday's
Most quiet need, by sun and candlelight.
I love thee freely, as men strive for Right;
I love thee purely, as they turn from Praise.
I love thee with the passion put to use
In my old griefs, and with my childhood's faith.
I love thee with a love I seemed to lose

# LOVE

With my lost saints,—I love thee with the breath,
Smiles, tears, of all my life!—and, if God choose,
I shall but love thee better after death.
                    —ELIZABETH BARRETT BROWNING.

We never know how much one loves till we know how much
he is willing to endure and suffer for us; and it is the suffering
element that measures love. The characters that are great, must,
of necessity, be characters that shall be willing, patient and strong
to endure for others. To hold our nature in the willing service of
another, is the divine idea of manhood, of the human character.
—HENRY WARD BEECHER.

Of all earthly music that which reaches farthest into heaven
is the beating of a truly loving heart.—HENRY WARD BEECHER.

That love for one from which there doth not spring
Wide love for all is but a worthless thing.
                    —JAMES RUSSELL LOWELL.

There is nothing so loyal as love.—ALICE CARY.

Where love is, there is God also.—LEO TOLSTOI.

Hope is like a harebell, trembling from its birth;
Love is like a rose, the joy of all the earth;
Faith is like a lily, lifted high and white,
Love is like a lovely rose; the world's delight.
Harebells and sweet lilies show a thornless growth,
But the rose with all its thorns excels them both.
                    —CHRISTINA GEORGINA ROSSETTI.

For our absent loved ones, we implore Thee,
That we may remain worthy of their love.
                    —ROBERT LOUIS STEVENSON.

To love as Christ loves is to let our love be a practical and
not a sentimental thing.—SIR CHARLES VILLIERS STANFORD.

Hide in your heart a bitter thought,
    Still it has power to blight;
Think Love, although you speak it not,
    It gives the world more light.
                    —ELLA WHEELER WILCOX.

# LOVE

Nobody will know what you mean by saying that "God is love" unless you act it as well.—LAWRENCE PEARSALL JACKS.

Love . . . is like a beautiful flower which I may not touch, but whose fragrance makes the garden a place of delight just the same.—HELEN KELLER.

Lacking the fundamental philosophy of love, the life of man becomes little more than a brutish adventure in time—and the peace and unity of nations little more than a dream and a delusion.—LOUIS BROMFIELD.

There is a land of the living and a land of the dead, and the bridge is love.—THORNTON WILDER.

The heart will commonly govern the head; and any strong passion, set the wrong way, will soon infatuate even the wisest of men; therefore, the first part of wisdom is to watch the affections.—DANIEL WATERLAND.

I am not one of those who do not believe in love at first sight, but I believe in taking the second look.—HENRY VINCENT.

Love is the dove of peace that soars out on the wings of the morning to greater spiritual heights. It is the angel's flight to a higher world of beauty, lifting life from its dust to meet the sunrise of God. It is beauty incarnated, kindness glorified, and goodness sanctified.—ROSALIE MILLS APPLEBY.

How often a new affection makes a new man. The sordid becomes liberal; the cowering heroic; the frivolous girl, the steadfast martyr of patience and ministration, transfigured by deathless love.—E. H. CHAPIN.

Love is the purification of the heart from self. It strengthens and ennobles the character, gives a higher motive and a nobler aim to every action of life, and makes both man and woman spring, noble and courageous; and the power to love truly and devotedly is the noblest gift, with which a human being can be endowed; but it is a sacred fire that must not be burned to idols.—GERALDINE ENDSOR.

# LOVE

Whatever of outward service or obedience we render to God or man, if love is withheld, the law is not fulfilled.—F. B. Mayer.

God hears no sweeter music than the cracked chimes of the courageous human spirit ringing in imperfect acknowledgment of His perfect love.—Joshua Loth Liebman.

By the law of love, above every other law, men ought to live. It provides the constraining dynamic for spiritual and moral achievement. God gave the law and to live by it is to live on the highest level of human experience.—Clifton J. Allen.

Keep love in your life, my friend,
    If you would have perfect joy;
Keep love, never let her depart—
    For who would his life destroy?
For life's no longer than love, my friend;
When love is no more, 'tis the journey's end,
And Regret and Fear will your way attend—
Keep love in your life, my friend.

Keep love in your life alway,
    Though tempted to bid her go;
Keep love the bride of your heart,
    If you would a true life know.
For life's no longer than love, I say;
With the end of love comes the close of day,
And the chill of death 'mid the shadows gray—
Keep love in your life alway.
                    —Thomas Curtis Clark.

To love abundantly is to live abundantly, and to love forever is to live forever.—Anonymous.

The love that kept us through the passing night
Will guide and keep us still.      —Anonymous.

Hidden and deep and never dry,
    Or flowing or at rest,
A living spring of love doth lie
    In every human breast.
All else may fail, that soothes the heart,
All, save that fount alone;

# LOVE

With that and life, we never part,
For life and love are one.
—ANONYMOUS.

Love is the key to the universe which unlocks all doors.—
ANONYMOUS.

Love is the only service that power cannot command and
money cannot buy.—ANONYMOUS.

If in the world one heart does beat,
    Does beat for me and only me,
Oh, then 'twere sweet, dear love, how sweet!
    To breathe—to be.

If in the world one voice alone,
    Does call for me, and only me,
How precious has this poor life grown,
    To be implored of thee!
—ANONYMOUS.

Love is the filling from one's own
    Another's cup;
Love is the daily laying down
    And taking up;
A choosing of the stony path
    Through each new day
That other feet may tread with ease
    A smoother way.
Love is not blind, but looks abroad
    Through other eyes;
And asks not, "Must I give?" but
    "May I sacrifice?"
Love hides its grief, that other hearts
    And lips may sing;
And burdened walks, that other lives
    May buoyant wing.
Hast thou a love like this
    Within thy soul?
'Twill crown thy life with bliss
    When thou dost reach the goal.
—ANONYMOUS.

# MAN

The Lord God formed man of the dust of the earth and breathed into his nostrils the breath of life and man became a living soul.—Gen. 2:7.

What is man that thou art mindful of him?—Heb. 2:6.

The way of a superior man is threefold; virtuous, he is free from anxieties; wise, he is free from perplexities; bold, he is free from fear.—Confucius.

Surely, if all the world was made for man, then man was made for more than the world.—Phillipe de Mornay, Seigneur du Plessis-Marly.

Whoever considers the study of anatomy, I believe will never be an atheist; the frame of man's body, and coherence of his parts, being so strange and paradoxical, that I hold it to be the greatest miracle of nature.—Edward Herbert, Lord of Cherbury.

> What a piece of work is man!
> How noble in reason!
> How infinite in faculties!
> In form and moving
> How express and admirable!
> In action, how like an angel!
> In apprehension, how like a god!
> —William Shakespeare.

The proper study of mankind is man.—Alexander Pope.

One can not always be a hero, but one can always be a man.—Johann Wolfgang von Goethe.

Show me the man you honor, and I will know what kind of a man you are, for it shows me what your ideal of manhood is, and what kind of a man you long to be.—Thomas Carlyle.

The older I grow, and I now stand on the brink of eternity —the more comes back to me that sentence in the Catechism I learned when a child, and the fuller and deeper its meaning becomes: "What is the chief end of man? To glorify God and enjoy him forever."—Thomas Carlyle.

# MAN

A man is like a bit of Labrador spur, which has no luster as you turn it in your hand until you come to a particular angle; then it shows deep and beautiful colors.—RALPH WALDO EMERSON.

The superior man is he who develops in harmonious proportions, his moral, intellectual, and physical nature. This should be the end at which men of all classes should aim, and it is this only which constitutes real greatness.—DOUGLAS WILLIAM JERROLD.

When faith is lost and honor dies, the man is dead.—JOHN GREENLEAF WHITTIER.

Man himself is the crowning wonder of creation; the study of his nature the noblest study the world affords.—WILLIAM EWART GLADSTONE.

In these two things the greatness of man consists: to have God so dwelling in us as to impart his character to us, and to have him so dwelling in us that we recognize his presence, and know that we are his, and he is ours. The one is salvation; the other, the assurance of it.—FREDERICK WILLIAM ROBERTSON.

I mean to make myself a man, and if I succeed in that, I shall succeed in everything.—JAMES A. GARFIELD.

Sweating slums, a sense of semi-slavery in labor must go. We must cultivate a sense of manhood by treating men as men.—DAVID LLOYD GEORGE.

We can only change the world by changing men.—CHARLES WELLS.

'Tis better that a man's own works than another man's words should praise him.—ROGER L'ESTRANGE.

Man is greater than a world—than systems of worlds; there is more mystery in the union of soul with body than in the creation of a universe.—HENRY GILES.

We read quite clearly the blueprint of our souls, and yet fail miserably to translate its perfect proportions into the reality of our lives. Spiritual complacency is the main sin of mankind. Have we ever been fervently and religiously grateful for every breath we draw? Have we ever seriously tried to dig up a piece of this old earth and to plant anew. Choose whatever language you wish and whatever terms you like best; make your conclusions as broad and as unorthodox as you please; even in this stream-lined, superbombed age, Godly men are needed!—GERHARD FRIEDRICH.

God send us men whose aim will be
Not to defend some ancient creed,
But to live out the laws of Right
In every thought, and word and deed.
God send us men alert and quick
His loft precepts to translate,
Until the laws of Christ become
The laws and habits of the State.
God send us men! God send us men!
Patient, courageous, strong and true;
With vision clear and mind equipped
His will to learn, His word to do.
God send us men with hearts ablaze,
All truth to love, all wrong to hate;
These are the patriots nations need,
These are the bulwarks of the State.
                    —F. J. GILMAN.

We need not worry so much about what man descends from —it's what he descends to that shames the human race.—ANONY-MOUS.

Nobody knows the age of the human race, but all agree that it is old enough to know better.—ANONYMOUS.

# MEDITATION

Let the words of my mouth and the meditations of my heart, be acceptable in thy sight, O Lord, my Strength and my Redeemer.—PSALM 19:14.

# MEDITATION

As he thinketh in his heart, so is he.—PROV. 23, 7.

A good man, out of the treasure of his heart, bringeth forth that which is good; and an evil man, out of the treasure of his heart, bringeth forth that which is evil: for of the abundance of the heart the mouth speaketh.—LUKE 7:45.

Let this mind be in you which was also in Christ Jesus.— PHIL. 2:5.

The happiness of your life depends upon the quality of your thoughts, therefore, guard accordingly; and take care that you entertain no notion unsuitable to virtue and reasonable nature.— MARCUS ANTONIUS.

The reflections on a day well spent furnish us with joys more pleasing than ten thousand triumphs.—THOMAS À KEMPIS.

They are never alone who are accompanied by noble thoughts. —SIR PHILIP SIDNEY.

In order to improve the mind, we ought less to learn than to contemplate.—RENÉ DESCARTES.

> Millions of spiritual creatures walk the earth
> Unseen, both when we wake and when we sleep.
> —JOHN MILTON.

> If thou thinkest twice before thou speakest once,
> Thou wilt speak twice the better for it.
> —WILLIAM PENN.

Toleration has never been the cause of civil wars; while, on the contrary, persecution has covered the earth with blood and carnage.—FRANCOIS VOLTAIRE.

The more accurately we search into the human mind, the stronger traces we everywhere find of the wisdom of Him who made it.—EDMUND BURKE.

God delights in true, earnest thinking.—TIMOTHY DWIGHT.

The closet and the study—these are the two corners of Eden left to the world and the two radiant points from which the light of heaven most streams out over the earth.—TIMOTHY DWIGHT.

# MEDITATION

Every man has some peculiar train of thought which he falls back upon when he is alone. This, to a great degree, moulds the man.—DUGALD STEWART.

Recollection is the only paradise from which we cannot be turned out.—JEAN PAUL RICHTER.

> To me the meanest flower that blows can give
> Thoughts that do often lie too deep for tears.
> —WILLIAM WORDSWORTH.

> . . . That blessed mood,
> In which the burden of the mystery,
> In which the heavy and the weary weight
> Of all this unintelligible world,
> Is lightened:—that serene and blessed mood,
> In which the affections gently lead us on,—
> Until, the breath of this corporeal frame
> And even the motion of our human blood
> Almost suspended, we are laid asleep
> In body, and become a living soul:
> While with an eye made quiet by the power
> Of harmony, and the deep power of joy,
> We see into the life of things.
> —WILLIAM WORDSWORTH.

The most important thought I ever had was that of my individual responsibility toward God.—DANIEL WEBSTER.

Evil is wrought by want of thought as well as by want of heart.—THOMAS HOOD.

It is the hardest thing in the world to be a good thinker without being a good self.—ANTHONY ASHLEY COOPER, EARL OF SHAFTESBURY.

There is a time in the lives of most of us, when despondent of all joy in an earthly future, and tortured by conflicts between inclinations and duty, we transfer all the passion and fervor of our troubled souls to enthusiastic yearnings for the divine love, looking to its mercy, and taking thence the only hopes that can cheer—the only strength that can sustain us.—EDWARD GEORGE BULWER-LYTTON.

# MEDITATION

Great men are they who see that spiritual is stronger than any material force—that thoughts rule the world.—Ralph Waldo Emerson.

Press on! for it is godlike to unloose the spirit and forget yourself in thought.—Nathaniel Parker Willis.

> Where'er a noble deed is wrought,
> Where'er is spoken a noble thought,
> Our hearts in glad surprise
> To higher levels rise.
> —Henry Wadsworth Longfellow.

Earth changes, but the soul and God stand sure.—Robert Browning.

Reflect upon your present blessings, of which every man has many; not on your past misfortune, of which all men have some.—Charles Dickens.

So it is that men sigh on, not knowing what the soul wants, but only that it needs something. Our yearnings are homesickness for heaven. Our sighings are sighings for God just as children that cry themselves to sleep away from home, and sob in their slumber, not knowing that they sob for their parents. The soul's inarticulate moanings are the affections, yearning for the Infinite, and having no one to tell them what it is that ails them.—Henry Ward Beecher.

It is not the number of books you read, nor the variety of sermons you hear, nor the amount of religious conversations in which you mix, but it is the frequency and earnestness with which you meditate on these things till the truth of them become your own and part of your being, that ensures your growth.—Frederick William Robertson.

Associate reverently, and as much as you can, with your loftiest thoughts.—Henry David Thoreau.

Great truths are portions of the soul of man; great souls are portions of eternity.—James Russell Lowell.

# MEDITATION

Great thoughts are blessed guests, and should be heartily welcomed, well fed and much sought after. Like rose leaves, they give out a sweet smell if laid up in the jar of memory.—CHARLES HADDON SPURGEON.

We thank Thee for this place in which we dwell; for the love which unites us; for the peace that is accorded us; for the hope with which we expect the morrow; for the wealth, the work, the food and the bright skies that make our lives delightful; for our friends in all parts of the earth, and our earthly helpers in this land. Help us to repay in service one to another the debt of Thine unmerited benefits and mercies. Grant that we may be set free from the fear of vicissitudes and death, may finish what remains of our course without dishonor to ourselves or hurt to others, and give at last rest to the weary.—ROBERT LOUIS STEVENSON.

Keep your mind on the great and splendid things you would like to do and then, as the days go gliding by you will find yourself unconsciously seizing the opportunities that are required for the fulfillment of your desire. Picture in your mind the able, earnest useful person you desire to be, and the thought you hold is hourly transforming you into that particular individual you so admire.—ELBERT HUBBARD.

Garner up pleasant thoughts in your lives; for pleasant thoughts make pleasant lives.—SIR GEORGE HUBERT WILKINS.

Christ had something to say about economics. He said, "lay not up for yourselves treasures on earth, but in heaven." Today, because we have laid up no treasures in heaven, we are in danger of losing what we have laid up on earth. Unless we rebuild God in our hearts we will never rebuild and reconstruct the world.—HUMPHREY BEEVER.

Knowledge is acquired by study and observation, but wisdom cometh by opportunity of leisure. The ripest thoughts come from a mind which is not always on the stretch, but fed, at times, by a wise passiveness.—WILLIAM MATHEWS.

The way we are going to think tomorrow depends largely on what we are thinking today.—DAVID LESLIE BROWN.

# MEDITATION

It is a psychological law that whatever we desire to accomplish we must impress upon the subjective or subconscious mind; that is, we must register a vow with ourselves, we must make our resolution with vigor, with faith that we can do the thing we want to do; we must register our conviction with such intensity that the great creative forces within us will tend to realize them. Our impressions will become expressions just in proportion to the vigor with which we register our vows to accomplish **our ambitions, to** make our visions realities.—SAMUEL MARSDEN.

Think on big things if you would grow
As splendid as an arched rainbow;
  No looking back remembering
  Old hurts or scars that prick and sting;
Forget yourself—small dreams forego.

If richer living you would know
Discard self-pity, vain ego;
  Bitterness won't let you sing—
  Think on big things.

If jealousy you will upthrow,
A kindly heart will overflow
  Into a philanthropic spring;
  Never let a petty thing
Tug at your thoughts like undertow;
  Think on big things!
                    —FAYE CARR ADAMS.

To live divinely is not to ignore the commonplace, but to ennoble it.—ANONYMOUS.

By meditation I can converse with God, solace myself on the bosom of the Saviour, bathe in the rivers of divine pleasure, tread the paths of my rest, and view the mansions of eternity.—ANONYMOUS.

What we are afraid to do before men, we should be afraid to think before God.—ANONYMOUS.

# MEMORY

The memory of the just is blessed.—PROV. 10:7.

A book of remembrance was written . . . for them that fear the Lord, and that thought on His name.—MAL. 3:16.

Memory is the cabinet of imagination, the treasury of reason, the registry of conscience, and the council chamber of thought.—SAINT BASIL.

The memory is a treasurer to whom we must give funds, if we would draw the assistance we need.—NICHOLAS ROWE.

The two offices of memory are collection and distribution.—SAMUEL JOHNSON.

The true art of memory is the art of attention.—SAMUEL JOHNSON.

It is a terrible thought, that nothing is ever forgotten: that not an oath is ever uttered that does not continue to vibrate through all time, in the wide-spreading current of sound; that not a prayer is lisped, that its record is not to be found stamped on the laws of nature by the indelible seal of the Almighty's will.—WILLIAM COWPER.

Recollection is the only paradise from which we cannot be turned out.—JEAN PAUL RICHTER.

A memory without a blot of contamination must be an inexhaustible source of pure refreshment.—CHARLOTTE BRONTE.

If you make children happy now, you will make them happy twenty years hence by the memory of it.—KATE DOUGLAS WIGGIN.

Remembrance is the sweetest flower
Of all this world perfuming,
For love doth guard it, Sun or Shower,
And Friendship keeps it blooming.
—CLIFTON BINGHAM.

Memory is one of the precious things of life, and if nourished long enough will become a veritable companion with us.—MAUDE MARCELL EVANS.

# MERCY

Have mercy on me, O God, according to the multitude of thy tender mercies.—PSALM 51:1a.

Let not mercy and truth forsake thee; bind them about thy neck; write them upon the table of thine heart.—PROV. 3:3.

Blessed are the merciful, for they shall obtain mercy.—MATT. 5:7.

Sweet mercy is nobility's true badge.—WILLIAM SHAKESPEARE.

How would you be, if he, who is the top of judgment, should but judge you as ye are. O, think on that, and mercy then will breathe within your lips, like man new made.—WILLIAM SHAKE-SPEARE.

> The quality of mercy is not strained,
> It droppeth as the gentle rain from heaven
> Upon the place beneath. It is twice blessed,
> It blesseth him that gives, and him that takes,
> 'Tis mightiest in the mightiest, it becomes
> The throned monarch better than his crown ...
> It is enthroned in the hearts of kings,
> It is an attribute of God himself ...
> —WILLIAM SHAKESPEARE.

Mercy is like the rainbow which God hath set in the clouds: it never shines after it is night. If we refuse mercy here, we shall have justice in eternity.—JEREMY TAYLOR.

Mercy more becomes the magistrate than the vindictive wrath which men call justice.—HENRY WADSWORTH LONGFELLOW.

We hand folks over to God's mercy, and show none ourselves.—GEORGE ELIOT.

Who will not mercy unto others show, how can he mercy ever hope to have.—HERBERT SPENCER.

> O God, how beautiful the thought,
>   How merciful the blest decree,
> That grace can always be found when sought,
>   And nought shut out the soul from thee.
> —ELIZA COOK.

# MERCY

Hate shuts her soul when dove-eyed Mercy pleads.—CHARLES SPRAGUE.

# MISFORTUNE

Cast thy burden on the Lord and He shall sustain thee; He shall never suffer the righteous to be moved.—PSALM 55:22.

All things work together for good to them who love the Lord.—ROM. 8:28.

Lest I should be exalted above measure through the abundance of the revelations, there was given me a thorn in the flesh, the messenger of Satan to buffet me, lest I should be exalted above measure.
For this thing I besought the Lord thrice, that it might depart from me.
And he said unto me, My grace is sufficient for thee: for my strength is made perfect in weakness.
Most gladly, therefore, will I rather glory in my infirmities, that the power of Christ may rest upon me.—2 COR. 12:7-9.

Difficulties are the things that show what men are.—EPICTETUS.

He who has endured vicissitudes with equanimity has deprived misfortune of its power.—SENECA.

Wise men ne'er sit and wail their loss but cheerily seek how to redress them.—WILLIAM SHAKESPEARE.

The longer we dwell on our misfortunes the greater is their power to harm us.—FRANCOIS VOLTAIRE.

Little minds are tamed and subdued by misfortune, but great minds rise above it.—WASHINGTON IRVING.

Our worst misfortunes never happen, and most miseries lie in anticipation.—HONORÉ DE BALZAC.

# MISFORTUNE

Perhaps when the light of heaven shows us clearly the pitfalls and dangers of the earth road that led to the heavenly city, our sweetest songs of gratitude will be not for the troubles we have conquered, but for those we have escaped.—AMELIA EDITH BARR.

Suffering accepted and vanquished will give you a security which may become the most exquisite fruit of your life.—DESIRE, CARDINAL MERCIER.

In every cloud is an angel's face.—JEROME KLAPKA JEROME.

It is not the will of God to give us more troubles than will bring us to live by faith on Him; He loves us too well to give us a moment of uneasiness for our good.—JULES ROMAINS.

Suffering is a choice instrument for shaping character, and without its touch the most delicate chasing on the vessel would be impossible.—IAN MACLAREN.

It is not what happens to you, but the way you take it that counts.—HILYS JASPER.

The less we parade our misfortunes the more sympathy we command.—O. DEWEY.

Most of our misfortunes are more supportable than the comments of our friends upon them.—C. C. COLTON.

Tribulation will not hurt you unless it hardens you—makes you sour, narrow and skeptical.—E. H. CHAPIN.

# MORALITY

Verily, verily I say unto thee, except a man be born again he cannot see the Kingdom of God.—JOHN 3:3b.

Follow that which is good.—I THES. 5:15.

Men are not made religious by performing certain actions which are externally good, but they must first have righteous principles, and then they will not fail to perform virtuous actions.—MARTIN LUTHER.

# MORALITY

To give a man a full knowledge of true morality, I would send him to no other book than the New Testament.—JOHN LOCKE.

The morality of the gospel is the noblest gift ever bestowed on man by God.—CHARLES LOUIS MONTESQUIEU.

The Christian religion is the only one that puts morality on its proper and right basis: the fear and love of God.—SAMUEL JOHNSON.

Reason and experience both forbid us to expect that national morality can prevail in exclusion of religious principle.—GEORGE WASHINGTON.

The great mistake of my life has been that I tried to be moral without faith in Jesus; but I have learned that true morality can only keep pace with trust in Christ as my Saviour.—GERRIT SMITH.

Religion without morality is a superstition and a curse, and morality without religion is impossible.—MARK HOPKINS.

Morality, taken as a part from religion, is but another name for decency in sin.—HORACE BUSHNELL.

Nothing really immoral is ever permanently popular. There does not exist in the literature of the world a single popular book that is immoral, two centuries after it is produced; for in the heart of nations the false does live so long, and the true is ethical to the end of time.—EDWARD GEORGE BULWER-LYTTON.

Morality without religion is only a kind of dead-reckoning—an endeavor to find our place on a cloudy sea by measuring the distance we have run, but without any observation of the heavenly bodies.—HENRY WADSWORTH LONGFELLOW.

Justification and sanctification are forever united.—MILTON VALENTINE.

The only morality that is clear in its course, pure in its precepts, and efficacious in its influence, is the morality of the gospel. All else, at last, is but idolatry—the worship of something of man's own creation, and that, imperfect and feeble like him-

self, and wholly insufficient to give him support and strength.—
JOHN SERGEANT.

The people of our nation and the people of the whole world
need to be gripped by the moral imperatives which grow out of
the nature of God, by a sense of right, by principles of truth, and
by ideals of decency. Nothing is more needed by this sinful world
than a revival of simple goodness and genuine uprightness.—
CLIFTON J. ALLEN.

The health of a community is an almost unfailing index of
its morals.—ANONYMOUS.

Morals without religion will wither and die, like seed sown
upon stony ground or among thorns.—ANONYMOUS.

# MUSIC

He hath put a new song in my mouth, even praise unto our
God.—PSALM 40:3.

I will sing with the spirit, and I will sing with the understanding.—I COR. 14:15.

> The man that hath no music in himself
> Nor is not moved with concord of sweet sounds
> Is fit for treasons, strategems, and spoils;
> The motions of his spirit are dull as night,
> And his affections dark as Erebus.
> Let no such man be trusted.
> —WILLIAM SHAKESPEARE.

I know a very wise man that believed if a man were permitted
to make all the ballads, he need not care who should make the
laws of the nation.—ANDREW FLETCHER.

> Of all the arts beneath the heaven
> That man has found or God has given,
> None draws the soul so sweet away

# MUSIC

As music's melting, mystic lay;
Slight emblem of the bliss above,
It soothes the spirit all to love.
                    —JAMES HOGG.

Music hath charms to soothe the savage breast,
To soften rocks, or bend a knotted oak.
                    —SIR WILLIAM CONGREVE.

Let me go where'er I will
I hear a sky-born music still;

\*   \*   \*

It is not only in the rose,
    It is not only in the bird,
Not only where the rainbow glows,
    Nor in the song of woman heard;
But in the darkest, meanest things.
There always, always something sings.
                    —RALPH WALDO EMERSON.

Music is the harmonious voice of creation; an echo of the
invisible world; one note of the divine concord which the entire
universe is destined one day to sound.—GIUSEPPE MAZZINI.

God sent his singers on earth
With songs of gladness and mirth
That they might touch the hearts of men
And bring them back to Heaven again.
                    —HENRY WADSWORTH LONGFELLOW.

The harp of Nature's advent strung
    Has never ceased to play;
The song the stars of morning sung
    Has never died away.
                    —JOHN GREENLEAF WHITTIER.

The song that nerves a nation's heart is in itself a deed.—
ALFRED TENNYSON.

There is no truer truth obtainable by man than comes of
music.—ROBERT BROWNING.

# MUSIC

Alas for those that never sing,
But die with all their music in them.
—OLIVER WENDELL HOLMES.

Life gives to every man a staff and a scale of notes. The song he sings is one of his own fashioning. The world will stop to hear it if be sweet. If it be brave, they will follow him; if it be a dirge, they will run away.—ALMA LEGGERT LONSDALE.

I heard a bird at break of day
Sing from the autumn trees
A song so mystical and calm
So full of certainties,
No man, I think, could listen long
Except upon his knees,
Yet this was but a simple bird
Alone, among the dead trees.
—WILLIAM A. PERCY.

Explain it as we may, a martial strain will urge a man into the front rank of battle sooner than an argument, and a fine anthem excite his devotion more certainly than a logical discourse.—JOSEPH TUCKERMAN.

Singing is the highest expression of music because it is the most direct expression of the emotions of the soul.—CLARA KATHLEEN ROGERS.

## SONGS IN THE NIGHT

### (JOB 35:10)

There are blessings that flow from the fountain
Of grace that are wondrously fair;
There are blessings of infinite beauty
That tell of the Shepherd's great care;
But of all that the Father hath given
To those who are dear in His sight,
There is one that excelleth all others:
He giveth us songs in the night.

231

# MUSIC

When the darkness of sin rolls upon us,
  And the soul is with sorrow pressed down,
And we longingly seek to find comfort
  But no peace on earth can be found;
When we cry out to Christ for His pardon
  And we feel the soul flooded with light
How the heart swells with praise to the Maker
  Who giveth us songs in the night.

When wild waves of doubt and temptation
  Like billows sweep over the soul,
And Sight cannot pierce the grim shadows,
  And Faith seems to lose her control,
O 'tis then that the dear loving Saviour
  Doth show forth the strength of His might
As He clothes us with sweet reassurance
  With the songs that He sends in the night.

There's rest for those who are weary;
  There's joy for those who are sad;
There's peace for those who are troubled;
  His presence makes lonely hearts glad.
But the marvelous gifts of His mercy
  Which quicken the soul with delight
And lift from the heart every burden
  Are the songs that He sends in the night.

—Virginia Ely.


The knower of the mystery of sound knows the mystery of the whole universe.—Ancient Prophet.


How many of us ever stop to think
Of music as a wondrous magic link
With God; taking sometimes the place of prayer,
When words have failed us 'neath the weight of care.
Music, that knows no country, race or creed,
But gives to each according to his need.

Anonymous.

232

# MUSIC

## I AM MUSIC

Servant and master am I; servant of those dead and master of those living. Through me, spirits speak the messages that make them nearby. I make the world weep and laugh, wonder and worship.

I tell the story of love, the story of hate, the story that saves and the story that destroys. I am the incense upon which prayers float to Heaven. I am the smoke which palls over the field of battle where men die with me on their lips.

I am close to the marriage altar and when the grave opens I stand nearby. I call the wanderer home, I rescue the soul from the depths; I open the lips of lovers and through me the dead whisper to the living.

One I serve as I serve all, and the king I make my slave as easily as I subject his slave. I speak through the birds of the air, the insects of the field, the crash of waters on rock ribbed shores, the sighing of the winds in the trees, and I am even heard by the soul that knows me in the clatter of the wheels on city streets.— ANONYMOUS.

Music is a soaring bird;
Ecstatic in its flight;
Music is the crooning heard
In tall pines' arms at night.
Music is the laughing sea
Embracing moon-white shores;
Music is the flashing key
Unlocking heaven's doors.
Music is the silver seine
Flung gaily in life's shoals;
Music is God's cool gray rain
On parched and thirsty souls.
—ANONYMOUS.

# NATURE

The heavens declare the glory of God; and the firmament showeth His handiwork.—PSALM 19:1.

# NATURE

He hath made everything beautiful in his time; also he hath set the world in their heart, so that no man can find out the work that God maketh from the beginning to the end.—Ecc. 3:11.

All things were made by him and without him was not anything made that was made.—John 1:3.

I follow nature as the surest guide, and resign myself with implicit obedience to her sacred ordinances.—Cicero.

Nature has perfections, in order to show that she is the image of God; and defects to show that she is only His image.—Blaise Pascal.

The course of nature is the art of God.—Edward Young.

> Extremes in nature equal ends produce;
> In man they join to some mysterious use.
> —Alexander Pope.

There is a signature of wisdom and power impressed on the works of God, which evidently distinguishes them from the feeble imitations of men. Not only the splendor of the sun, but the glimmering light of the glowworm proclaims his glory.—John Newton.

> To me more dear, congenial to my heart
> One native charm, than all the gloss of art.
> —Oliver Goldsmith.

Nature is but a name for an effect whose cause is God.—William Cowper.

> Not a flower
> But shows some touch, in freckle, streak or stain,
> Of His unrivall'd pencil. He inspires
> Their balmy odors, and imparts their hues,
> And bathes their eyes with nectar, and includes
> In grains as countless as the seaside sands
> The forms with which He sprinkles all the earth.
> —William Cowper.

> One impulse from the vernal wood
> May teach you more of man,

# NATURE

Of moral evil and of good
Than all the sages can.
—WILLIAM WORDSWORTH.

Knowing that Nature never did betray
The heart that loved her.
—WILLIAM WORDSWORTH.

Whatever you are by nature, keep to it; never desert your own
line of talent. Be what nature intended you for, and you will
succeed; be anything else and you will be ten thousand times
worse than nothing.—SIDNEY SMITH.

Earth with her thousand voices praises God.—SAMUEL TAYLOR
COLERIDGE.

It is truly a most Christian exercise to extract a sentiment of
piety from the works and appearance of nature. Our Saviour
expatiates on a flower and draws from it the delightful argument
of confidence in God.—THOMAS CHALMERS.

There is a serene and settled majesty in woodland scenery
that enters into the soul and delights and elevates it, and fills it
with noble inclinations.—WASHINGTON IRVING.

There is a pleasure in the pathless woods;
There is a rapture on the lonely shore;
There is society, where none intrudes,
By the deep sea, and music in its roar;
I love not man the less, but Nature more.
—GEORGE GORDON, LORD BYRON.

To him who in the love of Nature holds
Communion with her visible forms, she speaks
A various language.
—WILLIAM CULLEN BRYANT.

The groves were God's first temples.—WILLIAM CULLEN
BRYANT.

Nature admits no lie.—THOMAS CARLYLE.

Nature is the face of God. He appears to us through it, and
we can read his thoughts in it.—VICTOR HUGO.

# NATURE

The happiest man is he who learns from nature the lesson of worship.—RALPH WALDO EMERSON.

In the vaunted works of Art
The master-stroke is Nature's part.
—RALPH WALDO EMERSON.

Nature is a more powerful force than education; time will develop everything.—BENJAMIN DISRAELI.

I hold that we have a very imperfect knowledge of the works of Nature till we view them as works of God; not only as works of mechanism, but works of intelligence; not only as under laws, but under a law-giver, wise and good.—JAMES McCOSH.

Earth's crammed with Heaven
And every common bush afire with God.
But only he who sees takes off his shoes.
—ELIZABETH BARRETT BROWNING.

I trust in Nature for the stable laws
Of beauty and utility. Spring shall plant
And autumn garner to the end of time.
I trust in God—the right shall be the right
And other than the wrong, while He endures.
I trust in my own soul, that can perceive
The outward and the inward—Nature's good
and God's.
—ROBERT BROWNING.

I find earth not gray, but rosey,
Heaven not grim, but fair of hue.
Do I stoop? I pluck a posey;
Do a stand and stare? All's blue.
—ROBERT BROWNING.

Study Nature as the countenance of God.—CHARLES KINGSLEY.

Nature fits all her children with something to do.—JAMES RUSSELL LOWELL.

I saw God write a gorgeous poem this very morning. With the fresh sunbeam for a pencil, on the broad sheet of level snow, the diamond letters were spelled out one by one, till the whole was aflame with poetry.—PHILLIPS BROOKS.

It is something to make two blades of grass grow where only one was growing; it is much more to have been the occasion of the planting of an oak which shall defy twenty scores of winters, or of an elm which shall canopy with its green cloud of foliage half as many generations of mortal immortalities.—OLIVER WENDELL HOLMES.

Flowers always make people better, happier and more helpful; they are sunshine, food and medicine to the soul.—LUTHER BURBANK.

The mountains lie in curves so tender, I want to lay my arm about them as God does.—OLIVER TILFORD DARGAN.

Go to sleep at eight o'clock and get up with the robins. Never miss the bird orchestra at daylight. Everyone wonders and is carried away out of himself when for the first time he discovers morning.—E. P. POWELL.

> I like the fellowship of trees,
>     They are such wholesome things:
> They know not race nor creed nor class
> But share their best with all who pass,
> Not caring if their shade caress
>     The brow of kine or king.
>
> I like the language of the trees
>     They speak the whole day long:
> They know not craft, deceit nor guile
> But artless as a little child
> They tell their story, all the while
>     Unmindful of all wrong.
>
> I like the habits of the trees:
>     Tho' planted in the sod,
> They stay in their God-given space
> And coveting no other's place
> They serve the world with gentle grace
>     And glorify their God.
>                                   —VIRGINIA ELY.

# NATURE

This is my Father's world, this lovely place
   Where mountains hold their snowy peaks up high
Above the valleys, green with grain, and lace
   Is hung on leafy trees against the sky.
This is my Father's world and songbirds sing
   A deathless melody of joy and pain,
Purging their hearts of dreariness to bring
   Sweet notes of cheer to human hearts again.
Oh, he who loves a mountain's lofty peak—
   Or who sees valleys stretch to endless miles,
Knows in the splendid silence God will speak
   And in the virile greenness that He smiles.
This is my Father's world—His own design,
   But in His goodness He has made it mine!
            —FAYE CARR ADAMS.

# NEW YEAR

But the land, whither ye go to possess it, is a land of hills and valleys, and drinketh water of the rain of heaven:

A land which the Lord thy God careth for: the eyes of the Lord thy God are always upon it, from the beginning of the year even unto the end of the year.—DEUT. 11:11, 12.

Ye have not passed this way heretofore.—JOSH. 3:4.

    Beyond the dim unknown
  Standeth God within the shadow
  Keeping watch above his own.
      —JAMES RUSSELL LOWELL.

The Oriental shepherd was always ahead of his sheep. He was in front. Any attempt upon them had to take him into account. Now, God is down in front. He is in the tomorrows. It is tomorrow that fills men with dread. But God is there already, and all tomorrows of our life have to pass Him before they can get to us.—F. B. MAYER.

# NEW YEAR

The story of the past is told; the future may be writ in gold;
Sunshine and shadow have mingled in the year that has passed
    away;
Sunshine and shadow will mingle in the year that I meet today.
But hand in hand with the Master, I fear not what it will bring;
He knows, He cares, and He loves me, and God is in everything.
—ANONYMOUS.

> I asked the New Year for some message sweet,
> Some rule of life with which to guide my feet;
> I asked, and paused: he answered soft and low,
>     "God's will to know."
> "Will knowledge then suffice, New Year?" I cried:
> And, ere the question into silence died,
> The answer came, "Nay, but remember, too,
>     God's will to do."
> Once more I asked, "Is there no more to tell?"
> And once again the answer sweetly fell,
> "Yes! this thing, all other things above:
>     God's will to love."
> —ANONYMOUS.

# OBEDIENCE

And he took the book of the covenant, and read in the audience of the people: and they said, All that the Lord hath said will we do, and be obedient.—EXOD. 24:7.

When thou art in tribulation, and all these things are come upon thee, even in the latter days, if thou turn to the Lord thy God, and shalt be obedient unto his voice;

(For the Lord thy God is a merciful God;) he will not forsake thee, neither destroy thee, nor forget the covenant of thy fathers which he sware unto them.—DEUT. 4:30-31.

If ye be willing and obedient, ye shall eat the good of the land.—ISA. 1:19.

If ye love me, keep my commandments.—JOHN 14:15.

# OBEDIENCE

Obedience is the mother of success and is wedded to safety.
—AESCHYLUS.

We are born subjects and to obey God is perfect liberty. He that does this shall be free, safe and happy.—SENECA.

The first law that ever God gave to man was a law of obedience; it was a commandment pure and simple, wherein man had nothing to inquire after or to dispute, for as much as to obey is the proper office of a rational soul acknowledging a heavenly superior and benefactor. From obedience and submission spring all other virtues, as all sin does from self-opinion and self-will.
—MICHEL DE MONTAIGNE.

To obey God in some things and not in others shows an unsound heart. Childlike obedience moves toward every command of God, as the needle points where the loadstone draws.
—THOMAS WATSON.

> Of Man's first disobedience, and the fruit
> Of that forbidden tree, whose mortal taste
> Brought death into the world, and all our woe,
> With loss of Eden, till one greater Man
> Restore us, and regain the blissful seat,
> Sing, Heavenly Muse. . . .
>
> —JOHN MILTON.

Thirty years of our Lord's life are hidden in these words of the gospel: "He was subject unto them."—JACQUES BOSSUET.

> To do or not to do; to have or not to have,
>    I leave to Thee:
>       Thy only will be done in me;
> All my requests are lost in one,
> "Father, Thy will be done!"
>
> —CHARLES WESLEY.

One very common error misleads the opinion of mankind—that authority is pleasant and submission painful. In the general course of human affairs the very reverse of this is nearer the truth. Command is anxiety; obedience is ease.—WILLIAM PALEY.

# OBEDIENCE

It is vain thought to flee from the work that God appoints us, for the sake of finding a greater blessing, instead of seeking it where alone it is to be found—in loving obedience.—GEORGE ELIOT.

How will you find good? It is not a thing of choices; it is a river that flows from the foot of the invisible throne, and flows by the path of obedience.—GEORGE ELIOT.

Nothing is really lost by a life of sacrifice; everything is lost by failure to obey God's call.—HENRY PARRY LIDDON.

> That is best which God sends;
> It was His will; it is mine.
> —OWEN MEREDITH.

Obedience must be the struggle and desire of our life. Obedience, not hard and forced, but ready, loving and spontaneous; the doing of duty, not merely that the duty may be done, but that the soul in doing it may become capable of receiving and uttering God.—PHILLIPS BROOKS.

Doing the will of God leaves me no time for disputing about His plans.—GEORGE McDONALD.

God is too great to be withstood, too just to do wrong, too good to delight in any one's misery. We ought, therefore, quietly to submit to His dispensations as the very best.—BISHOP DANIEL WILSON.

Obedience to God is the most infallible evidence of sincere and supreme love to him.—NATHANIEL EMMONS.

No principle is more noble, as there is none more holy, than that of a true obedience.—HENRY GILES.

Patience, is an excellent remedy for grief, but submission to the hand of Him that sends it is a far better.—ANONYMOUS.

The ten commandments, which like a collection of diamonds, bear testimony to their own intrinsic worth, in themselves appeal to us as coming from a superhuman or divine source, and no conscientious or reasonable man has yet been able to find a flaw in them.—ANONYMOUS.

# OPPORTUNITY

The place whereon thou standest is holy ground.—Exod. 3:5.

I will tarry at Ephesus until Pentecost.
For a great door and effectual is opened unto me, and there are many adversaries.—I Cor. 16:8, 9.

Behold, I have set before thee an open door, and no man can shut it.—Rev. 3:8.

The wise man will make more opportunities than he finds. —Francis Bacon.

> Who seeks
> And will not take when once 'tis offered,
> Shall never find it more.
> —William Shakespeare.

> There is a tide in the affairs of men
> Which, taken at the flood, leads on to fortune:
> Omitted, all the voyage of their life
> Is bound in shallows and in miseries.
> —William Shakespeare.

Our opportunities to do good are our talents.—Cotton Mather.

It is common to overlook what is near by keeping the eye fixed on something remote. In the same manner present opportunities are neglected and attainable good is slighted by minds busied in extensive ranges, and intent upon future advantages. —Samuel Johnson.

How often do we sigh for opportunities of doing good, whilst we neglect the openings of Providence in little things, which would frequently lead to the accomplishment of most important usefulness!—George Crabbe.

The May of life blooms only once.—Friedrich Schiller.

Do not wait for extraordinary circumstances to do good; try to use ordinary situations.—Jean Paul Richter.

The secret of success in life is for a man to be ready for his opportunity when it comes.—Benjamin Disraeli.

# OPPORTUNITY

I will study and get ready and the opportunity will come. ABRAHAM LINCOLN.

...mit no greater folly than to sit by the roadside
...es along and invites you to ride with him to
...OHN B. GOUGH.

...stacle a stumbling block; another finds
WILLIAM LYON PHELPS.

...nity grasped and used produces at least one other
...y.—CHESTER A. SWOR.

...ife is not a collection bureau for power and pelf, but an
opportunity for service.—JOHN W. RALEY.

Trouble is only opportunity in work clothes.—HENRY J. KAISER.

If sorrow could enter heaven, if a sigh could be heard there, or a tear roll down the cheek of a saint in light, it would be for the lost opportunities, for the time spent in neglect of God which might have been spent for His glory.—EDWARD PAYSON.

Vigilance in watching opportunity; tact and daring in seizing upon opportunity; force and persistence in crowding opportunity to its utmost of possible achievement—these are the martial virtues which must command success.—AUSTIN PHELPS.

Weak men wait for opportunities; strong men make them. —ANDERSON M. BATEN.

Opportunity passes by those who are not prepared to avail themselves of it.—G. R. H. SHAFTO.

Great opportunities come to all, but many do not know they have met them. The only preparation to take advantage of them, is simple fidelity to what each day brings.—A. E. DUNNING.

The only way to keep an open door open is to enter that open door.—BAKER JAMES CAUTHEN.

If thou faint in the day of adversity, thy strength is small— too small to be worth talking about, for the day of adversity is its first real opportunity.—MALTBIE BABCOCK.

# OPPORTUNITY

The trouble with opportunity is that it always comes disguised as hard work.—ANONYMOUS.

God never shuts one door but that he opens another.—ANONYMOUS.

Life's great opportunities often open on the road of daily duties.—ANONYMOUS.

> Just where you stand in the conflict,
> There is your place!
> Just where you think you are useless,
> Hide not your face!
> God placed you there for a purpose,
> Whate'er it may be;
> Think you He has chosen you for it:
> Work loyally.
>
> —ANONYMOUS.

> Don't give me of tomorrow!
> Give me the man who'll say
> That when a good deed's to be done,
> "Let's do the deed today."
>
> —ANONYMOUS.

# OPTIMISM

Why is thy countenance fallen? If thou doest well, shalt thou not be accepted?—GEN. 4:6, 7.

The cynic is one who knows the price of everything and the value of nothing.—OSCAR WILDE.

The optimist is one who believes in God, in the right, and in his fellowman, and in himself. He believes that God and right ultimately will win. He lives to serve his fellowmen and makes the most of adverse circumstances.

He believes that this is a world of law and that the same righteous forces that won in the past will win today. He fills his soul with the good, and the beautiful and the cheerful things of life.

Out of these he produces the spirit of optimism—the spirit that makes "the teakettle sing when it is up to its neck in hotwater."—J. WHITCOMB BROUGHTER.

Artificial optimism alienates more friends than it makes.—F. C. ASPLEY.

Keep your face to the sunshine and you cannot see the shadows.—HELEN KELLER.

> Only thy restless heart keep still
>   And wait in cheerful hope; content
> To take whate'er His gracious will,
>   His all-discerning love hath sent;
> Nor doubt our inmost wants are known
>   To Him who chose us for His own.
>               —ANONYMOUS.

> Good Lawd sends me troubles,
>   And I got to wuk 'em out.
> But I look aroun' an' see
>   There's trouble all about.
> An' when I see my troubles
>   I jes' look up and grin
> To think ob all de troubles
>   Dat I ain't in!
>               —ANONYMOUS.

# PATIENCE

Fear ye not; stand still and see the salvation of the Lord.—EXOD. 14:13.

Sit still, my daughter, until thou know how the matter will fall.—RUTH 3:18.

They that wait upon the Lord shall renew their strength; they shall mount up with wings as eagles; they shall run and not be weary; they shall walk and not faint.—ISA. 40:31.

# PATIENCE

We glory in tribulation also; knowing that tribulation worketh patience.—Rom. 5:3.

Wherefore, seeing we also are compassed about with so great a cloud of witnesses, let us lay aside every weight and the sin which doth so easily beset us, and let us run with patience the race that is set before us, looking unto Jesus, the Author and Finisher of our Faith.—Heb. 12:1

Knowing this, that the trying of your faith worketh patience. But let patience have her perfect work, that ye may be perfect and entire, wanting nothing.—Jas. 1:3, 4.

Patience is so like fortitude that she seems either her sister or her daughter.—Aristotle.

He who hath heard the Word of God can bear His silences. —Saint Ignatius.

Genius is eternal patience.—Michelangelo.

How poor are they that have no patience;
What wound did ever heal but by slow degree.
—William Shakespeare.

Patience! why it is the soul of peace; of all the virtues, it is nearest kin to heaven; it makes men look like gods.—Thomas Dekker.

Patient waiting is often the highest way of doing God's will. —Jeremy Collier.

They also serve who only stand and wait.—John Milton.

He that can have patience can have what he will.—Benjamin Franklin.

Never think that God's delays are God's denials. Hold on; hold fast; hold out. Patience is genuine.—Georges L. Leclerc, Count de Buffon.

Patience is bitter, but its fruit is sweet.—Jean Jacques Rousseau.

# PATIENCE

It is not necessary for all men to be great in action. The greatest and sublimest power is often simple patience.—HORACE BUSHNELL.

There is one form of hope which is never unwise, and which certainly does not diminish with the increase of knowledge. In that form it changes its name and we call it Patience.—EDWARD GEORGE BULWER-LYTTON..

Patience is a necessary ingredient of Genius.—BENJAMIN DISRAELI.

> Let nothing disturb thee,
> Nothing affright thee;
> All things are passing;
> God never changeth:
> Patient endurance
> Attaineth to all things;
> Who God possesseth
> In nothing is wanting;
> Alone God sufficeth.
>           —HENRY WADSWORTH LONGFELLOW.

> Let us be content in work
> To do the thing we can, and not presume
> To fret because it's little.
>           —ELIZABETH BARRETT BROWNING.

There is no such thing as preaching patience into people unless the sermon is so long they have to practice it while they hear. No man can learn patience except by going out into the hurly-burly world, and taking life just as it blows. Patience is but lying to and riding out the gale.—HENRY WARD BEECHER.

There is no music in a "rest," but there's the making of music in it. And people are always missing that part of the life melody, always talking of perseverance and courage and fortitude; but patience is the finest and worthiest part of fortitude, and the rarest too.—JOHN RUSKIN.

> Serene I fold my hands and wait
> Nor care for wind or tide or sea;
> I rave no more 'gainst time or fate,
> For lo! my own shall come to me.

247

# PATIENCE

Serene I fold my hands and wait,
What'er the storms of life may be.
Faith guides me up to Heaven's gate
And Love will bring my own to me.
                          —JOHN BURROUGHS.

God's plans, like lilies
    Pure and white unfold:
We must not tear the close
    shut leaves apart;
Time will reveal the calyxes of gold.
                          —MAY RILEY SMITH.

Help me, dear Lord, this lesson sweet to learn:
To sit at thy pierced feet and only yearn
To love Thee better, Lord; and feel that still
Waiting is working, if it be Thy will.
                          —ANONYMOUS.

Hushing every muttered murmur,
Let your fortitude the firmer
    Gird your soul with strength,
While, no treason near her lurking,
Patience in her perfect working
    Shall be Queen at length.
                          —ANONYMOUS.

Patience is not passive; on the contrary, it is active; it is concentrated strength.—ANONYMOUS.

All hindrances are tests.—ANONYMOUS.


# PATRIOTISM

Blessed is the nation whose God is the Lord.—PSALM 33:12.
Righteousness exalteth a nation.—PROV. 14:34.

After what I owe to God, nothing should be more dear or more sacred to me than the love and respect I owe to my country.—JACQUES AUGUSTE DE THOU.

# PATRIOTISM

> Be just and fear not;
> Let all the ends thou aim'st at be thy country's,
> Thy God's and Truth's.
>> —WILLIAM SHAKESPEARE.

> I do love my country's good with a respect more tender
> And more holy and profound than mine own life.
>> —WILLIAM SHAKESPEARE.

> Who serves his country best has no need of ancestors.—
> FRANCOIS VOLTAIRE.

> Ill fares the land, to hastening ills a prey,
> Where wealth accumulates, and men decay.
> Princes and lords may flourish, or may fade;
> A breath can make them, as a breath has made:
> But a bold peasantry, their country's pride,
> When once destroyed, can never be supplied.
>> —OLIVER GOLDSMITH.

> With all her faults she is my country still.—EDMUND BURKE.

> Then join in hand, brave Americans all!
> By uniting we stand, by dividing we fall.
>> —JOHN DICKINSON.

> I am not a Virginian, but an American!—PATRICK HENRY.

> Breathes there the man, with soul so dead,
> Who never to himself hath said,
>> This is my own, my native land!
> Whose heart hath ne'er within him burned,
> As home his footsteps he hath turned,
>> From wandering on a foreign strand?
> If such there breathe, go, mark him well!
> For him no minstrel raptures swell;
> High though his titles, proud his name,
> Boundless his wealth, as wish can claim—
> Despite those titles, power and pelf,
> The wretch, concentered all in self,
> Living, shall forfeit fair renown,

# PATRIOTISM

And, doubly dying, shall go down
To the vile dust from whence he sprung,
Unwept, unhonored and unsung.
                    —SIR WALTER SCOTT.

Our country! In her intercourse with foreign nations may she always be in the right, but our country, right or wrong.—STEPHEN DECATUR.

America—the home of freedom, the hope of the down-trodden and oppressed among the nations of the earth.—DANIEL WEBSTER.

Let our object be our country, our whole country and nothing but our country.—DANIEL WEBSTER.

America has proved that it is practicable to elevate the mass of mankind—the laboring or lower class—to raise them to self-respect, to make them competent to act a part in the great right and the great duty of self-government; and she has proved that this may be done by education and the diffusion of knowledge. She holds out an example a thousand times more encouraging than ever was presented before to those nine-tenths of the human race who are born without hereditary fortune or hereditary rank.—DANIEL WEBSTER.

My country, 'tis of Thee,
Sweet land of Liberty,
    Of Thee I sing.
Land where my fathers died,
Land of the Pilgrim's pride,
From every mountain side,
    Let freedom ring!
            —SAMUEL F. SMITH.

No sound is breathed so potent to coerce
And to conciliate, as their names who dare
For that sweet motherland which gave them birth
    Nobly to do, nobly to die.
            —ALFRED LORD TENNYSON.

Of the whole sum of human life, no small part is that which consists of a man's relations to his country, and his feelings concerning it.—WILLIAM EWART GLADSTONE.

# PATRIOTISM

There are no points of the compass on the chart of true patriotism.—ROBERT CHARLES WINTHROP.

This is what I call the American idea—a government of the people, by the people and for the people. A government of the principles of eternal justice, and unchanging laws of God.—THEODORE PARKER.

America—half brother of the world.—PHILIP JAMES BAILEY.

He serves his party best who serves his country best.—RUTHERFORD B. HAYES.

A man's country is not a certain area of land, of mountains, rivers and woods, but it is a principle; and patriotism is loyalty to that principle.—GEORGE WILLIAM CURTIS.

> He serves his country best
> Who lives pure life and doeth righteous deeds,
> And walks straight paths, however others stray,
> And leaves his sons, an uttermost bequest,
> A stainless record, which all men may read.
> —SUSAN COOLIDGE.

Great countries have to deserve to live; they have to will to live; they have to struggle to live.—LYNN LANDRUM.

America—the home of the homeless all over the world.—ALFRED B. STREET.

If America ever sags, the world's hopes sag with her.—ARTHUR H. VANDENBERG.

> How shall I serve my father's land?
> There are no battles to be won,
> No deeds that heroes might have done
> No lives to give at her command.
>
> Nay, none of these—but lives to live,
> Within, of gentle soul and pure,
> Without, of zeal and courage sure,
> For all the best that life can give.

# PATRIOTISM

And then to crown the finished span
To honor country and her dead.
'Twere meed enough that it be said,
He lived a true American.
—M. A. DeWolf Howe, Jr.

Let not a man glory in this, that he loves his country;
Let him rather glory in this, that he loves his kind.
—Old Persian Proverb.

To love one's country, it is not necessary to hate others.—
Anonymous.

Patriotism is only vital when it is fully Christianized.—
Anonymous.

# PEACE

Mark the perfect man, and behold the upright; for the end of that man is peace—Psalm 37:37.

The Lord will bless His people with peace.—Psalm 29:11.

Great peace have they which love thy law; and nothing shall offend them.—Psalm 119:165.

When a man's ways please the Lord, he maketh even his enemies to be at peace with Him.—Prov. 16:7.

Thou wilt keep him in perfect peace whose mind is stayed on thee: because he trusteth in thee.—Isa. 26:3.

Blessed are the peacemakers, for they shall be called the children of God.—Matt. 5:9.

Peace I leave with you: my peace I give unto you. Not as the world giveth, give I unto you. Let not your heart be troubled, neither let it be afraid.—John 14:27.

To be spiritually minded is life and peace.—Rom. 8:6.

# PEACE

A mind from every evil thought set free
I count the noblest gift of Deity.
—AESCHYLUS.

In peace there's nothing so becomes a man
As modest stillness and humility;
But when the blast of war blows in our ears
Then imitate the action of the tiger:
Stiffen the sinews, summon up the blood.
—WILLIAM SHAKESPEARE.

I feel within me
A peace above all earthly dignities,
A still and quiet conscience.
—WILLIAM SHAKESPEARE.

'Tis death to me to be at enmity; I hate it, and desire all
men's love.—WILLIAM SHAKESPEARE.

Where peace
And rest can never dwell, hope never comes
That comes to all.
—JOHN MILTON.

The Pilgrim they laid in the large upper chamber, facing
the sunrising. The name of the chamber was Peace.—JOHN
BUNYAN.

Peace hath her victories
No less renown'd than war.
—JOHN MILTON.

Peace doth not dwell in outward things, but within the soul;
we may preserve it in the midst of the bitterest pain, if our will
remain firm and submissive. Peace in this life springs from ac-
quiescence, not in an exemption from suffering.—FRANCOIS DE LA
FENELON.

If we have not peace within ourselves, it is in vain to seek it
from outward sources.—FRANCOIS DE LA ROCHEFOUCAULD.

Nothing can bring you peace but yourself.—RALPH WALDO
EMERSON.

# PEACE

We love peace, but not peace at any price. There is a peace more destructive of the manhood of living men than war is destructive of his body. Chains are worse than bayonets.—DOUGLAS WILLIAM JERROLD.

> O the little birds sang east,
> And the little birds sang west,
> And I smiled to think God's greatness
> Flowed around our incompleteness,
> Found our restlessness, His rest.
> > —ELIZABETH BARRETT BROWNING

> Drop thy still dews of quietness till all our striving cease;
> > Take from our souls the strain and stress,
> > And let our ordered lives confess
> The beauty of thy Peace.
> > —JOHN GREENLEAF WHITTIER.

> What secret trouble stirs your heart?
> > Why all this fret and flurry?
> Dost thou not know that what is best
> In this too restless world is rest,
> > From over-work and hurry?
> > —HENRY WADSWORTH LONGFELLOW.

> God, give us Peace! not such as lulls to sleep,
> > But sword on thigh and brow with purpose knit
> And let our Ship of State to harbor sweep,
> > Her ports all up, her battle lantern lit,
> And her leashed thunders gathering for their leap.
> > —JAMES RUSSELL LOWELL.

Peace is always beautiful.—WALT WHITMAN.

I could not live in peace if I put the shadow of a wilful sin between myself and God.—GEORGE ELIOT.

The noblest mind the best contentment has.—HERBERT SPENCER.

God will keep no nation in supreme peace that will not do supreme duty.—WILLIAM McKINLEY.

# PEACE

You are not going to get peace with millions of armed men. The chariot of peace cannot advance over a road littered with cannon.—DAVID LLOYD GEORGE.

Without peace our property and possessions, much or little, are of no value, and without the Prince of Peace there can be no peace.—R. E. DUDLEY.

> If peace be in the heart,
> The wildest winter storm is full of solemn beauty,
> The midnight flash but shows the path of duty,
> Each living creature tells some new and joyous story,
> The very trees and stones all catch a ray of glory,
> If peace be in the heart.
> —CHARLES FRANCIS RICHARDSON.

There can be no greater service to mankind, and no nobler mission, than devotion to world peace. The course has been charted.—HARRY S. TRUMAN.

There are interests by the sacrifice of which peace is too dearly purchased. One should never be at peace to the shame of his own soul—to the violation of his integrity or of his allegiance to God.—E. H. CHAPIN.

Peace is such a precious jewel that I would give anything for it but truth.—MATTHEW HENRY.

No reconstructed society can be built on unreconstructed individuals. Personal unbalance never leads to social stability. And peace of mind is the indispensable prerequisite of individual and social balance.—JOSHUA LOTH LIEBMAN.

Peace is practical, and is bound at last to prevail.—LYNN LANDRUM.

An effective organization for world peace will be established not through political diplomats around a peace table, but through Christian teachers in all lands, teaching citizens in Sunday School and public school the sacredness of human life.— J. M. PRICE.

Nations have no existence apart from their people. If every person in the world loved peace, every nation would love peace.

# PEACE

If all men refused to fight one another, nations could not fight one another.—J. SHERMAN WALLACE.

Peace is the evening star of the soul, as virtue is its sun; and the two are never far apart.—C. C. COLTON.

> Peace does not mean the end of all our striving;
> Joy does not mean the drying of our tears;
> Peace is the power that comes to souls arriving
> Up to the light where God Himself appears.
> —G. A. STUDDART KENNEDY.

The good will that conditions peace must be positive and active. Men of good will must be the instruments and agents of Him who is out to bless all the families of the earth.—W. O. CARVER.

With God in charge of our defenses, there will be peace within.—T. T. FAICHNEY.

Promise yourself to be so strong that nothing can disturb your peace of mind.—ANONYMOUS.

# PERFECTION

Be ye therefore perfect even as your Father which is in heaven is perfect.—MATT. 5:48.

One that desires to excel should endeavor in those things that are in themselves excellent.—EPICTETUS.

He who stops being better stops being good.—OLIVER CROMWELL.

Try to put well into practice what you already know; and in so doing, you will, in good time, discover the hidden things you now inquire about. Practice what you know, and it will help to make clear what you do not know.—HARMENSZOON VAN RIJN REMBRANDT.

Perfection consists not in doing extraordinary things, but in doing ordinary things extraordinarily well.—ANTOINE ARNAULD.

# PERFECTION

Excellence is never granted to man but as a reward for labor. It argues no small strength of mind to persevere in habits of industry without the pleasure of perceiving those advances, which like the hand of a clock, whilst they make hourly approaches to their point, yet proceed so slowly as to escape observation.—SIR JOSHUA REYNOLDS.

If a man can write a better book, preach a better sermon or make a better mousetrap than his neighbor, though he build his house in the woods, the world will make a beaten path to his door.—RALPH WALDO EMERSON.

> In the elder days of Art
> Builders wrought with greatest care
> Each minute and unseen part;
> For the gods see everywhere.
> —HENRY WADSWORTH LONGFELLOW.

It takes less time to do a thing right than it does to explain why you did it wrong.—HENRY WADSWORTH LONGFELLOW.

Every difficulty slurred over will be a ghost to disturb your repose later on.—FREDERIC CHOPIN.

> What's come to perfection perishes;
> Things learned on earth we shall practice in heaven;
> Works done least rapidly, Art most cherishes.
> —ROBERT BROWNING.

> God is the perfect Poet
> Who in his person acts his own creation.
> —ROBERT BROWNING.

Human excellence, apart from God, is like the fabled flower which, according to the Rabbis, Eve plucked when passing out of Paradise. Severed from its native root, it is only the touching memorial of a lost Eden—sad while charming and beautiful, but dead.—SIR CHARLES VILLIERS STANFORD.

> Happy is he who walks the path of peace,
> With faith to guide his steps day after day;
> But happier, his earthly joys increase,
> Who leads another in the perfect way.
> —HERBERT HERSHEY.

# PERFECTION

We want an aim that can never grow vile and which cannot disappoint our hope. There is but one such on earth, and it is that of being like God. He who strives after union with perfect love must grow out of selfishness, and his success is secured in the omnipotent holiness of God.—SETH BROOKS.

If it be right, do it boldly; if it be wrong, leave it alone.—BERNARD GILPIN.

Every man is set upon an ascending line of human life. You never find God calling a man downwards, diminishing the volume of his manhood, checking his good aspirations, putting him down in the scale of his being. All the divine movement is an upward movement.—ANONYMOUS.

# PERSONALITY

God created man in his own image; in the image of God created He him.—GEN. 1:27.

Yet not I, but Christ liveth in me.—GAL. 2:20.

Beloved, now are we the sons of God, and it doth not yet appear what we shall be: but we know that, when he shall appear, we shall be like him: for we shall see him as he is.—I JOHN 3:2.

> His life was gentle, and the elements
> So mix'd in him that Nature might stand up
> And say to all the world, "This was a man!"
> —WILLIAM SHAKESPEARE.

The hand that hath made you fair hath made you good.—WILLIAM SHAKESPEARE.

> Her voice was ever soft,
> Gentle and low—an excellent thing in woman.
> —WILLIAM SHAKESPEARE.

> With thee conversing I forget all time,
> All seasons, and their change.
> —JOHN MILTON.

# PERSONALITY

The tones of human voice are mightier than strings of brass to move the soul.—FREDERICK KLOPSTOCK.

All the world cries: "We want a man." Don't look so far for this man. You have him right at hand—it is you, it is I, it is each one of us.—ALEXANDRE DUMAS.

> Men are polished through act and speech
>     Each by each,
> As pebbles are smoothed on the rolling beach.
>         —JOHN TOWNSEND TROWBRIDGE.

There are some men and women in whose company we are always at our best. All the best stops in our nature are drawn out, and we find a music in our souls never felt before.—WILLIAM HENRY DRUMMOND.

Whatever you dislike in another person, take care to correct in yourself.—THOMAS SPRATT.

The teachings of Jesus have brought reverence for personality which is at the basis of all right dealings with men.—J. M. PRICE.

The race advances only by the extra achievements of the individual. You are the individual.—CHARLES H. TOWNE.

> Be what thou seemeth; live thy creed;
> Hold up to earth the touch divine;
> Be what thou prayest to be made;
> Let the great Master's steps be thine.
> Sow love and taste its fruitage pure;
> Sow peace, and reap its harvest bright;
> Sow sunshine on the rock and moor,
> And find a harvest-home of light.
>         —HORATIUS BOMAR.

The investment of personality in the program of Christ is life's most valuable investment.—L. N. D. WELLS.

Your greatest contribution to the sum total of things is yourself.—ANONYMOUS.

If you are vain, you will color everything with your own vanities. If lustful, your heart and mind will be so loaded with the smoke and flames of passion that everything will appear distorted through them. If proud and opinionative, you will see nothing in the whole universe except the magnitude and importance of your own opinions.—ANONYMOUS.

When I met him I was looking down; when I left him I was looking up.—ANONYMOUS.

> Her air, her smile, her motions told
>   Of womanly completeness;
> A music as of household songs
>   Was in her voice of sweetness;
> Not fair alone in curve and line
>   But something more and better;
> The secret charm included art
>   In spirit not in letter—
> An inborn grace that nothing lacked
>   Of culture or appliance—
> The warmth of personal courtesy,
>   The charm of self-reliance.
>                       —ANONYMOUS.

# POSSIBILITIES

What is that in thine hand?—EXODUS 4:2.

All things are possible to him that believeth.—MARK 9:23.

With God, all things are possible.—MARK 10:27.

Longfellow could take a worthless sheet of paper, write a poem on it, and make it worth $6,000.00. That is genius.

Rockefeller can sign his name to a piece of paper and make it worth millions. That is capital.

Uncle Sam can take gold, stamp an eagle on it, and make it worth $20.00. That is money.

A mechanic can take material worth $5.00, and make an article worth $50.00. That is skill.

# POSSIBILITIES

An artist can take a fifty cent piece of canvas, paint a picture on it and make it worth $1,000.00. That is art.

God can take a worthless, sinful life, wash it in the blood of Christ, put His spirit in it and make it a blessing to humanity. That is salvation.—ANONYMOUS.

# POWER

All power is given unto me in heaven and in earth.—MATT. 28:20.

There is no power but of God.—ROM. 13:1.

The desire of power in excess caused angels to fall.—FRANCIS BACON.

> When impious men bear sway,
> The post of honor is a private station.
> —WILLIAM SHAKESPEARE.

Justice without power is inefficient; power without justice is tyranny. . . . Justice and power must therefore be brought together so that whatever is just may be powerful and whatever is powerful may be just.—BLAISE PASCAL.

All human power is a compound of time and patience.— HONORÉ DE BALZAC.

Power is so characteristically calm, that calmness in itself has the aspect of power, and forbearance implies strength.—EDWARD GEORGE BULWER-LYTTON.

> Self reverence, self-knowledge, self-control—
> These three alone lead life to sovereign power.
> —ALFRED TENNYSON.

> Give me the power to live for mankind;
> Make me the mouth for such as cannot speak;
> Eyes let me be to groping men and blind;
> A conscience to the base; and to the weak—
> Let me be hands and feet;
> And to the foolish, mind.
> —THEODORE PARKER.

261

# POWER

He who is firmly seated in authority soon learns to think security and not progress, the highest lesson of statecraft.—JAMES RUSSELL LOWELL.

I ask not wealth, but power to take
And use the things I have aright;
Not years, but wisdom that shall make
My life a profit and delight.

—PHOEBE CARY.

Immense power is acquired by assuring yourself in your secret reveries that you were born to control affairs.—ANDREW CARNEGIE.

You have powers you never dreamed of. You can do things you never thought you could do. There are no limitations in what you can do except the limitations in your own mind as to what you cannot do. Don't think you cannot. Think you can.—DARWIN P. KINGSLEY.

Power to its last particle is duty.—ALEXANDER MacLAREN.

Since nothing is settled until it is settled right, no matter how unlimited the power a man may have, unless he exercises it fairly and justly his actions will return to plague him.—FRANK VANDERLIP.

The price of power is responsibility for the public good.—WINTHROP W. ALDRICH.

Unused power slips imperceptibly into the hands of another. —KONRAD HEIDEN.

To know the pains of power, we must go to those who have it; To know the pleasure of power, we must go to those who seek it. The pains of power are real; its pleasures, imaginary.—C. C. COLTON.

Christ is the only transforming power there is and we strive in vain without Him whether we are building a life or a country.—ROSALIE MILLS APPLEBY.

# PRAISE

Bless the Lord, O my Soul: and all that is within me, bless his Holy Name.

Bless the Lord, O my soul, and forget not all his benefits.
—PSALM 103:1-2.

I will sing praise to my God while I have my being.
I will sing praise to my God while I have my being.
—PSALM 104.33.

All thy works shall praise thee.—PSALM 145:10.

Great and marvelous are thy works, Lord God Almighty; just and true are thy ways, thou King of saints.—REV. 15:3.

Praise our God all ye his servants, and ye that trust him, both small and great.—REV. 19:5.

I criticize by creation; not by finding fault.—CICERO.

Praise is the best auxiliary to prayer. He who most bears in mind what has been done for him by God will be most emboldened to ask for fresh gifts from above.—ANDREW MELVILLE.

It is a great happiness to be praised of them who are most praiseworthy.—SIR PHILIP SIDNEY.

Praise has different effects, according to the mind it meets with; it makes a wise man modest, but a fool more arrogant.—OWEN FELTHAM.

> Praise God from whom all blessings flow;
> Praise Him all creatures here below;
> Praise Him above, ye heavenly hosts;
> Praise Father, Son and Holy Ghost.
> —BISHOP THOMAS KEN.

I know of no manner of speaking so offensive as that of giving praise, and closing it with an exception.—RICHARD STEELE.

Man's first care should be to avoid the reproaches of his own heart, and next to escape the censure of the world. If the last interfere with the first, it should be entirely neglected.—But if not, there cannot be a greater satisfaction to an honest mind than to see its own approbation seconded by applauses of the public.—JOSEPH ADDISON.

# PRAISE

One of the most essential preparations for eternity is delight in praising God; a higher acquirement, I do think than even delight and devotedness in prayer.—THOMAS CHALMERS.

Now a little praise warms out of a man the good that is in him, as the sneer of contempt which he feels is unjust chills the ardor to excel.—EDWARD GEORGE BULWER-LYTTON.

There is not a person we employ who does not, like ourselves, desire recognition, praise, gentleness, forbearance, patience.— HENRY WARD BEECHER.

What a person praises is perhaps a surer standard, even, than what he condemns, of his character, information, and abilities.— JULIUS CHARLES HARE.

Applause is the spur of noble minds; the end and aim of weak ones.—C. C. COLTON.

All glory, laud and honor, to Thee, Redeemer, King,
To whom the lips of children, made sweet hosannas ring!
Thou art the King of Israel, Thou David's Royal Son,
Who in the Lord's name comest, the King and Blessed One.
                                        —ANONYMOUS.

Praise is sunshine; blame is rainstorm that beats down and bedraggles, even though at times necessary.—ANONYMOUS.

If you see anything that is worthy of praise, speak of it. Even if you cannot do a worthy deed yourself, commend one who does. Praise is a power for good; both God and man prize it. No prayer is complete without praise. The best worker, if his fellows fail to praise, fails doing as well as he can.—ANONYMOUS.

Criticism is seldom worth considering. Those who know more than you do know better than to criticize; they should rather encourage; and the criticism of those who know less than you do is not worth while.—ANONYMOUS.

# PRAYER

If I regard iniquity in my heart, the Lord will not hear me.—PSALM 66:18.

The Lord is nigh to all them that call upon him; to all that call upon Him in truth.—PSALM 145:18.

Lord, teach us to pray.—LUKE 11:1.

If ye abide in me and my words abide in you, ye shall ask what ye will and it shall be done unto you.—JOHN 15:7.

Pray to God at the beginning of all thy works that thou mayest bring them all to a good ending.—XENOPHON.

Trouble and perplexity drive me to prayer, and prayer drives away perplexity and trouble.—PHILIPP MELANCHTHON.

> We, ignorant of ourselves, beg often our own harms,
> Which the wise powers deny for our good;
> So we find profit by losing our prayers.
> —WILLIAM SHAKESPEARE.

Whatsoever we beg of God, let us also work for it.—JEREMY TAYLOR.

He who prays as he ought, will endeavor to live as he prays.—JOHN OWEN.

Prayer is a sincere, sensible, affectionate pouring out of the soul to God, through Christ in the strength and assistance of the Spirit, for such things as God has promised.—JOHN BUNYAN.

> Our vows are heard betimes! And Heaven takes care
> To grant, before we can conclude the prayer:
> Preventing angels met it half the way,
> And sent us back to praise, who came to pray.
> —JOHN DRYDEN.

> Satan trembles when he sees
> The least of saints upon his knees.
> —WILLIAM COWPER.

Prayer is not eloquence but earnestness.—HANNAH MORE.

All the duties of religion are eminently solemn and venerable in the eyes of children. But none will so strongly prove the sincerity of the parent—none so powerfully awaken the reverence of the child—none so happily recommend the instruction he receives, as family devotion, particularly those in which petitions for the children occupy a distinguished place.—TIMOTHY DWIGHT.

They never sought in vain that sought the Lord aright.—ROBERT BURNS.

The Lord's prayer contains the sum total of religion and morals.—ARTHUR WELLESLEY, DUKE OF WELLINGTON.

> He prayeth best who loveth best
> All things, both great and small;
> For the dear God who loveth us,
> He made and loveth all.
> —SAMUEL TAYLOR COLERIDGE.

I believe I should have been swept by the flood of French infidelity, if it had not been for one thing, the remembrance of the time when my sainted mother used to make me kneel by her side, taking my little hand in hers, and caused me to repeat the Lord's prayer.—JOHN RANDOLPH.

Let our prayers, like the ancient sacrifices, ascend morning and evening. Let our days begin and end with God.—WILLIAM ELLERY CHANNING.

I was never deeply interested in any object, I never prayed sincerely and earnestly for anything but it came at some time. No matter how distant the day, somehow, in some shape, probably the last I should have advised, it came—ADONIRAM JUDSON.

There are moments when whatever be the attitude of the body, the soul is on its knees.—VICTOR HUGO.

Let us be silent that we may hear the whisper of God.—RALPH WALDO EMERSON.

The Lord's prayer may be committed to memory quickly but it is slowly learned by heart.—JOHN F. D. MAURICE.

> Every chain that spirits wear
> Crumbles in the breath of prayer.
> —JOHN GREENLEAF WHITTIER.

# PRAYER

Prayer is not overcoming God's reluctance; it is laying hold of His highest willingness.—ARCHBISHOP RICHARD CHENEVIX TRENCH.

I have been driven many times to my knees by the overwhelming conviction that I had nowhere else to go. My own wisdom, and that of all about me, seemed insufficient for the day.—ABRAHAM LINCOLN.

> More things are wrought by prayer
> Than this world dreams of. Wherefore, let thy voice
> Rise like a fountain for me night and day.
> For what are men better than sheep or goats
> That nourish a blind life within the brain,
> If, knowing God, they lift not hands of prayer
> Both for themselves and those who call them friends?
> For so the whole round earth is every way
> Bound by gold chains about the feet of God.
> —ALFRED TENNYSON.

> They who have steeped their souls in prayer
> Can every anguish calmly bear.
> —RICHARD MONCKTON MILNES,
> LORD HOUGHTON.

> God answers sharp and sudden on some prayers,
> And thrusts the thing we have prayed for in our face,
> A gauntlet with a gift in it.
> —ELIZABETH BARRETT BROWNING.

If you do not wish for His Kingdom, don't pray for it, but if you do, you must do more than pray for it, you must work for it.—JOHN RUSKIN.

Faithful prayer always implies correlative exertion. No man can ask, honestly and hopefully to be delivered from temptation unless he has honestly and firmly determined to do the best he can to keep out of it.—JOHN RUSKIN.

I have lived to thank God that all of my prayers have not been answered.—JEAN INGELOW.

Who rises from prayer a better man, his prayer is answered.—GEORGE MEREDITH.

# PRAYER

Prayer, in its simplest definition, is merely a wish turned God-ward.—PHILLIPS BROOKS.

> Prayer is not artful monologue
> Of voice uplifted from the sod;
> It is Love's tender dialogue
> Between the soul and God.
> —JOHN RICHARD MORELAND.

If you would have God hear you when you pray, you must hear Him when he speaks.—THOMAS BENTON BROOKS.

Prayer crowns God with the honor and glory due to His name, and God crowns prayer with assurance and comfort. The most praying souls are the most assured souls.—THOMAS BENTON BROOKS.

> Dear Lord, who sought at dawn of day,
> In solitary woods to pray,
> In quietness we come to ask
> Thy presence for our daily task.
> —HARRY WEBB FARRINGTON.

> God answers prayer; sometimes, when hearts are weak,
> He gives the very gifts believers seek.
> But often faith must learn a deeper rest,
> And trust God's silence, when He does not speak;
> For he whose name is Love will send the best:
> Stars may burn out nor mountain walls endure
> But God is true; His promises are sure
> To those who seek. —M. G. PLANTZ.

God's way of answering the Christian's prayer for more patience, experience, hope and love often is to put him into the furnace of affliction.—RICHARD CECIL.

> Prayer is the soul's sincere desire,
> Uttered or unexpressed—
> The motion of a hidden fire,
> That trembles in the breast.

# PRAYER

Prayer is the burden of a sigh,
 The falling of a tear,
The upward glancing of an eye,
 When none but God is near.
                 —JAMES MONTGOMERY.

I know not by what methods rare,
But this I know: God answers prayer.
I know not if the blessing sought
Will come in just the guise I thought.
I leave my prayer to Him alone
Whose will is wiser than my own.
                 —ELIZA M. HICKOK.

We must remember that "No" can be an answer to prayer.—
KATIE PINSON.

Away in foreign fields they wondered how
 Their simple words had power—
At home the Christians, two or three had met
 To pray an hour.
Yes, we are always wondering, wondering how—
 Because we do not see
Someone—perhaps unknown and far away—
 On bended knee.        —ANONYMOUS.

In the morning, prayer is the key that opens to us the treasures of God's mercies and blessings; in the evening, it is the key
that shuts us up under His protection and safeguard.—ANONY-
MOUS.

O Thou by whom we come to God,
 The Life, the Truth, the Way—
The path of prayer Thyself hath trod,
 Lord, teach us how to pray.
                 —ANONYMOUS.

If Christians spent as much time praying as they do grum-
bling, they would have nothing to grumble about.—ANONYMOUS.

Thy shoes shall be iron and brass; and as thy days, so shall thy strength be.—DEUT. 33:25.

Thou art a great people, and hast great power: thou shalt not have one lot only:
But the mountain shall be thine.—JOSHUA 17:17-18.

If my people, which are called by my name, shall humble themselves, and pray, and seek my face, and turn from their wicked ways; then will I hear from heaven, and will forgive their sin, and will heal their land.—II CHRON. 7:14.

Be ye strong, therefore, and let not your hands be weak for your work shall be rewarded.—II CHRON. 15:7.

The eyes of the Lord run to and fro throughout the whole earth, to show himself strong in behalf of them whose heart is perfect toward him.—II CHRON. 16:9.

The Lord will be a refuge for the oppressed; a refuge in times of trouble.—PSALM 9:9.

He shall cover thee with his feathers, and under his wings shalt thou trust.—PSALM 91:4.

He shall give his angels charge over thee, to keep thee in all thy ways; they shall bear thee up in their hands, lest thou dash thy foot against a stone.—PSALM 91:11-12.

The Lord shall preserve thee from all evil: he shall preserve thy soul.
The Lord shall preserve thy going out and thy coming in from this time forth, and even forever more.—PSALM 121:7-8.

Though your sins be as scarlet, they shall be as white as snow; though they be red like crimson, they shall be as wool.—ISA. 1:18.

Then shall thy light break forth as the morning, and thine health shall spring forth speedily and thy righteousness shall go before thee; the glory of the Lord shall be thy reward.
And the Lord shall guide thee continually, and satisfy thy soul in drought, and make fat thy bones: and thou shalt be like a watered garden, and like a spring of water, whose waters fail not.—ISA. 58:8 & 11.

I will make thee an eternal excellency, a joy of many generations.—Isa. 60:15.

Thou shalt also be a crown of glory in the hand of the Lord,
and a royal diadem in the hand of thy God.

Thou shalt no more be termed Forsaken; neither shall thy
land any more be termed Desolate: but thou shalt be called
Hephzibah, and thy land Beulah: for the Lord delighteth in thee,
and thy land shall be married.

For as a young man marrieth a virgin, so shall thy sons marry
thee: and as the bridegroom rejoiceth over the bride, so shall thy
God rejoice over thee.—Isa. 62:3, 4, 5.

I will feed my flock, and I will cause them to lie down, saith
the Lord God.

I will seek that which was lost, and bring again that which
was driven away, and will bind up that which was broken, and
will strengthen that which was sick.—Ezek. 34:15-16.

Though I have afflicted thee, I will afflict thee no more.—
Nah. 1:12.

The just shall live by faith.—Hab. 2:4; Gal. 3:11; Heb. 10:38.

The earth shall be filled with the knowledge of the glory of
the Lord as the waters cover the sea.—Hab. 2:14.

They shall be mine, saith the Lord of hosts, in that day when
I make up my jewels; and I will spare them, as a man spareth
his own son that serveth him.—Mal. 3:17.

Ask, and it shall be given you; seek, and ye shall find; knock,
and it shall be opened unto you.—Matt. 7:7.

Come unto me, all ye that labor and are heavy laden, and I
will give you rest.

Take my yoke upon you, and learn of me; for I am meek and
lowly in heart: and ye shall find rest unto your souls.

For my yoke is easy, and my burden is light.—Matt. 11:28-30.

Believe on the Lord, Jesus Christ, and thou shalt be saved.—
Acts 16:31.

Be careful for nothing; but in every thing by prayer and sup-plication with thanksgiving let your requests be made known unto God.

And the peace of God, which passeth all understanding, shall keep your hearts and minds through Christ Jesus.—PHIL. 4:6-7.

We have not an high priest which cannot be touched with the feeling of our infirmities; but was in all points tempted like as we are, yet without sin.

Let us therefore come boldly unto the throne of grace, that we may obtain mercy, and find grace to help in time of need. —HEB. 4:15.

Whereby are given unto us exceeding great and precious promises: that by these ye might be partakers of the divine nature.—II PET. 1:4.

The Lord is not slack concerning his promise, as some men count slackness; but is longsuffering to usward, not willing that any should perish, but that all should come to repentance.—II PET. 3:9.

They shall walk with me in white.—REV. 3:4.


# PRINCIPLES

A double minded man is unstable in all his ways.—JAS. 1:8.

He who merely knows right principles is not equal to him who loves them.—CONFUCIUS.

Our principles are the springs of our actions; our actions, the springs of our happiness or misery. Too much care, therefore, cannot be taken in forming our principles.—JOHN SKELTON.

Always vote for a principle, though you vote alone, and you may cherish the sweet reflection that your vote is never lost.— JOHN QUINCY ADAMS.

Integrity in men is to be measured by their conduct, not by their professions.—JUNIUS.

# PRINCIPLES

Principle is a passion for truth and right.—WILLIAM HAZLITT.

Many men do not allow their principles to take root but pull them up every now and then, as children do the flowers they have planted, to see if they are growing.—HENRY WADSWORTH LONG-FELLOW.

Expedients are for the hour; principles for the ages.—HENRY WARD BEECHER.

One may be better than his reputation, but never better than his principles.—ANONYMOUS.

Better be poisoned in one's blood than to be poisoned in one's principles.—ANONYMOUS.

# PROGRESS

Speak to the children of Israel that they go forward.—EXOD. 14:15b.

Some falls are means the happier to rise.—WILLIAM SHAKE-SPEARE.

All that is human must retrograde if it does not advance.—EDWARD GIBBON.

Two principles govern the moral and intellectual world. One is perpetual progress, the other the necessary limitations to that progress. If the former alone prevailed there would be nothing steadfast and durable on earth, and the whole of social life would be the sport of winds and waves. If the latter had exclusive sway, or even if it obtained a mischievous preponderancy, everything would petrify or rot. The best ages of the world are those in which these two principles are the most equally balanced. In such ages every enlightened man ought to adopt both principles, and with one hand develop what he can, and with the other re-strain and uphold what he ought.—FRIEDRICH VON GENTZ.

Every age has its problems, by solving which humanity is helped forward.—HEINRICH HEINE.

# PROGRESS

Progress . . . the onward strides of God.—VICTOR HUGO.

Progress is the activity of today, and the assurance of tomorrow.—RALPH WALDO EMERSON.

The world owes all its onward impulses to men ill at ease. The happy man inevitably confines himself within ancient limits. —NATHANIEL HAWTHORNE.

> When the fight begins within himself,
> A man's worth something.
> —ROBERT BROWNING.

"Can any good come out of Nazareth?"—This is always the question of the wiseacres and knowing ones.—But the good, the new, comes from exactly that quarter whence it is not looked for, and is always something different from what is expected. Everything new is received with contempt for it begins in obscurity. It becomes a power unobserved.—LUDWIG FEUERBACH.

He is only advancing in life whose heart is getting softer, his blood warmer, his brain quicker, and his spirit entering into living peace.—JOHN RUSKIN.

Nothing is lost upon a man who is bent upon growth; nothing wasted on one who is always preparing for his work and his life by keeping eyes, mind and heart open to nature, men, books, experience. Such a man finds ministers to his education on all sides; everything cooperates with his passion for growth. And what he gathers serves him at unexpected moments in unforeseen ways.—HAMILTON WRIGHT MABIE.

The individual and the race are always moving; and as we drift into new latitudes new lights open in the heavens more immediately over us.—E. H. CHAPIN.

Intellectually, as well as politically, the direction of all true progress is toward greater freedom, and along an endless succession of ideas.—C. C. COLTON.

He that is good will infallibly become better, and he that is bad will certainly become worse; for vice, virtue and time are three things that never stand still.—C. C. COLTON.

# PROGRESS

The wisest man may be wiser today than he was yesterday, and tomorrow than he is today. Total freedom from change would imply total freedom from error; but this is the prerogative of Omniscience alone.—C. C. COLTON.

Works of true merit are seldom very popular in their own day; for knowledge is on the march and men of genius are the videttes that are far in the advance of their comrades. They are not with them, but before them; not in the camp, but beyond it.—C. C. COLTON.

The grandest of all laws is the law of progressive development.—Under it, in the wide sweep of things, men grow wiser as they grow older, and societies better.—E. G. BOVEE.

# PROVIDENCE

O Lord, thou hast searched me, and known me.

Thou knowest my downsitting and mine uprising, thou understandest my thought afar off.

Thou compassest my path and my lying down, and art acquainted with all my ways.

For there is not a word in my tongue, but, lo, O Lord, thou knowest it altogether.

Thou has beset me behind and before, and laid thine hand upon me.

Such knowledge is too wonderful for me; it is high, I cannot attain unto it.

Whither shall I go from thy spirit? or whither shall I flee from thy presence?

If I ascend up into heaven, thou art there: if I make my bed in hell, behold, thou art there.

If I take the wings of the morning, and dwell in the uttermost parts of the sea;

Even there shall thy hand lead me, and thy right hand shall hold me.

If I say, Surely the darkness shall cover me; even the night shall light about me.

# PROVIDENCE

Yea, the darkness hideth not from thee; but the night shinetl
as the day: the darkness and the light are both alike to thee.—
PSALM 139:1-12.

I have made the earth, and created man upon it: I, even my
hands, have stretched out the heavens, and all their hosts have I
commanded.—ISA. 45:12.

Who guides below and rules above, the great disposer and
mighty king; than He none greater, next to Him can be, or is,
or was; supreme, He singly fills the throne.—HORACE.

God's goodness hath been great to Thee.
Let never day or night unhallowed pass,
But still remember what the Lord hath done.
—WILLIAM SHAKESPEARE.

We must follow not force Providence.—WILLIAM SHAKESPEARE.

We cannot too often think there is a never-sleeping eye,
which reads the heart and registers our thoughts.—FRANCIS BACON.

In all thy actions, think God sees thee; in all his actions,
labor to see Him.—FRANCIS QUARLES.

My faith has no bed to sleep upon but omnipotency.—SAMUEL
RUTHERFORD.

What can escape the eye of God, all seeing,
Or deceive His heart, omniscient.
—JOHN MILTON.

God, veiled in majesty, alone gives light and life to all; bids
the great systems move, and changing seasons in their turns advance, unmoved, unchanged himself.—WILLIAM SOMERVILLE.

Who finds not Providence all good and wise,
Alike in what he gives and what he denies?
—ALEXANDER POPE.

God governs in the affairs of man; and if a sparrow cannot
fall to the ground without His notice, is it probable that an empire can rise without His aid.—BENJAMIN FRANKLIN.

God tempers the wind to the shorn lamb.—LAURENCE STERNE.

# PROVIDENCE

Providence has at all times been my only dependence, for all other resources seem to have failed us.—GEORGE WASHINGTON.

> Yes, thou art ever present, Power Divine;
> Not circumscribed by time,
> Nor fixed by space,
> Confined to altars, nor to temples bound,
> In wealth, in want, in freedom, or in chains,
> In dungeons or on thrones, the faithful find thee.
> —HANNAH MORE.

God is everywhere, the God who framed mankind to be one mighty family, himself our Father, and the world our home.—SAMUEL TAYLOR COLERIDGE.

In the huge mass of evil as it rolls and swells, there is ever some good working toward deliverance and triumphs.—THOMAS CARLYLE.

Every blade of grass in the field is measured; the green cups and the colored crowns of every flower are curiously counted; the stars of the firmament wheel in cunningly calculated orbits; even the storms have their laws.—WILLIAM G. BLAIKIE.

By going a few minutes sooner or later, by stopping to speak with a friend on the corner, by meeting this man or that, or by turning down this street instead of the other, we may let slip some impending evil, by which the whole current of our lives would have been changed. There is no possible solution in the dark enigma but the one word, "Providence."—HENRY WADSWORTH LONGFELLOW.

Cast all your care on God! That anchor holds.—ALFRED TENNYSON.

One on God's side is a majority.—WENDELL PHILLIPS.

Some one has said that in war Providence is on the side of the strongest regiments. And I have noticed that Providence is on the side of clear heads and honest hearts; and wherever a man walks faithfully in the ways that God has marked out for him, Providence, as the Christian says,—luck as the heathen says,—

will be on that man's side. In the long run you will find that God's providence is in favor of those that keep His laws, and against those that break them.—HENRY WARD BEECHER.

Resignation and faith behold God in the smallest hair that falls; and the happiest life is that of him who has bound together all the affairs of life, great and small, and intrusted them to God.—JOHN WHITE ALEXANDER.

> God never forsook at need
> The soul that trusted Him indeed.
> —G. NEWMARK.

One cannot think that any holy earthly things will cease when we shall join the angels of God in Heaven. Love here must shadow our love there, deeper, because more spiritual.—ANONYMOUS.


# PRUDENCE

The wisdom of the prudent is to understand his way.—PROV. 14:8.

A prudent man foreseeth evil.—PROV. 27:12.

Woe unto them that are wise in their own eyes, and prudent in their own sight.—ISA. 5:21.

No other protection is wanting provided you are under the guidance of prudence.—JUVENAL.

The richest endowments of the mind are temperance, prudence and fortitude. Prudence is a universal virtue, which enters into the composition of all the rest; and where she is not, fortitude loses its name and nature.—FRANCOIS VOLTAIRE.

Those who, in the confidence of superior capacities or attainments, neglect the common maxims of life, should be reminded that nothing will supply the want of prudence; but that negligence and irregularity, long continued, will make knowledge useless, wit ridiculous and genius contemptible.—SAMUEL JOHNSON.

# PRUDENCE

Prudence is a duty which we owe ourselves, and if we will be so much our own enemies as to neglect it, we are not to wonder if the world is deficient in discharging their duty to us; for when a man lays a foundation of his own ruin, others too often are apt to build upon it.—HENRY FIELDING.

Prudence is a quality incompatible with vice, and can never be effectively enlisted in its cause.—EDMUND BURKE.

If the prudence of reserve and decorum dictates silence in some circumstances, in others prudence of a higher order may justify us in speaking our thoughts.—EDMUND BURKE.

> Beware of desperate steps! The darkest day,
> Live till tomorrow, will have passed away.
> —WILLIAM COWPER.

The rules of prudence, in general, like the laws of the stone tablets, are for the most part prohibitive. Thou shalt not, is their characteristic formula; and it is an especial part of Christian prudence that it should be so.—SAMUEL TAYLOR COLERIDGE.

Without prudence, fortitude is madness.—SAMUEL G. GOODRICH.

Prudence is a conformity to the rules of reason, truth and decency, at all times, in all circumstances. It differs from wisdom only in degree; wisdom being nothing but a more consummate habit of prudence; and prudence a lower degree or weaker habit of wisdom.—JAMES M. MASON.

Let prudence always attend your pleasures; it is the way to enjoy the sweets of them, and not be afraid of the consequences. —ANONYMOUS.

# PURITY

He that loveth pureness of heart, for the grace of his lips the king shall be his friend.—PROV. 22:11.

Blessed are the pure in heart, for they shall see God.—MATT. 5:8.

# PURITY

To the pure, all things are pure.—TITUS 1:15.

Whatsoever things are pure . . . think on these things.—PHIL. 4:8.

Only a heart without a stain knows perfect ease.—JOHANN WOLFGANG VON GOETHE.

Modesty is the conscience of the body.—HONORÉ DE BALZAC.

Man is the only animal that blushes, or needs to.—MARK TWAIN (pseud. of SAMUEL L. CLEMENS).

Purity is the power without which a girl can never run the royal race to which she is destined.—ROSALIE MILLS APPLEBY.

# PURPOSE

Choose you this day whom ye will serve.—JOSH. 24:15.

Thine ears shall hear a word behind thee, saying, This is the way, walk ye in it.—ISA. 30:21.

A man's true greatness lies in the consciousness of an honest purpose in life, founded on a just estimate of himself and everything else, on frequent self-examinations, and a steady obedience to the rule which he knows to be right, without troubling himself about what others may think or say, or whether they do or do not that which he thinks and says and does.—MARCUS AURELIUS.

It is better by a noble boldness to run the risk of being subject to half of the evils we anticipate, than to remain in cowardly listlessness for fear of what may happen.—HERODOTUS.

Who does the best his circumstances allow, does well, acts nobly; angels could do no more.—EDWARD YOUNG.

Firmness of purpose is one of the most necessary sinews of character, and one of the best instruments of success. Without it genius wastes its efforts in a maze of inconsistencies.—LORD CHESTERFIELD.

# PURPOSE

Attempt great things for God; expect great things from God. —WILLIAM CAREY.

When a man has not a good reason for doing a thing, he has one good reason for letting it alone.—SIR WALTER SCOTT.

Great minds have purposes; others have wishes.—WASHINGTON IRVING.

The man without a purpose is like a ship without a rudder—a waif, a nothing, a no man. Have a purpose in life, and, having it, throw such strength of mind and muscle into your works as God has given you.—THOMAS CARLYLE.

The man who succeeds above his fellows is the one who early in life clearly discerns his object, and towards that object habitually directs his powers. Even genius itself is but fine observation strengthened by fixity of purpose. Every man who observes vigilantly and resolves steadfastly grows unconsciously into genius. —EDWARD GEORGE BULWER-LYTTON.

I have brought myself by long meditation to the conviction that a human being with a settled purpose must accomplish it, and that nothing can resist a will which will stake even existence upon its fulfillment.—BENJAMIN DISRAELI.

The secret of success is constancy in purpose.—BENJAMIN DISRAELI.

Determine that the thing can and shall be done, and then we shall find the way.—ABRAHAM LINCOLN.

Once to every man and nation comes a moment to decide,
In the strife of Truth with Falsehood, for the good or evil side.
—JAMES RUSSELL LOWELL.

The greatest thing in this world is not so much where we are, but in what direction we are moving—OLIVER WENDELL HOLMES.

There is no road to success but through a clear, strong purpose.—T. T. MUNGER.

More men fail through lack of purpose than through lack of talent.—W. A. ("BILLY") SUNDAY.

# PURPOSE

Achievements ordinarily follow in due course when a person, after planning his work, works his plan.—ELSIE BOWMAN.

He who would be a mover of the world must not be moved by the world.—ANONYMOUS.

# QUIETNESS

In quietness and in confidence shall be your strength.—ISA. 30:15.

I have oft regretted my speech—never my silence.—PUBLIUS SYRUS.

True silence is the rest of the mind, and is to the spirit what sleep is to the body, nourishment and refreshment. It is a great virtue; it covers folly, keeps secrets, avoids disputes, and prevents sin.—WILLIAM PENN.

> The gods approve
> The depth and not the tumult of the soul.
> —WILLIAM WORDSWORTH.

> Tranquility; thou better name
> Than all the family of Fame.
> —SAMUEL TAYLOR COLERIDGE.

What sweet delights a quiet life affords.—HENRY DRUMMOND.

> There is in stillness oft a magic power
> To calm the breast when struggling passions lower,
> Touched by its influence, in the soul arise
> Diviner feelings, kindred with the skies.
> —JOHN HENRY, CARDINAL NEWMAN.

> Drop Thy still dews of quietness,
>    Till all our strivings cease;
> Take from our souls the strain and stress,
> And let our ordered lives confess
>    The beauty of Thy peace.
> —JOHN GREENLEAF WHITTIER.

# QUIETNESS

Well timed silence hath more eloquence than speech.—MARTIN FARQUHAR TUPPER.

A consistent Christian may not have rapture. He has that which is much better than rapture—calmness. God's serene and perpetual presence.—FREDERICK WILLIAM ROBERTSON.

Solitude is as needful to the imagination as society is wholesome for the character—JAMES RUSSELL LOWELL.

Be silent and safe—silence never betrays you.—JOHN BOYLE O'REILLY.

> O Golden Silence, bid our souls be still,
>> And on the foolish fretting of our care
>> Lay thy soft touch of healing unaware.
>>> —JULIA CAROLINE DORR.

Talent grows in the silence—OLD PROVERB.

> "He giveth quietness," O Elder Brother,
>> Whose homeless feet have pressed our path of pain,
> Whose hands have borne the burden of our sorrow,
>> That in our losses we might find our gain.
>>> —ANONYMOUS.

> I need wide spaces in my heart
> Where Faith and I can go apart
>> And grow serene.
> Life gets so choked by busy living,
> Kindness so lost in fussy giving
>> That Love slips by unseen.
>>> —ANONYMOUS.


# REDEMPTION

Ye shall be redeemed without money.—ISA. 52:3.

Thou shalt know that I, the Lord, am thy Saviour and thy Redeemer.—ISA. 60:16b.

# REDEMPTION

Behold the Lamb of God which taketh away the sin of the world.—JOHN 1:29.

When the fullness of time was come, God sent forth his Son, made of a woman, made under the law,

To redeem them that were under the law, that we might receive the adoption of sons.—GAL. 4:4, 5.

By his own blood he entered in once into the holy place, having obtained eternal redemption for us.—HEB. 9:12.

Ye know that ye were not redeemed with corruptible things, as silver and gold . . . But with the precious blood of Christ, as of a lamb without blemish and without spot.—I PET. 1:18, 19.

> Alas! Alas!
> Why, all the souls that were, were forfeit once;
> And He that might the vantage best have took,
> Found out the remedy.
> —WILLIAM SHAKESPEARE.

And now, without redemption, all mankind must have been lost, adjudged to death and hell by doom severe.—JOHN MILTON.

> When I survey the wondrous cross
> On which the Prince of Glory died,
> My richest gain I count but loss
> And pour contempt on all my pride.
> —ISAAC WATTS.

By Christ's purchasing redemption, two things are intended: his satisfaction and his merit; the one pays our debt, and so satisfies; the other procures our title, and so merits. The satisfaction of Christ is to free us from misery; the merit of Christ is to purchase happiness for us.—JONATHAN EDWARDS.

Underneath all the arches of Bible history, throughout the whole grand temple of the Scriptures, these two voices ever echo —Man is ruined! Man is redeemed!—C. D. FOSS.

> I take, O Cross, thy shadow
> For my abiding place;
> I ask no other sunshine
> Than the sunshine of His face;

# REDEMPTION

Content to let the world go by,
To know no gain nor loss,
My sinful self my only shame—
My glory all the cross.
—Elizabeth C. Clephane.

Justification is God's own bridge which stretches across the pit of iniquity and leads to our heavenly home. The Word tells us that God is the architect of the bridge, that He fashioned it through grace, that its cornerstone is redemption through the blood of Christ, and that its approach is by faith alone.—Charles J. Woodbridge.

The whole structure of man and of the world is moulded to be the theatre of the redemption of the sinner. Not in Eden, but on Calvary and in heaven, which is the child of Calvary, we see realized the whole idea of God.—I. B. Brown.

The work of redemption is the most glorious of all the works of God; it will forever remain the grand mirror to reflect the brightest beams of the divine glory.—Nathaniel Emmons.

Redemption is the science and the song of all eternity. Archangels, day and night, into its glories look. The saints and elders around the throne, old in the years of heaven, examine it perpetually.—Robert Pollock.

It cost more to redeem than to create us. In creation there was but "speaking a word"; in redeeming us there was "shedding of blood."—Anonymous.

# RELIGION

If any man among you seem to be religious, and bridleth not his tongue, but deceiveth his own heart, this man's religion is vain. Pure religion and undefiled before God and the Father is this: To visit the fatherless and widows in their affliction, and to keep himself unspotted from the world.—Jas. 1:26-27.

Unless we place our religion and our treasure in the same thing, religion will always be sacrificed.—Epictetus.

# RELIGION

A city may as well be built in the air, as a commonwealth or kingdom be either constituted or preserved without the support of religion.—PLUTARCH.

It is no good reason for a man's religion that he was born and brought up in it; for then a Turk would have as much reason to be a Turk as a Christian a Christian.—WILLIAM CHILLINGWORTH.

No sciences are better attested than the religion of the Bible. —SIR ISAAC NEWTON.

Religion would not have any enemies if it were not an enemy to their vices.—JEAN BAPTISTE MASSILLON.

If men are so wicked with religion, what would they be without it?—BENJAMIN FRANKLIN.

True religion is the foundation of society, the basis on which all true civil governments rest, and from which power derives its authority, laws their efficacy, and both their sanction. If it once is shaken by contempt, the whole fabric cannot be stable or lasting—EDMUND BURKE.

Educate children without religion and you make a race of clever devils out of them.—ARTHUR WELLESLEY, DUKE OF WELLINGTON.

Religion cannot pass away. The burning of a little straw may hide the stars of the sky, but the stars are there, and will reappear. —THOMAS CARLYLE.

An every-day religion—one that loves the duties of our common walk; one that makes an honest man; one that accomplishes an intellectual and moral growth in the subject; one that works in all weather and improves all opportunities, will best and most healthily promote the growth of a church and the power of the gospel.—HORACE BUSHNELL.

I say the whole earth and all the stars in the sky are for religion's sake.—WALT WHITMAN.

What I want is, not to possess religion but to have a religion that shall possess me.—CHARLES KINGSLEY.

# RELIGION

It has been said that true religion will make a man a more thorough gentleman than all the courts of Europe. And it is true that you may see simple laboring men as thorough gentlemen as any duke, simply because they have learned to fear God; and fearing him, to restrain themselves, which is the very root and essence of all good breeding.—CHARLES KINGSLEY.

You cannot legislate the human race into heaven.—CHARLES PARKHURST.

God looks with approval and man turns with gratitude to every one who shows by a cheerful life that religion is a blessing for this world and the next.—HENRY VAN DYKE.

The very helpfulness of the world today is in itself a repudiation of that self-sufficient and self-confident view of life that the world in its progressive development has outgrown the need of religion. It is religion which gives the world what it most needs—a standard of right living, a cause to maintain and defend, a leader to follow and a law to obey.—JOHN GRIER HIBBEN.

True religion is the life we live; not the creed we profess.—J. F. WRIGHT.

There are three modes of bearing the ills of life: by indifference, which is the most common; by philosophy, which is the most ostentatious; and by religion, which is the most effectual.—C. C. COLTON.

Where true religion has prevented one crime, false religions have offered pretexts for a thousand.—C. C. COLTON.

If we make religion our business, God will make it our blessedness.—H. G. J. ADAM.

Religion is equally the basis of private virtue and public faith: of happiness of the individual and prosperity of the nation.—W. BARROW.

The flower of youth never appears more beautiful than when it bends toward the sun of righteousness.—MATTHEW HENRY.

Science and religion no more contradict each other than light and electricity.—WILLIAM HIRAM FAULKES.

# RELIGION

Religion consists not so much in joyous feelings as in constant devotedness to God, and laying ourselves out for the good of others.—GEORGE E. STEWART, JR.

Wherever there has been an established religion it has eventuated in one of two things: either the absorption of the Church by the State or the absorption of the State by the Church. Either of the two makes a hybrid monstrosity! Both are bad, and neither is right.—GEORGE E. STEWART, JR.

It is natural to be religious; it is supernatural to be Christian.
—ANONYMOUS.

A man's religion should be as broad as his life. The man who has the right concept of religion will not speak of his business life, his social life, his religious life, but will make a practical application of his religion in all phases of his activities.—T. B. MASTON.

True religion extends alike to the intellect and the heart. Intellect is in vain if it lead not to emotion, and emotion is vain if it is not enlightened by intellect; and both are vain if not guided by truth and leading to duty.—TRYON EDWARDS.

A man who puts aside his religion because he is going into society, is like one taking off his shoes because he is about to walk upon thorns.—RICHARD CECIL.

Let your religion be seen. Lamps do not talk but they do shine. A lighthouse sounds no drums, it beats no gong; yet, far over the waters, its friendly light is seen by the mariner.—THEODORE L. CUYLER.

It is a part of my religion never to hurt any man's feelings.
—W. D. HOWARD.

The man proclaims his religion in his life and shows it in his face; worships God in the nobleness of his life, and shows his reverence in the love of man and of animals; reveals it in tolerance, kindness, gentleness and strength. Our love of mankind is the measure of our love of God; our faith in the eternal goodness, eternal progress, is the test of our religion.—ANONYMOUS.

# REPENTANCE

I am not come to call the righteous but sinners to repentance. —MATT. 9:13.

John did baptize in the wilderness, and preach the baptism of repentance for the remission of sins.—MARK 1:4.

Except ye repent ye shall all likewise perish.—LUKE 13:3.

Repent ye, therefore, and be converted that your sins may be blotted out.—ACTS 3:19.

Godly sorrow worketh repentance.—II COR. 7:10.

True repentance is to cease from sin.—SAINT AMBROSE.

There is one case of death bed repentance recorded—that of the penitent thief, that none should despair; and only one that none should presume.—SAINT AUGUSTINE.

To do so no more is the truest repentance.—MARTIN LUTHER.

You cannot repent too soon, because you do not know how soon it may be too late.—THOMAS FULLER.

Repentance is a hearty sorrow for our past misdeeds, and a sincere resolution and an endeavor to the utmost of our power, to conform all our actions to the law of God. It does not consist in one single act of sorrow, but in doing works meet for repentance; in a sincere obedience to the law of Christ for the remainder of our lives.—JOHN LOCKE.

Repentance hath a purifying power and every tear is of the cleansing virtue; but these penitential clouds must be still kept dropping; one shower will not suffice; for repentance is not one single action but a course.—ROBERT SOUTH.

True repentance has a double aspect; it looks upon things past with a weeping eye, and upon the future with a watchful eye.—ROBERT SOUTH.

Repentance is the heart's sorrow, and a clear life ensuing. —WILLIAM SHAKESPEARE.

A true repentance shuns the evil itself
More than the external suffering or the shame.
                                        —WILLIAM SHAKESPEARE.

# REPENTANCE

Our greatest glory consists not in never falling, but in rising every time we fall.—OLIVER GOLDSMITH.

When the soul has laid down its faults at the feet of God, it feels as though it had wings.—EUGENIE DE GUÉRIN.

Of all acts of man, repentance is the most divine. The greatest of all faults is to be conscious of none.—THOMAS CARLYLE.

Repentance may begin instantly, but reformation often requires a sphere of years.—HENRY WARD BEECHER.

Mere sorrow, which weeps and sits still, is not repentance. Repentance is sorrow converted into action; into a movement toward a new and better life.—MARVIN RICHARDSON VINCENT.

There is a greater depravity in not repenting of sin when it has been committed, than in committing it at first. To deny, as Peter did, is bad; but not to weep bitterly, as he did, when we have denied, is worse.—EDWARD PAYSON.

The repentance consists in the heart being broken for sin and broken from sin. Some often repent, yet never reform; they resemble a man travelling in a dangerous path, who frequently starts and stops, but never turns back.—B. THORNTON.

It is one thing to mourn for sin because it exposes us to hell, and another to mourn for it because it is an infinite evil; one thing to mourn for it because it is injurious to ourselves, and another to mourn for it because it is wrong and offensive to God. It is one thing to be terrified; another, to be humbled.—GARDINER SPRING.

True repentance hates the sin, and not merely the penalty; and it hates the sin most of all because it has discovered and felt God's love.—W. M. TAYLOR.

Repentance, to be of any avail, must work a change of heart and conduct.—THEODORE L. CUYLER.

Late repentance is seldom true, but true repentance is never too late.—R. VENNING.

To repent is to alter one's way of looking at life; it is to take God's point of view instead of one's own.—ANONYMOUS.

# RESIGNATION

And so will I go in unto the king, which is not according to the law: and if I perish, I perish.—ESTHER 4:16.

> White Captain of my soul, lead on;
> I follow Thee, come dark or dawn.
> Only vouchsafe three things I crave:
> Where terror stalks, help me be brave!
> Where righteous ones can scarce endure
> The siren call, help me be pure!
> Where vows grow dim, and men dare do
> What once they scorned, help me be true
> —ROBERT FREEMAN.

I will absolutely surrender to God every unsurrendered area of my life.—PAUL MORRISON.

Christ has no way to reach His imperial place at the heart of mankind save as you and I open up a path for His sovereign feet. —PAUL MORRISON.

> Although my body be confined
>    To ways of quietness and rest,
> My spirit sings within
> And God's white wings of destiny
>    Beat high within my breast.
>
> For spirit does not need the feet
>    Of earth to climb some splendid crest
> Of peace and light;—restricted lives
> Restrained from tasks held dear,
>    With richer gain are blest.
>
> For so it is that God Himself is found,
>    His love shines brightest in the path of pain
> And what was loss,—whatever life denies,—
> Is found in Him to be
>    The greater gain.
>
> So I shall sing, tho' soon or late,
>    I am restored to love's glad tasks,
> And while I wait, a higher love,
> A deeper knowledge of His will,
>    Is all I ask.          —ZULA EVELYN COON.

# RESIGNATION

The designs of the kingdom of God become visible when Christ works through us.—L. R. VAN SICKLE.

> God of our fathers, be the God
> Of their succeeding race.
> —JESSE H. ARNUP.

> He placed me in a little cage
> Away from gardens fair;
> But I must sing the sweetest song
> Because He placed me there.
> Not beat my wings against the gate,
> If it's my Maker's will,
> But raise my voice to heaven's gate,
> And sing the louder still.
> —ANONYMOUS.

# RESOLUTION

As for me and my house, we will serve the Lord.—JOSH. 24:15b.

I will pay my vows unto the Lord now in the presence of all his people.—PSALM 116:18.

> Love work;
> Turn a deaf ear to slander;
> Be considerate in correcting others;
> Do not be taken up by trifles;
> Do not resent plain speaking;
> Meet offenders half-way;
> Be thorough in thought;
> Have an open mind;
> Do your duty without grumbling.
> —MARCUS AURELIUS.

Resolved, to live with all my might while I do live;
Resolved, never to lose one moment of time, to improve in the most profitable way I possibly can.
Resolved, never to do anything which I should despise or think meanly of in another.

# RESOLUTION

Resolved, never to do anything out of revenge.
Resolved, never to do anything which I should be afraid
to do if it were the last hour of my life.

—JONATHAN EDWARDS.

Hold yourself responsible for a higher standard than anybody else
expects of you;
Never excuse yourself;
Never pity yourself;
Be a hard master on yourself, and be lenient to everybody else.

—HENRY WARD BEECHER.

Nothing relieves and ventilates the mind like a resolution.
—JOHN BURROUGHS.

I will this day try to live a simple, sincere and serene life;
repelling promptly every thought of discontent, anxiety, dis-
couragement, impurity and self-seeking; cultivating cheerfulness,
magnanimity, charity, and the habit of holy silence; exercising
economy in expenditure, carefulness in conversation, diligence
in appointed service, fidelity to every trust, and a childlike trust
in God.—JOHN M. VINCENT.

Promise yourself:
To be so strong that nothing can disturb your peace of mind;
To talk health, happiness and prosperity;
To make your friends feel that there is something in them;
To look on the sunny side of everything;
To think only of the best;
To be just as enthusiastic about the success of others as you are
about your own;
To forget the mistakes of the past and profit by them;
To wear a cheerful countenance and give a smile to everyone
you meet;
To be too large for worry, too noble for anger, too strong
for fear, and too happy to permit the presence of trouble.

—CHRISTIAN D. LARSON.

# RESPONSIBILITY

They made me the keeper of the vineyards; but mine own vineyard have I not kept.—SONG OF SOL. 1:6.

I sat where they sat.—EZEK. 3:15.

Ye have not chosen me, but I have chosen you, and ordained you, that ye should go and bring forth fruit, and that your fruit should remain.—JOHN 15:16.

Be ready always to give an answer to every man that asketh you a reason of the hope that is in you with meekness and fear.—I PET. 3:15.

Responsibility walks hand in hand with capacity and power.—JOHN G. HOLLAND.

Responsibility gravitates to the power that can carry out that responsibility. If you alone can do what ought to be done, then that oughtness rests on you. You can't dodge it. It is yours.—LYNN LANDRUM.

God becomes a reality to us when He lays upon us a commission.—JOHN OXENHAM.

Ability involves responsibility.—ALEXANDER MACLAREN.

# REVERENCE

Moses, Moses . . . Draw not nigh hither: put off thy shoes from off thy feet, for the place whereon thou standest is holy ground.—EXOD. 3:4-5.

Honor thy father and thy mother: that thy days may be long upon the land.—EXOD. 20:12.

Ye shall keep my sabbaths and reverence my sanctuary: I am the Lord.—LEV. 19:30.

God is greatly to be feared in the assembly of the saints, and to be had in reverence of all them that are about him.—PSALM 89:7.

# REVERENCE

Remove not the ancient landmark, which thy fathers have set.—Prov. 22:28.

Rather let my head stoop to the block
Than these knees bow to any, save to the God of heaven.
—William Shakespeare.

The soul of the Christian religion is reverence.—Johann Wolfgang von Goethe.

We treat God with irreverence by banishing Him from our thoughts, not by referring to His will on slight occasions.—John Ruskin.

He that has no pleasure in looking up is not fit so much as to look down.—Washington Allston.

Reverence is the very first element of religion; it cannot but be felt by every one who has right views of the divine greatness and holiness, and of his own character in the sight of God. —Charles Simmons.

Reverence is one of the signs of strength; irreverence one of the surest indications of weakness. No man will rise high who jeers at sacred things. The fine loyalties of life must be reverenced or they will be foresworn in the day of trial.—Anonymous.

# RIGHTEOUSNESS

The eyes of the Lord run to and fro throughout the whole earth, to show himself strong in behalf of them whose heart is perfect toward him.—II Chron. 16:9.

The righteous shall inherit the land, and dwell therein forever.—Psalm 37:29.

The Lord God is a sun and a shield: the Lord will give grace and glory: no good thing will he withhold from them that walk uprightly.—Psalm 84:11.

# RIGHTEOUSNESS

They that be wise shall shine as the brightness of the firmament; and they that turn many to righteousness as the stars for ever and ever.—DAN. 12:3.

Blessed are they which do hunger and thirst after righteousness: for they shall be filled.—MATT. 5:6.

When good men die their goodness does not perish,
But lives though they are gone. As for the bad,
All that was theirs dies and is buried with them.
>—EURIPIDES.

And oft, though wisdom wake, suspicion sleeps
At wisdom's gate, and to simplicity
Resigns her charge, while goodness thinks no ill
Where no ill seems.
>—JOHN MILTON.

True piety hath in it nothing weak, nothing sad, nothing constrained. It enlarges the heart; it is simple, free and attractive.
—FRANCOIS DE LA FENELON.

For never, never wicked man was wise.—ALEXANDER POPE.

After long experience in the world, I affirm before God that I never knew a rogue who was not unhappy.—JUNIUS.

Sin may be clasped so close we cannot see its ugly face.— ARCHBISHOP RICHARD CHENEVIX TRENCH.

Because right is right, to follow right
Were wisdom in the scorn of consequence.
>—ALFRED TENNYSON.

When a man does a noble act, date him from that. Forget his faults. Let his noble act be the standpoint from which you regard him.—HENRY WHITNEY BELLOWS.

Among the many strange servilities mistaken for pieties one of the least lovely is that which hopes to flatter God by despising the world and villifying human nature.—GEORGE HENRY LEWES.

Every noble life leaves the fiber of itself interwoven in the work of the world.—JOHN RUSKIN.

# RIGHTEOUSNESS

There is one evident, indubitable manifestation of the Divinity, and that is the laws of right which are made known to the world through Revelation.—LEO TOLSTOI.

Always do right. This will gratify some people and astonish the others.—MARK TWAIN, *pseud. of* SAMUEL L. CLEMENS.

Where truth and right are concerned we must be firm as God. —THOMAS ANSTEY GUTHRIE.

No man is justified in doing evil on the grounds of expediency. —THEODORE ROOSEVELT.

Sin is the most unmanly thing in God's world. You never were made for sin and selfishness. You were made for love and obedience.—JOHN G. HOLLAND.

Right attitudes and right actions right most things, including life itself.—B. C. FORBES.

All wickedness is weakness.—ANONYMOUS.


# SABBATH

Remember the sabbath day, to keep it holy.—EXOD. 20:8.

This is the day which the Lord hath made; we will rejoice and be glad in it.—PSALM 118:24.

If thou turn away thy foot from the sabbath, from doing thy pleasure on my holy day; and call the sabbath a delight, the holy of the Lord honorable; and shalt honour him, not doing thine own ways, nor finding thine own pleasure, nor speaking thine own words.
Then shalt thou delight thyself in the Lord; and I will cause thee to ride upon the high places of the earth, and feed thee with the heritage of Jacob thy father: for the mouth of the Lord hath spoken it.—ISA. 58:13, 14.

A corruption of morals usually follows a profanation of the Sabbath.—SIR WILLIAM BLACKSTONE.

# SABBATH

The keeping of one day in seven holy, as a time of relaxation and refreshment as well as public worship is of inestimable benefit to a state, considered merely as a civil institution.—SIR WILLIAM BLACKSTONE.

> Safely through another week
> God has brought us on our way;
> Let us now a blessing seek,
> Waiting in His courts today.
> Day of all the week the best.
> Emblem of eternal rest.
> —JOHN NEWTON.

I feel as if God had, by giving the Sabbath, given fifty-two springs in every year.—SAMUEL TAYLOR COLERIDGE.

I never knew a man escape failures in either mind or body, who worked seven days a week.—SIR ROBERT PEEL.

The longer I live the more highly do I estimate the Christian Sabbath, and the more grateful do I feel to those who impress its importance on the community.—DANIEL WEBSTER.

Where there is no Christian Sabbath, there is no Christian morality; and without this, free institutions cannot long be sustained.—JOHN McLEAN.

Nothing draws along with it such a glory as the Sabbath. Never has it unfolded without some witness and welcome, some song and salutation. It has been the coronation day of martyrs—the first day of saints. It has been, from the first day till now, the sublime day of the Church of God; still the out going of its morning and evening rejoice. Let us, then, remember the Sabbath day to keep it holy.—JAMES HAMILTON.

Sunday is the core of our civilization, dedicated to thought and reverence. It invites to the noblest solitude and to the noblest society.—RALPH WALDO EMERSON.

O what a blessing is Sunday, interposed between the waves of worldly business like the divine path of the Israelites through the sea.—BISHOP SAMUEL WILBERFORCE.

# SABBATH

Sunday is the golden clasp that binds together the volume of the weeks.—HENRY WADSWORTH LONGFELLOW.

Sunday is like a stile between the fields of toil, where we can kneel and pray, sit and meditate.—HENRY WADSWORTH LONG-FELLOW.

As we keep or break the Sabbath, we nobly save or meanly lose the last best hope by which man rises.—ABRAHAM LINCOLN.

Through the week we go down into the valleys of care and shadow. Our Sabbaths should be hills of light and joy in God's presence; and so as time rolls by we shall go on from mountain top to mountain top, till at last we catch the glory of the gate, and enter in to go no more out forever.—HENRY WARD BEECHER.

Without a Sabbath, no worship; without worship, no religion; and without religion, no permanent freedom.—CHARLES FORBES, COUNT DE MONTALEMBERT.

The green oasis, the little grassy meadow in the wilderness; where, after the weekday's journey, the pilgrim halts for refreshment and repose.—CHARLES READE.

I never knew one man or woman who steadily avoided the house of prayer and public worship on the Lord's day, who did not come to grief, and bring other people to grief.—HENRY WHITNEY BELLOWS.

He who ordained the Sabbaths loves the poor.—JAMES RUSSELL LOWELL.

The Sabbath is God's special present to the working man, and one of its chief objects is to prolong his life, and preserve efficient his working tone. The savings bank of human existence is the weekly Sabbath.—WILLIAM G. BLAIKIE.

Hail, hallowed day, that binds a yoke on vice, gives rest to toil, proclaims God's holy truth, blesses the family, secures the state, prospers communities, nations exalts, pours life and light on earth and points the way to heaven.—TRYON EDWARDS.

Break down Sunday, close the churches, open the bars and the theatres on that day, and where would values be? What was real estate worth in Sodom?—H. L. WAYLAND.

# SABBATH

He that remembers not to keep the Christian Sabbath at the beginning of the week will be in danger of forgetting, before the end of the week, that he is a Christian.—Ewing Turner.

Sabbath days, when rightly observed, are to Time what the mountains are to the earth—eminences from which we may survey glorious prospects, while the earth is beneath our feet.—Anonymous.

The law of the Sabbath is the key stone of the arch of public morals; take it away and the whole structure falls.—Anonymous.

# SACRIFICE

Neither will I offer burnt offerings unto the Lord my God of that which doth cost me nothing.—II Sam. 24:24.

> Brave conqueror; for so you are,
> That war against your own affections
> and the huge army of the world's desires.
> —William Shakespeare.

Self denial is a kind of holy association with God.—Robert Boyle.

There never did and never will exist anything permanently noble and excellent in the character which is a stranger to the exercise of resolute self-denial.—Sir Walter Scott.

Contempt of all outward things that come in competition with duty fulfills the ideal of human greatness. It is sanctioned by conscience, that universal and eternal lawgiver, whose chief principle is, that everything must be yielded up for right.—William Ellery Channing.

In vain do they talk of happiness who never subdued an impulse in obedience to a principle. He who never sacrificed a present to a future good, or a personal to a general one, can speak of happiness only as the blind speak of color.—Horace Mann.

# SACRIFICE

One secret act of self-denial, one sacrifice of inclination to duty, is worth all the mere good thoughts, warm feelings, passionate prayers in which idle people indulge themselves.—JOHN HENRY, CARDINAL NEWMAN.

The very act of faith by which we receive Christ is an act of utter renunciation of self and all its works as a ground of salvation.—MARK HOPKINS.

Self-denial is indispensable to a strong character, and the loftiest kind thereof comes only of a religious stock—from consciousness of obligation and dependence on God.—THEODORE PARKER.

Self-denial does not belong to religion as characteristic of it; it belongs to human life. The lower nature must always be denied when you are trying to rise to a higher sphere.—HENRY WARD BEECHER.

That which especially distinguishes a high order of man from a lower and which constitutes human goodness and nobleness, is self-forgetfulness, self-sacrifice, and disregard for personal pleasure, personal indulgence, personal advantage, remote or present, because some other line of conduct is more right.—JAMES ANTHONY FROUDE.

The altar of sacrifice is the touchstone of character.—O. P. CLIFFORD.

He who would be a saviour must somewhere and somehow have been upon a cross.—LETITIA BURD COWMAN.

They that deny themselves for Christ shall enjoy themselves in Christ.—JAMES M. MASON.

Self-denial is the result of a calm, deliberate, invincible attachment, to the highest good, flowing forth in the voluntary renunciation of everything inconsistent with the glory of God or the good of our fellowmen.—GARDINER SPRING.

> I sinned. Then straightaway, post haste, Satan flew
> Before the presence of the most high God
> And made a railing accusation there.
> He said: "This soul, this thing of clay and sod

# SACRIFICE

Has sinned. 'Tis true that he has named Thy name;
But I demand his death, for Thou hast said:
'The soul that sinneth it shall die'. Shall not
Thy sentence be fulfilled? Is Justice dead?
Send now this wretched sinner to his doom;
What other thing can righteous ruler do?"

And so he did accuse me day and night,
And every word he spoke, O God, was true!

Then quickly One rose up from God's right hand,
Before whose glory angels veil their eyes.
He spoke: "Each jot and tittle of the law
Must be fulfilled; the guilty sinner dies!
But wait; his guilt was all transferred to me
And I have paid his penalty!
Behold my side, my hands, my feet!
One day I was made sin for him, and died that he
Might be presented guiltless at Thy throne!"

Then Satan fled away. Full well he knew
That he could not prevail against such love,
Since every word my dear Lord spoke was true!
—MARTHA SNELL NICHOLSON.


# SECURITY

I give unto them eternal life; and they shall never perish,
neither shall any man pluck that out of my hand.—JOHN 10:28.

Keep through thine own name those whom thou hast given
me.—JOHN 17:11.

I know whom I have believed, and am persuaded that he is
able to keep that which I have committed unto him against that
day.—II TIM. 1:12.

When you have accomplished your daily task, go to sleep in
peace; God is awake.—VICTOR HUGO.

# SECURITY

The problem involves a spiritual recrudescence and improvement of human character that will synchronize with our almost matchless advance in science, art, literature and all material developments of the past two thousand years. It must be of the spirit if we are to save the flesh.—GENERAL DOUGLAS MACARTHUR.

There can be no security in this world until men and nations put God right in the center and at the very heart of life.—LYN CLAYBROOK.

We know not what the future holds, but we do know who holds the future.—WILLIS J. RAY.

# SELF CONTROL

Keep thy heart with all diligence; for out of it are the issues of life.—PROV. 4:23.

He that is slow to anger is better than the mighty; and he that ruleth his spirit than he that taketh a city.—PROV. 16:32.

He that hath knowledge spareth his words: and a man of understanding is of an excellent spirit.
Even a fool, when he holdeth his peace, is counted wise.—PROV. 17:27-28.

He that hath no rule over his own spirit is like a city that is broken down, and without walls.—PROV. 25:28.

Ye are bought with a price: therefore glorify God in your body, and in your spirit, which are God's.—I. COR. 6:20.

Every man that striveth for the mastery is temperate in all things. . . . Now they do it to obtain a corruptible crown; but we an incorruptible. . . . I keep under my body, and bring it into subjection: lest that by any means, when I have preached to others, I myself should be a castaway.—I COR. 9:25, 27.

Deliberate much before you say or do anything, for it will not be in your power to recall what is said or done.—EPICTETUS.

# SELF CONTROL

He that lays down precepts for governing our lives and moderating our passions, obliges humanity not only in the present, but for all future generations.—SENECA.

He can never speak well who knows not how to hold his peace.—PLUTARCH.

> Wouldst thou have thy flesh obey the spirit?
> Then let thy spirit obey thy God.
> Thou must be governed that thou mayst govern.
> —SAINT AUGUSTINE.

> To mourn a mischief that is past and gone
> Is the best way to bring a fresh mischief on.
> —WILLIAM SHAKESPEARE.

Better conquest never canst thou make than warn thy constant and thy nobler parts against giddy, loose suggestion.—WILLIAM SHAKESPEARE.

The brain may devise laws for the blood, but a hot temper leaps o'er a cold decree.—WILLIAM SHAKESPEARE.

A man must first govern himself ere he be fit to govern a family; and his family, ere he be fit to bear the government in the commonwealth.—SIR WALTER RALEIGH.

Conquer thyself. Till thou hast done this, thou art but a slave; for it is almost as well to be subjected to another's appetite as to thine own.—ROBERT BURTON.

He who reigns himself and rules his passions, desires and fears is more than a king.—JOHN MILTON.

The constancy of sages is nothing but the art of locking up their agitation in their hearts.—FRANCOIS DE LA ROCHEFOUCAULD.

> Of all bad things by which mankind are cursed.
> Their own bad tempers surely are the worst.
> —RICHARD CUMBERLAND.

Let not any one say that he cannot govern his passions, nor hinder them from breaking out and carrying him to action; for what he can do before a prince or a great man, he can do alone, or in the presence of God, if he will.—JOHN LOCKE.

# SELF CONTROL

The most precious of all possessions, is the power over ourselves; power to withstand trial, to bear suffering, to front danger; power over pleasure and pain; power to follow our convictions, however resisted by menace and scorn; the power of calm reliance in scenes of darkness and storms. He that has not a mastery over his inclinations; he that knows not how to resist the importunity of present pleasure or pain, for the sake of what reason tells him is fit to be done, wants the true principle of virtue and industry, and is in danger of never being good for anything.—JOHN LOCKE.

I entreat you, give no place to despondency. This is a dangerous temptation—a refined, not a gross temptation of the adversary. Melancholy contracts and withers the heart, and renders it unfit to receive the impressions of grace. It magnifies and gives a false coloring to objects, and thus renders your burdens too heavy to bear. God's designs regarding you, and His methods of bringing about these designs, are infinitely wise.—MME. JEANNE MARIE GUYON.

Complaisance renders a superior amiable, an equal agreeable, and an inferior acceptable. It soothes distinction, sweetens conversation and makes every one in the company pleased with himself. It produces good nature and mutual benevolence, encourages the timorous, soothes the turbulent, humanizes the fierce, and distinguishes a society of civilized persons from a confusion of savages.—JOSEPH ADDISON.

One of the most important, but one of the most difficult things for a powerful mind is to be its own master. A pond may lie quiet in a plain; but a lake wants mountains to compass and hold it in.—JOSEPH ADDISON.

It is the man who is cool and collected, who is master of his countenance, his voice, his actions, his gestures, of every part, who can work upon others at his pleasure.—DENNIS DIDEROT.

I will be lord over myself. No one who cannot master himself is worthy to rule and only he can rule.—JOHANN WOLFGANG VON GOETHE.

> But hushed be every thought that springs
> From out the bitterness of things.
> —WILLIAM WORDSWORTH.

# SELF CONTROL

A self controlled mind is a free mind, and freedom is power. I call that mind free which jealously guards its intellectual rights and powers. I call that mind free which resists the bondage of habit, which does not live on its old virtues but forgets what is behind, and rejoices to pour forth in fresh and higher exertions. —WILLIAM ELLERY CHANNING.

Self-control is promoted by humility. Pride is a fruitful source of uneasiness.—LYDIA HUNTLEY SIGOURNEY.

Over the times thou hast no power. To redeem a world sunk in dishonesty has not been given thee. Solely over one man therein thou hast a quiet, absolute, uncontrollable power. Him redeem and make honest.—THOMAS CARLYLE.

There are moments in life when the heart is so stirred with emotion,
That if by chance it be shaken, or into its depths, like a pebble,
Drops some careless word, it overflows, and its secret
Spilt on the ground, like water, it can never be gathered together.
                    —HENRY WADSWORTH LONGFELLOW.

Self-reverence, self-knowledge, self-control,—
These three alone lead life to sovereign power.
                    —ALFRED TENNYSON.

For want of self-restraint many men are engaged all their lives in fighting with difficulties of their own making, and rendering success impossible by their own cross-grained ungentleness; while others, which may be much less gifted, make their way and achieve success by simple patience, and self control.—SAMUEL SMILES.

It is by presence of mind in untried emergencies that the native metal of a man is tested.—JAMES RUSSELL LOWELL.

The worst of slaves is he whom passion rules.—PHILLIPS BROOKS.

Every temptation that is resisted, every noble aspiration that is encouraged, every sinful thought that is repressed, every bitter word that is withheld, adds its little item to the impetus of that great movement which is bearing humanity onward toward a richer life and higher character.—JOHN FISKE.

# SELF CONTROL

To have what we want is riches; but to be able to do without is power.—GEORGE McDONALD.

Self control is more often called for than self-expression. —WILLIAM WISTAR COMFORT.

Complaisance pleases all; prejudice, none; adorns wit; renders humor agreeable, augments friendship; redoubles love; and united with justice and generosity, becomes the secret chain of the society of mankind.—M. DE SOUDERI.

We can be truest and best blessings to others only when we live victoriously ourselves. We owe it, therefore, to the needy, sorrowing tempted world about us to keep our inner life calm, quiet, strong, restful and full of love in whatever we must live. The one secret is to abide in Christ.—J. R. MILLER.

> If a wren can cling to a spray a-swing
> In a mad May wind and sing and sing
>     As if she'd burst for joy;
> Why can not I, contented lie
> In His quiet arms, beneath the sky
>     Unmoved by earth's alloy?
>                 —F. B. MAYER.

Those who wish to transform the world must be able to transform themselves.—KONRAD HEIDEN.

That man is sure to win who can command the situation instead of allowing the situation to control him.—HOLLIS BURKE FRISSELL.

The most difficult of arts is that of companionship to a loved one who is ill. Devotion alone is not enough. You must possess the tact of self-control, to show thoughtfulness without solicitude, attention without anxiety; you must exhibit sympathy, but hide all worry. Only one man in a hundred can fill the trying position, and only one woman in ten.—ANONYMOUS.

The eagle that soars in the upper air does not worry itself as to how it is to cross the river.—ANONYMOUS.

# SELF CONTROL

Composure is often the highest result of power.—ANONYMOUS.

Prove that you can control yourself and you are an educated man; without this, all other education is good for nothing.—ANONYMOUS.

# SERVICE

Who then is willing to consecrate his service this day unto the Lord?—I CHRON. 29:5b.

The useful and beautiful are never separated.—PERIANDER OF CORINTH.

> . . . That best portion of a good man's life,
> His little, nameless, unremembered acts
> Of kindness and of love.
> —WILLIAM WORDSWORTH.

Every man is useful to his kind by the very fact of his existence.—THOMAS CARLYLE.

> "Get me some great task, ye gods, and I will show you
> my Spirit!"
> "No, no", says the good Heaven, "Plod and Plough."
> —RALPH WALDO EMERSON.

> All service ranks the same with God
> There is no last or first.
> —ROBERT BROWNING.

No one is useless in this world who lightens the burden of it for any one else.—CHARLES DICKENS.

It is not the possession of extraordinary gifts that makes extraordinary usefulness, but the dedication of what we have to the service of God.—FREDERICK WILLIAM ROBERTSON.

The weakest among us has a gift, however seemingly trivial, which is peculiar to him, and which worthily used, will be a gift to his race forever.—JOHN RUSKIN.

# SERVICE

When generous acts bloom from unselfish thought
The Lord is with us though we know it not.
— LUCY LARCOM.

The measure of a man is not the number of his servants, but in the number of people whom he serves.— PAUL D. MOODY.

So long as we love we serve; so long as we are loved by others I would almost say that we are indispensable; and no man is useless while he has a friend.— ROBERT LOUIS STEVENSON.

Every task, however simple
Sets the soul that does it, free;
Every deed of love and mercy
Done to man, is done to me.
— HENRY VAN DYKE.

Honest toil is holy service,
Faithful work is praise and prayer.
— HENRY VAN DYKE.

We have committed the Golden Rule to memory; let us now commit it to life.— EDWIN MARKHAM.

God loves to see in me not His servant, but Himself, who serves all.— RABINDRANATH TAGORE.

To tolerate misery among men without feeling the call to remedy it is to fall under the reprobation—"Inasmuch as ye did it not—ye did it not to me."— BISHOP CHARLES GORE.

We are not here to play, to dream, to drift,
We have hard work to do, and loads to lift;
Shun not the struggle, face it, 'tis God's gift.
— MALTBIE B. BABCOCK.

That which constitutes the supreme worth of life is not wealth, not ease, nor fame—not even happiness, but service. Nothing at last counts but service, and that always counts.— ALFRED W. MARTIN.

The paths our bravest ones have trod, O make us brave
to go,
That we may give our lives to God in serving man below;

# SERVICE

So hence shall flow fresh strength and grace as from a
full-fed spring,
And make the world a better place and life a worthier
thing.                               —WILLIAM DeWITT HOWE.


# SINCERITY

Fear the Lord, and serve him in sincerity and in truth.—JOSH.
24:14.

This I pray . . . That ye may approve things that are excellent; that ye may be sincere and without offence till the day of
Christ.—PHIL. 1:9,10.

Sincerity and truth are the basis of every virtue.—CONFUCIUS.

The shortest and surest way to life with honor in the world
is to be in reality what we would appear to be; all human virtues increase and strengthen themselves by the practice and experience of them.—SOCRATES.

His words are bonds, his oaths are oracles;
His love sincere, his thoughts immaculate;
His tears, pure messengers sent from his heart;
His heart, as far from fraud as heaven from earth.
                          —WILLIAM SHAKESPEARE.

Inward sincerity will of course influence the outward deport-
ment; where the one is wanting, there is great reason to suspect
the absence of the other.—LAURENCE STERNE.

Sincerity is the indispensable ground of all conscientiousness,
and by consequence of all heartfelt religion.—IMMANUEL KANT.

O what a tangled web we weave
When first we practice to deceive!
                —SIR WALTER SCOTT.

There is no wisdom like frankness.—BENJAMIN DISRAELI.

Candor is the brightest gem of criticism.—BENJAMIN DISRAELI.

A word in earnest is better than a speech.—CHARLES DICKENS.

# SINCERITY

It is often said it is no matter what a man believes if he is only sincere. But let a man sincerely believe that seed planted without ploughing is as good as with; that January is as favorable for seed sowing as April; and that cockle seed will produce as good harvest as wheat, and is it so?—HENRY WARD BEECHER.

No man can produce great things who is not thoroughly sincere in dealing with himself.—JAMES RUSSELL LOWELL.

The diligent fostering of a candid habit of mind, even in trifles, is a matter of high moment both to character and opinions. —JOHN HOWARD HOWSON.

I make it my rule to lay hold of light and embrace it, wherever I see it, though held forth by a child or an enemy.—HENRY THOMAS EDWARDS.

Sincerity, a deep, genuine, heart-felt sincerity is a trait of true and noble manhood.—ANONYMOUS.


# SOLITUDE

They wandered in the wilderness in a solitary way; they found no city to dwell in. . . . And he led them forth by the right way, that they might go to a city of habitation. . . . For he satisfieth the longing soul, and filleth the hungry soul with goodness. —PSALM 107:4, 7, 9.

I called him alone, and blessed him.—ISA. 51:2.

In the morning, rising up a great while before day, he went out, and departed into a solitary place, and there prayed.—MARK 1:35.

> And Wisdom's self
> Oft seeks to sweet retired solitude,
> Where with her best nurse Contemplation
> She plumes her feathers and lets grow her wings,
> That in the various bustle of resort
> Were all-to ruffled, and sometimes impair'd.
> —JOHN MILTON.

# SOLITUDE

A wise man is never less alone than when he is alone.—Jonathan Swift.

Few are the faults we flatter when alone.—Edward Young.

Conversation enriches the understanding, but solitude is the school of genius.—Edward Gibbon.

> By all means, use some time to be alone;
> Salute thyself—see what thy soul doth wear;
> Dare to look in thy chest, for 'tis thine own,
> And tumble up and down what thou findest there.
> —William Wordsworth.

> There is a pleasure in the pathless woods;
> There is a rapture in the lonely shore;
> There is society, where none intrude,
> By the deep sea, and music in its roar.
> —George Gordon, Lord Byron.

If from society we learn to live, it is solitude should teach us how to die.—George Gordon, Lord Byron.

> I love tranquil solitude
> And such society
> As is quiet, wise and good.
> —Percy Bysshe Shelley.

Silence is the element in which great things fashion themselves together, that at length they may emerge, full formed and majestic, into the daylight of life. . . . In thy own mean perplexities, do thou thyself but hold thy tongue for one day; on the morrow how much clearer are thy purposes and duties.—Thomas Carlyle.

What would a man do if he were compelled to live always in the sultry heat of society, and could never better himself in the cool of solitude.—Nathaniel Hawthorne.

Converse with men makes sharp the glittering wit, but God to man doth speak in solitude.—John Stuart Blackie.

I never found the companion that was so companionable as solitude.—Henry David Thoreau.

# SOLITUDE

Solitude is as needful to the imagination as society is wholesome for the character.—JAMES RUSSELL LOWELL.

Consider what Saint Augustine said,—that he sought God within himself. Settle yourself in solitude, and you will come upon Him in yourself.—SAINT THERESA.

It is the mark of a superior man that left to himself, he is able endlessly to amuse, interest and entertain himself out of his personal stock of meditations, ideas, criticisms, philosophy, humor and what not.—GEORGE JEAN NATHAN.

One hour of thoughtful solitude may nerve the heart for days of conflict.—JAMES G. PERCIVAL.

Lonesomeness is part of the cost of power. The higher you climb, the less you can hope for companionship. The heavier and the more immediate the responsibility, the less can a man delegate his tasks or escape his own mistakes.—SHAILER MATTHEWS.

Solitude shows us what we should be; society shows us what we are.—RICHARD CECIL.

> At cool of day, with God I walk
> My garden's grateful shade;
> I hear his voice among the trees
> And I am not afraid.
> —ANONYMOUS.

There is power in the aggregate which the solitude can not find.—ANONYMOUS.

> If chosen men had never been alone
> In deepest silence open-doored to God,
> No greatness ever had been dreamed or done.
> —ANONYMOUS.

> We wander in a "solitary way,"
> No matter what or where our lot may be;
> Each heart, mysterious even to itself,
> Must live its inner life in solitude.
> And would you know the reason why this is?
> It is because the Lord desires our love.

# SOLITUDE

In every heart He wishes to be first:
He therefore keeps the secret key Himself
To open all its chambers, and to bless
With perfect sympathy, and holy peace,
Each solitary soul which comes to Him.
—Anonymous.

# SORROW

Sorrow is better than laughter: for by the sadness of the countenance the heart is made better.—Eccles. 7:3.

Blessed are they that mourn: for they shall be comforted.—Matt. 5:4.

The deeper the sorrow the less tongue it hath.—The Talmud.

If it were possible to heal sorrow by weeping and to raise the dead with tears, gold were less prized than grief.—Sophocles.

An excess of sorrow is as foolish as profuse laughter; while, on the other hand, not to mourn at all is insensibility.—Seneca.

Light griefs do speak, while sorrow's tongue is bound.—Seneca.

He that hath pity on another man's sorrow shall be free from it himself; and he that delighteth in and scorneth the misery of another shall one time or other fall into it himself—Sir Walter Raleigh.

Give sorrow words: the grief that does not speak
Whispers the o'er-fraught heart and bids it break.
—William Shakespeare.

The robb'd that smiles, steals something from the thief;
He robs himself that spends a bootless grief.
—William Shakespeare.

The true way of softening one's troubles is to solace those of others.—Mme. de Maintenon.

314

# SORROW

Sorrows gather around great souls as storms do around mountains; but like them, they break the storm and purify the air of the plain beneath them.—JEAN PAUL RICHTER.

Has it never occurred to us, when surrounded by sorrows, that they may be sent to us only for our instruction, as we darken the eyes of birds when we wish them to sing.—JEAN PAUL RICHTER.

Grief should be the instructor of the wise; sorrow is knowledge; they who know the most must mourn the deepest o'er the fatal truth.—GEORGE GORDON, LORD BYRON.

Tears hinder sorrow from becoming despair.—LEIGH HUNT.

> Be still, sad heart! and cease repining;
> Behind the clouds, the sun's still shining;
> Thy fate is the common fate of all,
> Into each life some rain must fall,
>   Some days must be dark and dreary.
>     —HENRY WADSWORTH LONGFELLOW.

Pain is no evil unless it conquer us.—CHARLES KINGSLEY.

Wherever souls are being tried and ripened, in whatever commonplace and homely way, there God is hewing out the pillars for His temple.—PHILLIPS BROOKS.

> Never a tear bedims the eye
> That time and patience will not dry.
>     —FRANCIS BRET HARTE.

These touches of manhood, of nature, of sorrow, of price, of generosity and pity, which make the whole world kin, tell us specifically and with emphasis that we are of one family and should be of one household forever.—HENRY WATTERSON.

The soul would have no rainbow had the eye no tears.—JOHN VANCE CHENEY.

Where there is sorrow, there is holy ground.—OSCAR WILDE.

To withhold from a child some knowledge—apportioned to his understanding—of the world's sorrows and wrongs is to cheat him of his kinship with humanity.—AGNES REPPLIER.

Set about doing good to somebody. Put on your hat and visit the sick and poor of your neighborhood; inquire into their circumstances and minister to their wants. Seek out the desolate, and afflicted, and oppressed, and tell them of the consolation of religion. I have often tried this method, and have always found it the best medicine for a heavy heart.—SYDNEY HOWARD.

This world is so full of care and sorrow that it is a gracious debt we owe to one another to discover the bright crystals of delight hidden in somber circumstances and irksome tasks.—HELEN KELLER.

Sorrow is only one of the lower notes in the oratorio of our blessedness.—A. J. GORDON.

Often the clouds of sorrow reveal the sunshine of His face.—HILYS JASPER.

It is the veiled angel of sorrow who plucks away one thing and another that bound us here in ease and security, and in vanishing of those dear objects, indicates the true home of our affections and our peace.—E. H. CHAPIN.

Out of sufferings have emerged the strongest souls; the most massive characters are seamed with scars; martyrs have put on their coronation robes glittering with fire, and through their tears have the sorrowful first seen the gates of heaven.—E. H. CHAPIN.

Despise not thy school of sorrow, O my Soul; it will give thee a unique part in the universal song.—GEORGE MATHESON.

The happiest, sweetest, tenderest homes are not those where there has been no sorrow, but those which have been overshadowed with grief, and where Christ's comfort was accepted. The very memory of the sorrow is a gentle benediction that broods ever over the household, like the silence that comes after prayer. There is a blessing sent from God in every burden of sorrow.—J. R. MILLER.

> Alas by some degree of woe
> We every bliss must gain;
> The heart can ne'er a transport know
> That never feels a pain.
> —GEORGE LYTTLETON.

# SORROW

The capacity of sorrow belongs to our grandeur; and the loftiest of our race are those who have had the profoundest griefs because they have had the profoundest sympathies.—HENRY GILES.

To forecast our sorrows is only to increase the suffering without increasing our strength to bear them. Many of life's noblest enterprises might never have been undertaken if all the difficulties and defeats could be foreseen.—THEODORE L. CUYLER.

> Not until each loom is silent
> And the shuttles cease to fly,
> Will God unroll the pattern
> And explain the reason why
> The dark threads are as needful
> In the Weaver's skilful hand
> As the threads of gold and silver
> For the pattern which He planned.
> —ANONYMOUS.

There is something vitally wrong with the blood of a man who reveals the same unhealed wound year after year. For it is the impulse of a healthful nature to heal wounds. So is there something radically wrong in the makeup of the person who shows you the same cankering sorrow year after year, for it is also the wish and purpose of progressive nature that we should outgrow our griefs. He who does not has a right to our pity.—ANONYMOUS.

> O learn one truth, in all its fair completeness:
> A sorrow's crown of thorns, if worn aright,
> With calm humility and patient sweetness
> Becomes a crown of light!—ANONYMOUS.

> I walked a mile with Pleasure,
> She chatted me all the way,
> But I was none the wiser
> For what she had to say.

> I walked a mile with Sorrow,
> And ne'er a word said she,
> But O the things I learned from her
> When Sorrow walked with me.
> —ANONYMOUS.

# SORROW

The cry of man's anguish went up to God,
    "Lord, take away pain!
The shadow that darkens the world Thou hast made,
    The close-coiling chain
That strangles the heart, the burdens that weigh
    On wings that would soar,
Lord, take away pain from the world Thou hast made,
    That it love Thee the more."

Then answered the Lord to the cry of His world:
    "Shall I take away pain,
And with it the power of the soul to endure,
    Made strong by the strain?
Shall I take away pity, that knits heart to heart
    And sacrifice high?
Will ye lose all your heroes that lift from the fire
    White brows to the sky?
Shall I take away love that redeems with a price
    And smiles at its loss?
Can ye spare from your lives that would climb up to Me
    The Christ of the Cross?"    —ANONYMOUS.

Blessed to us is the night, for it reveals to us the stars.—ANONYMOUS.

# STEADFASTNESS

Thou shalt be steadfast, and shalt not fear.—JOB 11:15.

Will ye also go away?—JOHN 6:67.

Stand, therefore, having your loins girt about with truth, and having on the breastplate of righteousness;

And your feet shod with the preparation of the gospel of peace;

Above all, taking the shield of faith, wherewith ye shall be able to quench all the fiery darts of the wicked.

And take the helmet of salvation, and the sword of the Spirit, which is the word of God.—EPH. 6:14-17.

# STEADFASTNESS

Hold fast that which is good.—I THES. 5:21.

That those things which cannot be shaken may remain.—HEB. 12:27.

It is only persons of firmness that can have real gentleness. Those who appear gentle are, in general, only weak characters, which easily change into asperity.—FRANCOIS DE LA ROCHEFOUCAULD.

When firmness is sufficient, rashness is unneccessary.—NAPOLEON BONAPARTE.

The greatest firmness is the greatest mercy.—HENRY WADSWORTH LONGFELLOW.

Steadfastness is a noble quality, but unguided by knowledge or humility it becomes rashness or obstinacy.—J. SWARTZ.

# STEWARDSHIP

Am I my brother's keeper?—GEN. 4:9b.

Who knoweth whether thou art come to the Kingdom for such a time as this?—ESTHER 4:14b.

It is required in stewards, that a man be found faithful.—I COR. 4:2.

There is no portion of our time that is our time, and the rest God's; there is no portion of our money that is our money, and the rest God's money. It is all His; He made it all, gives it all, and He has simply trusted it to us for His service. A servant has two purses, the Master's and his own, but we have only one.—ADOLPHE MONOD.

Men are often like knives with many blades; they know how to open one and only one; all the rest are buried in the handle, and they are no better than they would have been if they had been made with but one blade. Many men use but one or two faculties out of the score with which they are endowed.—HENRY WARD BEECHER.

# STEWARDSHIP

Rulers have the right to exist only if they become the trustees and servants of the people.—MOHANDAS K. GANDHI.

Strange is our situation here upon earth. Each of us comes for a short visit, not knowing why, yet sometimes seeming to divine a purpose. From the standpoint of daily life, however, there is one thing we do know; that man is here for the sake of other men—above all for those upon whose smiles and well-being our own happiness depends, and also for the countless unknown souls with whose fate we are connected by a bond of sympathy. Many times a day I realize how much my own outer and inner life is built upon the labors of my fellow men, both living and dead, and how earnestly I must exert myself in order to give in return as much as I have received. My peace of mind is often troubled by the depressing sense that I have borrowed too heavily from the work of other men.—ALBERT EINSTEIN.

We are not to judge thrift solely by the test of saving or spending. If one spends what he should prudently save, that certainly is to be deplored. But if one saves what he should prudently spend, that is not necessarily to be commended. A wise balance between the two is the desired end.—OWEN D. YOUNG.

As to all that we have and are, we are but stewards of the Most High God. On all our possessions,—on our time, and talents and influence, and property, He has written "occupy for me, till I shall come." To obey his instruction and serve him faithfully is the true test of obedience and discipleship.—CHARLES SIMMONS.

Stewardship is the acceptance from God of personal responsibility for all of life and life's affairs.—ROSWELL C. LONG.

There's a stewardship of waiting,
    Lord, may I most patient be
As I'm waiting for the answer
    That I know will come from Thee.

There's a stewardship of trusting,
    Keep my faith both strong and sure;
Lord, I know it often falters,
    Thou canst make it to endure.

# STEWARDSHIP

There's a stewardship of singing
  Though the waiting may seem long,
Though the trust may seem to weaken,
  And the heart may lose its song.

All these things are simple service,
  Service for my Lord and King,
Take them, Lord, though they be little,
  They're the best that I can bring.
           —ZULA EVELYN COON.

Our children, relations, friends, honors, houses, lands, and endowments, the goods of nature and fortune, nay, even of grace itself, are only lent. It is our misfortune, and our sin to fancy they are given. We start, therefore, and are angry when the loan is called in. We think ourselves masters, when we are only stewards, and forget that to each of us it will one day be said, "Give an account of thy stewardship."—BISHOP THOMAS H. HORNE.

There's never a rose in all the world
  But makes some green spray sweeter;
There's never a wind in all the sky
  But makes some bird wing fleeter;
There's never a star but brings to heaven
  Some silver radiance tender;
And never a rosy cloud but helps
  To crown the sunset splendor;
No robin but may thrill some heart,
  His dawn like gladness voicing;
God gives to all some small sweet way
  To set the world rejoicing.
           —ANONYMOUS.

# STRENGTH

Be strong, and quit yourselves like men.—I SAM. 4:9.

In thine hand is power and might; and in thine hand it is to make great, and to give strength unto all.—I CHRON. 29:12.

# STRENGTH

God is our refuge and strength, a very present help in trouble.
—Psalm 46:1.

Thy God hath commanded thy strength.—Psalm 68:28.

Blessed is the man whose strength is in thee.—Psalm 84:5.

They that wait upon the Lord shall renew their strength; they shall mount up with wings as eagles; they shall run, and not be weary; they shall walk, and not faint.—Isa. 40:31.

Not by might, nor by power, but by my spirit, saith the Lord. —Zech. 4:6.

Nothing is so strong as gentleness; nothing so gentle as real strength.—Saint Francis de Sales.

The strength of a country is the strength of its religious convictions.—Calvin Coolidge.

> This is my grief
> And I must bear it;
> As the green shafts of corn
> Gain strength from earth and sun and storm,
> So must my strength be kept through grief.
> Born of the earth,
> I, too, must know the saber of wind,
> Disquieting hours and grief;
> But knowing God,
> Sustenance comes;
> There is no life nor beauty
> That has not come by pain;
> And there can be no grief
> But through His conquering strength
> Will find the gain.
>
> —Faye Carr Adams.

No two things differ more than hurry and dispatch. Hurry is the mark of a weak mind, dispatch of a strong one. A weak man in office, like a squirrel in a cage, is laboring eternally, but to no purpose, and is in constant motion without getting on a job; like a turnstile, he is in everybody's way, but stops nobody; he talks a great deal, but says very little; looks into everything but sees nothing; has a hundred irons in the fire, but very few of them are hot, and with those few that are, he only burns his fingers.—C. C. COLTON.


# SUCCESS

I can do all things through Christ which strengtheneth me.— PHIL. 4:13.

> Prosperity is not without many fears and distastes,
> And adversity is not without comforts and hopes.
> —FRANCIS BACON.

Nothing is impossible to the willing heart.—THOMAS HEY-WOOD.

> 'Tis not in mortals to command success,
> But we'll do more . . . we'll deserve it.
> —JOSEPH ADDISON.

They never fail who die in a great cause.—GEORGE GORDON, LORD BYRON.

Perseverance gives power to weakness, and opens to poverty the world's wealth. It spreads fertility over the barren landscape, and bids the choicest fruits and flowers spring up and flourish in the desert abode of thorns and briers.—SAMUEL GRISWOLD GOODRICH.

Adversity is sometimes hard upon a man; but for one man who can stand prosperity there are a hundred that will stand adversity.—THOMAS CARLYLE.

> Not in the clamor of the crowded street
> Not in the shouts and plaudits of the throng,
> But in ourselves are triumph and defeat.
> —HENRY WADSWORTH LONGFELLOW.

Great results cannot be achieved at once, and we must be satisfied to advance in life as we walk—step by step.—SAMUEL SMILES.

# SUCCESS

If you can sit at set of sun
And count the deeds that you have done
    And counting find
One self-denying act, one word
That eased the heart of him that heard—
    One glance most kind,
Which fell like sunshine where he went,
Then you may count that day well spent.
                    —ROBERT BROWNING.

The men who I have seen succeed best in life have always been cheerful and hopeful men, who went about their business with a smile on their faces, and took the changes and chances of this mortal life like men, facing rough and smooth alike as it comes.—CHARLES KINGSLEY.

Yet they, believe me, who await
No gifts from chance, have conquered Fate.
                    —MATTHEW ARNOLD.

These three things—work, will, success—fill human existence. Will opens the door to success, both brilliant and happy. Work passes these doors, and at the end of the journey success comes in to crown one's efforts.—LOUIS PASTEUR.

No life is wasted unless it ends in sloth, dishonesty and cowardice.—THOMAS HUXLEY.

To find his place and fill it is success for a man.—PHILLIPS BROOKS.

To achieve success not by heritage but by individual effort is the greatest joy in life.—JOHN P. MORGAN.

Success doesn't happen. It is organized, pre-empted, captured by concentrated common sense!—FRANCES E. WILLARD.

The three great essentials to achieve anything worth while are, first, hard work; second, stick-to-itiveness; third, common sense.—THOMAS EDISON.

Some defeats are only installments to victory.—JACOB A. RIIS.

The true blessedness of a man is not to arrive, but to travel. —ROBERT LOUIS STEVENSON.

324

# SUCCESS

There are two remedies that, in proper combination, have never failed for any situation. They will save us when the numerous others that are proposed and being tried have run their course, if we will apply them. The first of these is the more essential, and without it, the other can do no good. It is faith—faith in a power higher than ourselves, with wisdom and resources infinitely greater than those which belong to man. Faith in God, and in the teachings of His Son, Jesus Christ. The other lies in the application of what is known as common sense.—ALEX ACHESON.

Every thought you let yourself think; every emotion you permit yourself to enjoy, leaves its mark and helps either to make you insufficient for life or to give you some greater sufficiency. —WINIFRED RHOADES.

He has achieved success who has lived well, laughed often and loved much; who has gained the respect of intelligent men, and the love of little children; who has filled his niche and accomplished his task; who has left the world better than he found it, whether by an improved poppy, a perfect poem, or a rescued soul; who has never lacked appreciation of earth's beauty, or failed to express it; who has always looked for the best in others, and given the best he had; whose life was an inspiration; whose memory a benediction.—THOMAS STANLEY.

A long time ago a noted specialist said that his secret of success as a physician was keeping the patient's head cool and his feet warm. And it is just now becoming generally known that "a hot head" and "cool feet" are enough to bring disaster to even a well man.—O. BYRON COOPER.

It is surprising to observe how much more anybody may become by simply being always in His place.—SALINA WATCHMAN.

Everybody finds out, sooner or later, that all success worth having is founded on Christian rules of conduct.—H. M. FIELD.

I do not believe in that word Fate. It is the refuge of every self-confessed failure.—ANDREW SOUTAR.

# SUCCESS

The difficult we do at once. The impossible takes a little longer.—MOTTO OF THE U. S. ARMY ENGINEERS.

To have grown wise and kind is real success.—ANONYMOUS.

If you wish for success in life, make perseverance your bosom friend, experience your wise counsellor, caution your elder brother, and hope your guardian genius.—ANONYMOUS.

Every man has the secret of becoming rich who resolves to live within his means.—ANONYMOUS.


# SYMPATHY

When Mary was come where Jesus was, and saw him, she fell down at his feet, saying unto him, Lord, if thou hadst been here, my brother had not died. When Jesus therefore saw her weeping, and the Jews also weeping which came with her, he groaned in the spirit, and was troubled. . . . Jesus wept. Then said the Jews, Behold how he loved him!—JOHN 11:32-36.

Be ye kind one to another, tenderhearted, forgiving one another, even as God for Christ's sake hath forgiven you.—EPH. 4:32.

Remember them that are in bonds, as bound with them; and them which suffer adversity, as being yourselves also in the body. —HEB. 13:3.

Shun the proud man that is ashamed to weep.—EDWARD YOUNG.

A tender hearted and compassionate disposition, which inclines men to pity and feel for the misfortune of others, and which is, even for its own sake, incapable of involving any man in ruin and misery, is of all tempers of mind the most amiable; and though it seldom receives honor, is worthy of the highest. —HENRY FIELDING.

Next to love, sympathy is the divinest passion of the human heart.—EDMUND BURKE.

# SYMPATHY

With the soul that ever felt the sting of sorrow, sorrow **is a** sacred thing.—WILLIAM COWPER.

Let us cherish sympathy. It prepares the mind for receiving the impressions of virtue; and without it there can be no true politeness.—JAMES BEATTIE.

Love is loveliest when embalmed in tears.—SIR WALTER SCOTT.

There is a sacredness in tears. They are not the mark of weakness but of power. They speak more eloquently than ten thousand tongues. They are the messengers of overwhelming grief, of deep contrition, of unspeakable love.—WASHINGTON IRVING.

Our sympathy is never very deep unless founded on our own feelings. We pity, but do not enter into the grief which we have never felt.—LETITIA E. LANDON (L. E. L.).

If we could read the secret history of our enemies, we should find in each man's life sorrow and suffering enough to disarm all hostility.—HENRY WADSWORTH LONGFELLOW.

The only true knowledge of our fellowmen is that which enables us to feel with him . . . which gives us a fine ear for the heart-pulses that are beating under the mere clothes of circumstances and opinion.—GEORGE ELIOT.

> And see how everywhere
> Love comforts, strengthens, helps and saves us all;
> What opportunities of good befall
> To make life sweet and fair.
> —CELIA THAXTER.

Sympathy is a thing to be encouraged apart from humane consideration, because it supplies us with the materials for wisdom.—ROBERT LOUIS STEVENSON.

> I treasure more than I despise
> My tendency to sin,
> Because it helps me sympathize
> With all my erring kin.
> He who has nothing in his soul
> That links him to the sod.

# SYMPATHY

Knows not the joy of self-control
That lifts him up to God.
So I am glad my heart can say
When others slip and fall:
Altho' I safely passed that way,
I understand it all.

—ELLA WHEELER WILCOX.

He that lacks time to mourn, lacks time to mend.
Eternity mourns that. 'Tis an ill cure
For life's worst ills, to have no time to feel them.
Where sorrow's held intrusive and turned out,
There Wisdom will not enter, not true Power
Nor aught that dignified humanity.

—SIR HENRY TAYLOR.

To rejoice in another's prosperity, is to give content to your own lot; to mitigate another's grief, is to alleviate or dispel your own.—TRYON EDWARDS.

How long, oh how long will it take us to learn that there are only two things in life that really count—one is character and the other is human sympathy.—ANONYMOUS.

When all our hopes are gone,
'Tis well our hands must still keep toiling on
For others' sake;
For strength to bear is found in duty done;
And he is blest indeed who learns to make
The joy of others cure his own heartache.

—ANONYMOUS.

Who are the blest?
They who have kept their sympathies awake,
And scattered joy for more than custom's sake—
Steadfast and tender in the hour of need,
Gentle in thought, benevolent in deed;
Whose looks have power to make dissension cease—
Whose smiles are pleasant, and whose words are peace.

—ANONYMOUS.

# TEMPERANCE

Every inordinate cup is unbless'd,
and the ingredient is the devil.
—WILLIAM SHAKESPEARE.

In my youth I never did apply
Hot and rebellious liquors in my blood.
Therefore my age is as a lusty winter,
Frosty but kindly.
—WILLIAM SHAKESPEARE.

O thou invisible spirit of wine, if thou hast no name to be known by, let us call thee devil!—WILLIAM SHAKESPEARE.

What is a drunken man like? Like a drowned man, a fool and a madman; one draught above heat makes him a fool; the second maddens him; and the third drowns him.—WILLIAM SHAKESPEARE.

It were better for a man to be subject to any vice than to drunkenness; for all other vanities and sins are recovered, but a drunkard will never shake off the delight of beastliness; for the longer it possesseth a man, the more he will delight in it, and the older he groweth the more he shall be subject to it.—SIR WALTER RALEIGH.

Beware of drunkenness, lest all good men beware of thee. Where drunkenness reigns, there reason is an exile, virtue a stranger, and God an enemy; blasphemy is wit, oaths are rhetoric and secrets are proclamations.—FRANCIS QUARLES.

Inflaming wine, pernicious to mankind!—ALEXANDER POPE.

Temperance puts wood on the fire, meal in the barrel, flour in the tub, money in the purse, credit in the country, contentment in the house, clothes on the children, vigor in the body, intelligence in the brain, and spirit in the whole constitution.
—BENJAMIN FRANKLIN.

Some of the domestic evils of drunkenness are houses without windows, gardens without fences, fields without tillage, barns without roofs, children without clothing, principles, morals or manners.—BENJAMIN FRANKLIN.

# TEMPERANCE

Temperance and labor are the two best physicians of man; labor sharpens the appetite and temperance prevents him from indulging to excess.—JEAN JACQUES ROUSSEAU.

The habit of intemperance by men in office has occasioned more injury to the public and more trouble to men than all other causes; and, were I to commence my administration again, the first question I would ask respecting a candidate for office would be, "Does he use ardent spirits?"—THOMAS JEFFERSON.

Since the creation of the world there has been no tyrant like Intemperance and no slaves so cruelly treated as his.—WILLIAM LLOYD GARRISON.

By abstaining from most things it is surprising how many things we enjoy.—WILLIAM G. SIMMS.

We lead but one life here on earth. We must make that beautiful. And to do this, health and elasticity of mind are needful; and whatever endangers or impedes these must be avoided.—HENRY WADSWORTH LONGFELLOW.

I cannot consent to place in the control of others one who cannot control himself.—ROBERT E. LEE, who never promoted a man who drank.

The saloon is a cancer on humanity, eating at its vitals and threatening its destruction.—ABRAHAM LINCOLN.

Temperance is the preservation of divine order in the body. —THEODORE PARKER.

If we could sweep intemperance out of the country there would be hardly enough poverty left to give healthy exercise to the charitable impulses.—PHILLIPS BROOKS.

> Drink has drained more blood,
> Hung more crepe,
> Sold more houses,
> Plunged more people into bankruptcy,
> Armed more villians,
> Slain more children,
> Snapped more wedding rings,
> Defiled more innocence,

# TEMPERANCE

Blinded more eyes,
Twisted more limbs,
Dethroned more reason,
Wrecked more manhood,
Dishonored more womanhood,
Broken more hearts,
Blasted more lives,
Driven more suicide, and
Dug more graves
   than any other poisoned scourge that ever
   swept its death-dealing waves across the world.
                              —EVANGELINE BOOTH.

My medical experience has taught me that the effect of alcohol is temporary, evanescent; that the drug (for such it is) does not real good, and that a dangerous habit is thus easily engendered which may be most difficult to eradicate, a habit which may utterly ruin the patient—body, soul and spirit, making it far better if he had died at once of his disease while under the doctor's care.—DR. HOWARD KELLY.

All my life I have lived in the presence of fine and beautiful men, going to their death through alcohol. I call it the greatest trap that life has set for the feet of genius.—UPTON SINCLAIR.

When I have a good time, I want to know about it.—LADY NANCY ASTOR.

My chief quarrel with the drugs that enslave is that they do enslave—that they take away freedom of choice, so that the man who becomes an addict renounces usually forever the inestimable privilge of being master of himself.—DR. HENRY SMITH WILLIAMS.

Temperance is to the body what religion is to the soul—the foundation of health, strength and peace.—TRYON EDWARDS.

A drunkard is the annoyance of modesty; the trouble of civility; the spoil of wealth; the distraction of reason. He is the brewer's agent; the tavern and alehouse benefactor; the beggar's companion; the constable's trouble; his wife's woe; his children's sorrow; his neighbor's tax; his own shame. In short he is a spirit of unrest, a thing below a beast and a monster of a man.— T. ADAMS.

# TEMPERANCE

The sight of a drunkard is a better sermon against that vice than the best sermon that was ever preached on that subject.
—SARAH E. SAVILLE.

The drunkard drinks alcohol to escape the hard realities of life. His wife does not escape, his children do not escape, society does not escape, and in the end the drunkard does not escape.
—ANONYMOUS.

# TEMPTATION

There hath no temptation taken you but such as is common to man: but God is faithful, who will not suffer you to be tempted above that ye are able; but will with the temptation also make a way to escape, that ye may be able to bear it.—I COR. 10:13.

[He] was in all points tempted like as we are, yet without sin.
—HEB. 4:15.

Blessed is the man that endureth temptation: for when he is tried, he shall receive the crown of life, which the Lord hath promised to them that love him.—JAS. 1:12.

Resist the devil, and he will flee from you.—JAS. 4:7.

When devils will their blackest sins put on
They do suggest at first with heavenly shows.
—WILLIAM SHAKESPEARE.

Most dangerous is that temptation
That doth goad us on to sin, in loving virtue.
—WILLIAM SHAKESPEARE.

There is no vice so simple but assumes
Some mark of virtue in its outward parts.
—WILLIAM SHAKESPEARE.

It is one thing to be tempted,
And another thing to fall.
—WILLIAM SHAKESPEARE.

# TEMPTATION

Temptations, when we meet them at first, are as the lion that reared upon Samson; but if we overcome them, the next time we see them we shall find a nest of honey within them.—John Bunyan..

God is better served in resisting a temptation to evil than in many formal prayers.—William Penn.

In so far as you approach temptation to a man, you do him an injury; and if he is overcome, you share his guilt.—Samuel Johnson.

Whoever yields to temptation debases himself with a debasement from which he can never rise. A man can be wronged and live; but the unrestricted, unchecked impulse to do wrong is the first and second death.—Horace Mann.

No degree of temptation justifies any degree of sin.—Nathaniel Parker Willis.

Every moment of resistance to temptation is a victory.—Frederick William Faber.

No one can ask honestly or hopefully to be delivered from temptation, unless he has himself honestly and firmly determined to do the best he can to keep out of it.—John Ruskin.

Some temptations come to the industrious, but all temptations attack the idle.—Charles Haddon Spurgeon.

Learn to say "No!" It will be of more use to you than to be able to read Latin.—Charles Haddon Spurgeon.

Temptation rarely comes in working hours. It is in their leisure time that men are made or marred.—W. T. Taylor.

God chooses that men should be tried, but let a man beware of tempting his neighbor. God knows how and how much, and where and when. Man is his brother's keeper, and must keep him according to his knowledge.—George McDonald.

To pray against temptation, and yet to rush into occasion, is to thrust your fingers into the fire, and then pray they might not be burnt.—Thomas Secker.

# TEMPTATION

To attempt to resist temptation, abandon our bad habits, and to control our dominant passions in our own unaided strength, is like attempting to check by a spider's thread the progress of a ship borne along before wind and tide.—BENJAMIN WAUGH.

To realize God's presence is the one sovereign remedy against temptation.—ANONYMOUS.

Many so-called innocent amusements are but contrivances of the devil to make us forget God.—ANONYMOUS.

# TIME

I must work the works of him that sent me, while it is day: the night cometh, when no man can work.—JOHN 9:4.

If all the years were playing holidays, to sport would be as tedious as to work.—WILLIAM SHAKESPEARE.

> See golden days, fruitful of golden deeds
> With joy and love triumphing.
> —JOHN MILTON.

Spend your time in nothing which you know must be repented of; in nothing on which you might not pray for the blessing of God; in nothing which you could not review with a quiet conscience on your dying bed; in nothing which you might not safely and properly be found doing if death should surprise you in the act.—RICHARD BAXTER.

> Happy the man, and happy he alone,
> He who can call today his own;
> He who, secure within, can say,
> Tomorrow, do thy worst,
> For I have liv'd today.
> —JOHN DRYDEN.

The morning hour has gold in its hand.—BENJAMIN FRANKLIN.

> One today is worth two tomorrows;
> What I am to be I am now becoming.
> —BENJAMIN FRANKLIN.

# TIME

Dost thou love life? Then do not squander time, for that is the stuff life is made of.—BENJAMIN FRANKLIN.

Lose the day loitering. 'Twill be the same story
Tomorrow, and the next more dilatory.

For indecision brings its own delays,
And days are lost lamenting o'er lost days.

Are you in earnest? Seize this very minute!
What you can do, or think you can, begin it!
Boldness has genius, power and magic in it!

Only engage, and when the mind grows heated,
Begin it, and the work will be completed.
—JOHANN WOLFGANG VON GOETHE.

So here hath been dawning
Another blue day;
Think, will thou let it
Slip useless away?
—THOMAS CARLYLE.

Time is a great physician.—BENJAMIN DISRAELI.

Look not mournfully into the past; it returns no more; wisely improve the present, and go forth into the shadowy future without fear and with a manly heart.—HENRY WADSWORTH LONGFELLOW.

Let every corner of this day
Become an altar, Lord for Thee.
A quiet place where I can pray
And hear Thee talk to me.

The bright expectancy of dawn
Will not endure the noon day heat
Unless refreshing strength is drawn
Where altars touch Thy feet.
—SYBIL LEONARD ARMES.

'Tis not for man to trifle; life is brief,
And sin is here.
Our age is but the falling of a leaf,
A dropping tear.

# TIME

We have no time to sport away the hours;
All must be earnest in a world like ours.
Not many lives, but only one have we,
    Only, only one.
How earnest should that one life be,
    That narrow span;
Day after day spent in blessed toil.
              —HORATIUS BOMAR.

I see not a step before me as I tread on another year;
But I've left the Past in God's keeping—the Future
    His mercy shall clear;
And what looks dark in the distance may brighten as I draw near.

                * * *

So I go on, not knowing, I would not if I might;
I would rather walk with God in the dark, than to go alone in the
    light.
              —MARY GARDINER BRAINARD.

Life seems too little when life is past,
And the memories of sorrow flee so fast,
And the woes which were bitter to you and to me
Shall vanish as raindrops which fall in the sea;
And all that has hurt us shall be made good,
And the puzzles which hindered be understood,
And the long, hard march through the wilderness bare
Seem but a day's journey when once we are there.
              —SUSAN COOLIDGE.

Time worketh, let me work too;
Time undoeth; let me do;
Busy as time my work I'll ply
Till I rest in the rest of eternity.

Sin worketh; let me work too;
Sin undoeth; let me do;
Busy as sin my work I'll ply
Till I rest in the rest of eternity.

# TIME

Death worketh; let me work too;
Death undoeth; let me do.
Busy as Death my work I'll ply
Till I rest in the rest of eternity.
—ROLAND Q. LEAVELL.

No man ever sank under the burden of the day. It is when tomorrow's burden is added to the burden of today that the weight is more than a man can bear. Never load yourselves so. If you find yourselves so loaded, at least remember this: it is your own doing, not God's. He begs you to leave the future to Him, and mind the present.—GEORGE MCDONALD.

I shall try to remember all this day that I am a divine creation with infinite possibilities.—BENJAMIN EITELGEORGE.

Time is so precious that it is dealt out to us only in the smallest possible fractions—a tiny moment at a time.—IRISH PROVERB.

Now let Him who blows out our candle light
Defend our dreams from perils of the night.
—ANONYMOUS.

O soul, this day is thine to imitate!
Be thou a day clothed in the living light!
Rise to thy task, and, be it small or great,
Shine on it till thy smile has made it bright;
Smile, smile on all thy duties, and beyond!
Thy life, like day, shall walk in robes of gold.
—ANONYMOUS.

Take time to work—it is the price of success;
Take time to think—it is the source of power;
Take time to play—it is the secret of perpetual youth;
Take time to read—it is the foundation of wisdom;
Take time to worship—it is the highway to reverence;
Take time to be friendly—it is the road to happiness;
Take time to dream—it is hitching our wagon to a star;
Take time to love and be loved—it is the privilege of the gods.
—ANONYMOUS.

The soul is dyed the color of the leisure hours.—ANONYMOUS.

# TIME

The best things are nearest—breath in your nostrils; light in your eyes, flowers at your feet, duties at your hand, the path of God just before you. Then do not grasp at the stars, but do life's plain, common work as it comes, certain that daily duties and daily bread are the sweetest things of life.—ANONYMOUS.

Look well to this day!
For it is life; the very life of life.
In its brief course lie all the verities
    And realities of your existence.
The bliss of growth, the glory of action,
The splendor of beauty;
For yesterday is only a dream,
Tomorrow only a vision;
But today, well lived, makes of every yesterday
A dream of happiness and of every tomorrow
    A vision of hope.
Look well, therefore, to this day.
                            —ANONYMOUS.

Every day remember that you have a God to glorify; a Saviour to imitate; a soul to save; your body to mortify; virtue to acquire; heaven to seek; eternity to meditate upon; temptations to resist; the world to guard against; and perhaps death to meet.—ANONYMOUS.

All the time which God allows us is just enough for the work which God allots us.—ANONYMOUS.

Live full today, and let no pleasure pass untasted—
    And no transcient beauty scorn;
Fill well the storehouse of the soul's delight
    With light of memory—
Who knows? Tomorrow may be—Night.
                            —ANONYMOUS.

We have to live but one day at a time, but we are living for eternity in that one day.—ANONYMOUS.

# TRUTH

Keep thy tongue from evil, and thy lips from speaking guile. —PSALM 34:13.

His truth shall be thy shield.—PSALM 91:4.

These are the things that ye shall do; Speak ye every man the truth to his neighbor; execute the judgment of truth and peace in your gates.—ZECH. 8:16.

Ye shall know the truth and the truth shall make you free. —JOHN 8:32.

When he, the Spirit of truth, shall come, he will guide you into all truth.—JOHN 16:13.

Truth is always the strongest argument.—SOPHOCLES.

What we have in us of the image of God is the love of truth and justice.—DEMOSTHENES.

Truth is the highest thing that man can keep.—GEOFFREY CHAUCER.

Truth has a quiet breast.—WILLIAM SHAKESPEARE.

No pleasure is comparable to the standing upon the vantage ground of truth.—FRANCIS BACON.

Truth is as impossible to be soiled by any outward touch as the sunbeam.—JOHN MILTON.

Though all the winds of doctrine were let loose to play upon the earth, so Truth be in the field, we do ingloriously, by licensing and prohibiting, to misdoubt her strength. Let her and Falsehood grapple; who ever knew Truth put to the worst in a free and open encounter?—JOHN MILTON.

The most natural beauty in the world is honesty and moral truth; for all beauty is truth. True features makes the beauty of the face; and true proportions the beauty of architecture; and true measures that of harmony and music.—ANTHONY ASHLEY COOPER, EARL OF SHAFTESBURY.

# TRUTH

There are two peculiarities in the truths of religion: a divine beauty which renders them lovely, and a holy majesty which makes them venerable. And there are two peculiarities in errors: an impiety which renders them horrible, and an impertinence which renders them ridiculous.—Blaise Pascal.

Truth is always consistent with itself, and needs nothing to help it out; it is always at hand and sits upon our lips, and is ready to drop out before we are aware; whereas a lie is troublesome, and sets a man's invention on the rack, and one trick needs a great many more of the same kind to make it good.—Archbishop John Tillotson.

> Truth has such a face and such a mien,
> As to be lov'd needs only to be seen.
> —John Dryden.

He that hath truth on his side is a fool as well as a coward if he is afraid to own it because of other man's opinions.—Daniel Defoe.

Be truthful; be accurate. We always weaken when we exaggerate.—Jean Francois de La Harpe.

I have seldom known any one who deserted truth in trifles that could be trusted in matters of importance.—William Paley.

Search for the truth is the noblest occupation of man; its publication is a duty.—Mme. de Staël.

There is nothing so powerful as truth—and often nothing so strange.—Daniel Webster.

When two truths seem to directly oppose each other, we must not question either, but remember there is a third—God—who reserves to himself the right to harmonize them.—Mme. Soymonoff Swetchine.

The grand character of truth is its capability of enduring the test of universal experience, and coming unchanged out of every possible form of fair discussion.—Sir John Frederick Herschel.

# TRUTH

Truth crushed to earth will rise again;
The eternal years of God are hers;
But Error wounded writhes in pain,
And dies amid her worshippers.
—WILLIAM CULLEN BRYANT.

Can there be a more horrible object in existence than an eloquent man not speaking the truth.—THOMAS CARLYLE.

Keep one thing forever in view—the truth; and if you do this, though it may seem to lead you away from the opinion of men, it will assuredly conduct you to the throne of God.—HORACE MANN.

There is no fit search after truth which does not, first of all, begin to live the truth which it knows.—HORACE BUSHNELL.

Every violation of truth is a stab at the health of human society.—RALPH WALDO EMERSON.

The grandest homage we can pay to truth is to use it.—RALPH WALDO EMERSON.

A lie which is half a truth is ever the blackest of lies. A lie which is all a lie may be met and fought with outright; but a lie which is part a truth is a harder matter to fight.—ALFRED TENNYSON.

Truth never yet fell dead in the streets; it has such affinity with the soul of man, the seed, however broadcast, will catch somewhere and produce itself a hundredfold.—THEODORE PARKER.

Truth lies in character. Christ did not simply speak the truth; he was Truth—Truth through and through, for truth is a thing not of words but a life and being.—FREDERICK WILLIAM ROBERTSON.

He who has truth at his heart need never fear the want of persuasion on his tongue.—JOHN RUSKIN.

Who speaks the truth stabs Falsehood to the heart.—JAMES RUSSELL LOWELL.

# TRUTH

Truth forever on the scaffold;
Wrong forever on the throne;
Yet the scaffold sways the future
And beyond the dim unknown,
Standeth God among the shadows
Keeping watch above his own.
                    —JAMES RUSSELL LOWELL.

Truth is not only violated by falsehood; it may be equally outraged by silence.—HENRI FREDERIC AMIEL.

Truth is the heart of morality.—THOMAS HUXLEY.

If you tell the truth, you have infinite power supporting you; but if not, you have infinite power against you.—GENERAL CHARLES ("CHINESE") GORDON.

Sin has many tools, but a lie is the handle that fits them all.
—OLIVER WENDELL HOLMES.

Every truth has practical consequences, and these are the test of Truth.—WILLIAM JAMES.

In the mountains of truth, you never climb in vain. Either you already reach a higher point today, or you exercise your strength in order to be able to climb higher tomorrow.—FRIEDRICH W. NIETZSCHE.

Only he who lives in truth finds it. The deepest truth is not born of conscious striving, but comes in the quiet hour when a noble nature gives itself into the keeping of life, to suffer, to feel, to think, and to act as it is moved by wisdom not its own.—HAMILTON WRIGHT MABIE.

Honesty of thought and speech and written word is a jewel, and they who curb prejudice and seek honorably to know and speak the truth are the only builders of a better life.—JOHN GALSWORTHY.

There is no problem in dealing with error if truth is presented intelligently and in love.—W. R. WHITE.

# TRUTH

God has revealed many truths which he has not explained. We will just have to be content to let Him know some things we do not and take Him at His word.—B. A. Copass.

If you find truth anywhere in the world, seize upon it, for real truth cannot contradict the Bible.—W. Douglas Hudgins.

Our recognition and apprehension of the highest truth is essentially an affair of the heart, far more than of the head.—J. B. Kieffer.

Doctrine is truth, and you can not preach the truth without preaching doctrine.—L. M. Joines.

The greatest friend of truth is time; her greatest enemy is prejudice.—C. C. Colton.

Much of the glory and sublimity of truth is connected with its mystery. To understand everything we must be as God.— Tryon Edwards.

Falsehood may have its hour, but it has no future.—Francois D. Pressense.

There is no progress in fundamental truth. We may grow in the knowledge of its meaning, and in the modes of its application, but its great principles will forever be the same.—W. Radcliff.

You cannot pound an idea into the human mind. An idea is a flower. You can shake its perfume on the air, but that requires no bluster. An idea is a jewel. You can twirl it before the people, that the light of every facet may fall upon their eyes, but that requires no muscle. If you want to get a great truth into the human heart, tip it with a gentle tone.—Charles E. Jefferson.

To love truth because truth is the essence of refinement and to be true to one's self is to be moral.—Anonymous.

There is no defeat in truth, save from within;
Unless you're beaten there, you're bound to win.
—Anonymous.

# UNSELFISHNESS

He that hath a bountiful eye shall be blessed; for he giveth of his bread to the poor.—PROV. 22:9.

He who civilly shows the way to one who has missed it, is as one who lighted another's lamp from his own lamp—it nonetheless gives light to himself when it burns for the other.—CICERO.

We shall never acquire any great capacity for joy, the blessed peace of God will never possess our mind and heart, as long as we shrink from self-denial.—AUZIAS MARCH.

Reach that which is of God in every one.—GEORGE FOX.

The most delicate, the most sensible of all pleasures consists in promoting the pleasures of others.—JEAN DE LABRUYÈRE.

Learn the luxury of doing good.—OLIVER GOLDSMITH.

> The man may last but never lives
> Who much received but nothing gives;
> Whom none can love, whom none can thank—
> Creation's blot—Creation's blank.
> —THOMAS GIBBONS.

There never did, and never will, exist anything permanently noble and excellent in the character which is a stranger to the exercise of self-denial.—SIR WALTER SCOTT.

It is only with renunciation that life, properly speaking, can be said to begin . . . In a valiant suffering for others, not in a slothful making others suffer for us, did nobleness ever lie.—THOMAS CARLYLE.

Selfishness is the greatest curse of the human race.—WILLIAM EWART GLADSTONE.

What we have done for ourselves alone dies with us; what we have done for others and the world remains and is immortal.—ALBERT PIKE.

The man who has lived for himself has the privilege of being his own mourner.—HENRY WARD BEECHER.

If you want to be miserable, think much about yourself; about what you want, what you like, what respect people ought to pay you, and what people think of you.—CHARLES KINGSLEY.

344

# UNSELFISHNESS

That which we look on with unselfish love,
And true humility is surely ours,
Even as a lake looks at the stars above
And makes within itself a heaven of stars.
　　　　　—MARY GARDINER BRAINARD.

We only begin to realize the value of our possessions when we commence to do good to others with them.—SIR JOSEPH COOK.

The greatest difficulty with the world is not its inability to produce, but its unwillingness to share.—ROY L. SMITH.

We cannot serve ourselves until we serve others also.—LYNN LANDRUM.

Remain not folded in thy pleasant joys
Within the narrow circle of thy walls,
Content if thine are blessed. Cold is thy fire
If on the hearth-stone only; and thy bread
Bitter, which feeds alone thy selfish blood;
Thy house a prison, if it holds thy world,
　　　Thy heaven a fiction.　　　—F. R. ABBE.

We live for others in the inevitable condition of our being. To accept the situation gladly is to find it crowned with its own joy.—ANONYMOUS.

Lord, keep me big enough to work with other people and let them get the credit.—ANONYMOUS.

One smile can glorify the day,
　One word new hope impart;
The least disciple need not say
There are no alms to give away
　If love be in the heart.
　　　　　—ANONYMOUS.

# VICTORY

Thanks be to God, which giveth us the victory through our Lord Jesus Christ.—I COR. 15:57.

# VICTORY

I have fought a good fight, I have finished my course, I have kept the faith:

Henceforth there is laid up for me a crown of righteousness, which the Lord, the righteous judge, shall give me at that day. —II TIM. 4:7, 8.

To him that overcometh will I grant to sit with me in my throne.—REV. 3:21.

The first and best victory is to conquer self; to be conquered by self is, of all things, the most shameful and vile.—PLATO.

There are some defeats more triumphant than victories.— MICHEL DE MONTAIGNE.

> An enterprise, when fairly once begun
> Should not be left till all that ought is won.
> —WILLIAM SHAKESPEARE.

In victory the hero seeks the glory, not the prey.—SIR PHILIP SIDNEY.

> Who overcomes
> By force, hath overcome but half his foe.
> —JOHN MILTON.

Great minds have purposes; others have wishes. Little minds are tamed and subdued by misfortune, but great minds rise above them.—WASHINGTON IRVING.

They conquer who believe they can. He has not learned the lesson of life who does not each day surmount a fear.—RALPH WALDO EMERSON.

> Well to suffer is divine.
> Pass the watchword down the line—
> Pass the countersign, Endure!
> Not to him who rashly dares,
> But to him who nobly bears
> Is the Victor's garland sure.
> —JOHN GREENLEAF WHITTIER.

# VICTORY

Herosim is the brilliant triumph of the soul over the flesh, . . . over fear . . . fear of poverty, of suffering, of calumny, of illness, of loneliness, and of death. There is no real piety without heroism. Heroism is the dazzling and glorious concentration of courage.—HENRI FREDERIC AMIEL.

> Defeat may serve as well as victory
> To shake the soul and let the glory out.
> When the great oak is straining in the wind,
> The boughs drink in new beauty, and the trunk
> Sends down a deeper root on the windward side.
> Only the soul that knows the mighty grief
> Can know the mighty rapture. Sorrows come
> To stretch out spaces in the heart for joy.
>                                   —EDWIN MARKHAM.

God can work wonders if He can get a suitable man; men can work wonders if they can get God to lead them.—E. M. BOUNDS.

Life, after all, contains only one great problem—that of so adjusting yourself to the inevitable that you can keep your peace of mind and your self respect. The greatest victory of life is the conquest of worry. The greatest discovery a man can make is how to escape envy and hate.—DOUGLAS FREEMAN.

God's greatest victories are won on the battle-fields that have seen our biggest defeats.—ANONYMOUS.

A great help in overcoming mistakes is to acknowledge them. —ANONYMOUS.

> Heroes are forged on anvils hot with pain
> And splendid courage comes but with the best.
>                                   —ANONYMOUS.

He who has resolved to conquer or die is seldom conquered. —ANONYMOUS.

You don't have to know how to sing; it's the feeling as though you want to that makes the day a successful one.—ANONYMOUS.

347

# VICTORY

No man can choose what coming hours may bring
To him of need, of joy, of suffering,
But what his soul shall bring into each hour
To meet its challenge—that is in his power.
                                    —ANONYMOUS.


# VIRTUE

Follow . . . holiness, without which no man shall see the Lord.
—HEB. 12:14.

Pure religion and undefiled before God and the Father is
this . . . to keep . . . unspotted from the world.—JAS. 1:27.

Silver and gold are not the only coin; Virtue, too, passes current all over the world.—EURIPIDES.

One ought to seek out virtue for its own sake, without being
influenced by fear or hope, or by any external influence.—DI-
OGENES.

Never esteem anything as of advantage to thee that shall
make thee break thy word or lose thy self respect.—MARCUS
AURELIUS.

Every virtue gives a man a degree of facility in some kind:
honesty gives a man a good report; justice, estimation; prudence,
respect; courtesy and liberality, affection; temperance gives
health; fortitude, a quiet of mind, not to be moved by any adversity.—SIR FRANCIS WALSINGHAM.

Virtue is bold, and goodness never fearful.—WILLIAM SHAKE-
SPEARE.

> Whose virtue and whose general graces speak
> That which none else can utter.
>                     —WILLIAM SHAKESPEARE.

There's nothing ill can dwell in such a temple:
If ill spirit have so fair a house,
Good things will starve to dwell with it.
                    —WILLIAM SHAKESPEARE.

348

# VIRTUE

The only impregnable citadel of virtue is religion; for there is no bulwark of more morality which some temptation may not overtop, or undermine and destroy.—SIR PHILIP SIDNEY.

Virtue is like a rich stone—best plain set.—FRANCIS BACON.

Good company and good discourse are the very sinews of virtue.—IZAAK WALTON.

Virtue could see to do what virtue would,
By her own radiant light, though sun and moon
Were in the flat sea sunk.
                    —JOHN MILTON.

Mortals, who would follow me,
Love virtue, she alone is free:
She can teach you how to climb
Higher than the spherey clime;
Or if virtue feeble were,
Heaven itself would stoop to her.
                    —JOHN MILTON.

Abash'd the devil stood,
And felt how awful goodness is, and saw
Virtue in her shape how lovely.
                    —JOHN MILTON.

'Tis chastity, my brother, chastity:
She that has that is clad in complete steel.
                    —JOHN MILTON.

So dear to heav'n is saintly chastity,
That when a soul is found sincerely so,
A thousand liveried angels lackey her,
Driving far off each thing of sin and guile,
And in clear dream and solemn vision
Tell her of things that no gross ear can hear,
Till oft converse with heav'nly habitants
Begin to cast a beam on th' outward shape.
                    —JOHN MILTON.

# VIRTUE

I would be virtuous for my own sake, though nobody were to know it; as I would be clean for my own sake, though nobody were to see me.—ANTHONY ASHLEY COOPER, EARL OF SHAFTESBURY.

The virtue of a man ought to be measured not by his extraordinary exertions, but by his every day conduct.—BLAISE PASCAL.

Virtue, though in rags, will keep me warm.—JOHN DRYDEN.

Were there but one virtuous man in the world, he would hold up his head with confidence and honor; he would shame the world, and not the world him.—ROBERT SOUTH.

To be innocent is to be not guilty; but to be virtuous is to overcome our evil feeling and intentions.—WILLIAM PENN.

When men grow virtuous in old age they are merely making an offering to God of the devil's leavings.—JONATHAN SWIFT.

Sweet are the slumbers of virtuous men.—JOSEPH ADDISON.

Know then this truth (enough for man to know) —
"Virtue alone is happiness below."
                    —ALEXANDER POPE.

Vice is a monster of so frightful mien,
As to be hated needs but to be seen;
Yet seen too oft, familiar with her face,
We first endure, then pity, then embrace.
                    —ALEXANDER POPE.

Virtue is not to be considered in the light of mere innocence, or abstaining from harm; but as the exertion of our faculties in doing good.—BISHOP JOSEPH BUTLER.

Virtue is a state of war, and to live in it we have always to combat with ourselves.—JEAN JACQUES ROUSSEAU.

Perfect virtue is to do unwitnessed what we should be capable of doing before the world.—FRANCOIS DE LA ROCHEFOUCAULD.

Chastity enables the soul to breathe a pure air in the foulest places. . . . Her sway over the senses makes her queenly: her light and peace render her beautiful.—JOSEPH JOUBERT.

# VIRTUE

Guilt, though it may attain temporal splendor, can never confer real happiness; the evil consequences of our crimes long survive their commission, and, like the ghosts of the murdered, forever haunt the steps of the malefactor; while the paths of virtue, though seldom those of worldly greatness, are always those of pleasantness and peace.—SIR WATER SCOTT.

Virtue consists in doing our duty in the various relations we sustain to ourselves, to our fellowmen, and to God, as it is made known by reason, revelation and Providence.—ARCHIBALD ALEXANDER.

I would rather be right than to be President.—HENRY CLAY.

Blessed is the memory of those who have kept themselves unspotted from the world! Yet more blessed and more dear the memory of those who have kept themselves unspotted in the world!—ANNA JAMESON.

Virtue is the habitual sense of right, and the habitual courage to act up to the sense of right, combined with benevolent sympathies, and the charity which thinketh no evil. The union of the highest conscience and highest sympathy fulfils my notion of virtue.—ANNA JAMESON.

Virtue is an angel; but she is a blind one and must ask of knowledge to show her the path that leads to her goal.—HORACE MANN.

What the world calls virtue, without Christ, is a name and a dream. The foundation of all human excellence must be laid deep in the blood of the Redeemer's cross and in the power of His resurrection.—FREDERICK WILLIAM ROBERTSON.

To be contented with the divine discontent, and to be ashamed with the noble shame, is the very germ of the first upgrowth of all virtue.—CHARLES KINGSLEY.

A man defines his standing at the court of chastity by his views of women . . . he cannot be any man's friend, nor his own, if not hers.—A. BRONSON ALCOTT.

Purity lives and derives its life solely from the Spirit of God.—JULIUS CHARLES HARE.

# VIRTUE

Any practice that destroys a man's character is a vice.—ROBERT QUILLEN.

He that is good will infallibly become better, and he that is bad will as certainly become worse; for vice, virtue and time are three things that never stand still.—C. C. COLTON.

Virtue is uniform and fixed, because she looks for approbation only from Him who is the same yesterday, today and forever.—C. C. COLTON.


# VISION

Where there is no vision, the people perish.—PROV. 29:18.

Whereupon, O King Agrippa, I was not disobedient unto the heavenly vision.—ACTS 26:19.

Open your eyes and the whole world is full of God.—JAKOB BOEHME.

He alone is an acute observer who can observe acutely without being observed.—JOHANN KASPAR LAVATER.

'Tis looking downward makes one dizzy.—ROBERT BROWNING.

All religion, all art, all finance, all business, every ship at sea, every bridge that spans the gulf, and every discovery in the great world of science owes its origin, its inception, and its first impulse to the exercise of that strange gift, imagination—a power to make images.—FRANCIS PARKES CADMAN.

Poor eyes limit your sight; poor vision limits your deeds.—FRANKLIN FIELD.

A vision without a task is a dream;
A task without a vision is drudgery;
A vision and a task is the hope of the world.
—ANONYMOUS.

# WAR

Scatter thou the people that delight in war.—PSALM 68:30.

He shall judge among the nations, and shall rebuke many people: and they shall beat their swords into plowshares, and their spears into pruninghooks: nation shall not lift up sword against nation, neither shall they learn war any more.—ISA. 2:4.

War loves to seek its victims in the young.—SOPHOCLES.

> War's a game which were their subjects wise
> Kings would not play at.—WILLIAM COWPER.

To be prepared for war is one of the most effectual means of preserving peace.—GEORGE WASHINGTON.

War is but an organized barbarism and an inheritance of the savage state, however disguised or ornamented.—LOUIS BONAPARTE.

What a fine looking thing is war! Yet, dress it as we may, dress and feather it, daub it with gold, huzza it, and sing swaggering songs about it, what is it but murder in uniform!—DOUGLAS WILLIAM JERROLD.

Fondly do we hope, fervently do we pray, that this mighty scourge of war will speedily pass away.—ABRAHAM LINCOLN.

As long as war is regarded as wicked it will always have its fascination. When it is looked upon as vulgar, it will cease to be popular.—OSCAR WILDE.

I learned that war was a profit-making business and that there are men in the world who stir up war for profit. It is a terrible thing to think of. War is man-made—it is not natural; it never settles anything.—HENRY FORD.

War is a futile thing; it neither insures peace nor composes difficulties. Arms have never yet saved a nation from war, nor have they given security to either strong or weak nations against attack.—RAMSAY MACDONALD.

War is not an act of God but a crime of man.—CORDELL HULL.

It is not enough to try to prevent war; something must be done to remove its causes.—SIR SAMUEL HOARE.

# WAR

What is the use of new inventions and new knowledge if they lead us only to the dark age?—REAR ADMIRAL RICHARD E. BYRD.

All we have to do to preserve the heroic in men is to set them fighting their real enemies; and the real enemies of mankind are ignorance, disease, superstition and war.—FREDERICK K. STAMM.

Build friendships not battleships for national defense.—ANONYMOUS.

It is in peace that our commerce flourishes most, and that our taxes are most easily paid.—ANONYMOUS.

# WEALTH

And Jacob vowed a vow, saying, If God will be with me, and will keep me in this way that I go, and will give me bread to eat, and raiment to put on,

So that I come again to my father's house in peace; then shall the Lord be my God:

And this stone, which I have set for a pillar, shall be God's house: and of all that thou shalt give me I will surely give the tenth unto thee.—GEN. 28:20, 21, 22.

But thou shalt remember the Lord thy God: for it is he that giveth thee power to get wealth.—DEUT. 8:18.

> The rich and the poor meet together:
> the Lord is the maker of them all.
> —PROV. 22:2.

There is a sore evil which I have seen under the sun, namely, riches kept for the owners thereof to their hurt.—ECC. 5:13.

Lay not up for yourselves treasures upon earth, where moth and rust doth corrupt, and where thieves break through and steal:

But lay up for yourselves treasures in heaven, where neither moth nor rust doth corrupt, and where thieves do not break through nor steal.—MATT. 6:19, 20.

# WEALTH

For what is a man profited if he shall gain the whole world, and lose his own soul?—MATT. 16:26.

A man's life consisteth not in the abundance of things which he possesseth.—LUKE 12:15.

The love of money is the root of all evil.—I TIM. 6:10.

Prosperity makes friends; adversity tries them.—PUBLIUS SYRUS.

He is richest who is content with the least, for content is the wealth of nature.—SOCRATES.

Riches, like glory or health, have no more beauty or pleasure than their possessor is pleased to lend them.—MICHEL DE MONTAIGNE.

Seek not proud wealth but such as thou mayest get justly, use soberly, distribute cheerfully and leave contentedly, yet have not any abstract or friarly contempt of it.—FRANCIS BACON.

Mammon, the least erected spirit that fell
From heaven; for ev'n in heaven his looks and thoughts
Were always downward bent, admiring more
The riches of heaven's pavement, trodden gold,
Than aught divine or holy else enjoy'd
   In vision beatific.
          —JOHN MILTON.

Money was made not to command our will,
But all our lawful pleasures to fulfill;
Shame and woe to us, if we our wealth obey—
The horse doth with the horseman run away.
          —ABRAHAM COWLEY.

To purchase Heaven has gold the power?
Can gold remove the mortal hour?
In life can love be bought with gold?
Are friendship's pleasures to be sold?
No—all that's worth a wish—a thought,
Fair virtue gives unbribed, unbought.
Cease then on trash thy hopes to bind,
Let nobler views engage thy mind.
          —SAMUEL JOHNSON.

# WEALTH

Money and time are the heaviest burdens of life, and the unhappiest of all mortals are those who have more of either than they know how to use.—SAMUEL JOHNSON.

Riches exclude only one inconvenience, and that is poverty.—SAMUEL JOHNSON.

Men are seldom more innocently employed than when they are honestly making money.—SAMUEL JOHNSON.

The way to wealth is as plain as the way to market. It depends chiefly on two words, industry and frugality; that is, waste neither time nor money, but make the best use of both. Without industry and frugality, nothing will do; and with them, everything.—BENJAMIN FRANKLIN.

Wealth is not his that has it, but his that enjoys it.—BENJAMIN FRANKLIN.

The use of money is all the advantage there is in having it.—BENJAMIN FRANKLIN.

If thou art rich, then show the greatness of thy fortune; or what is better, the greatness of thy soul, in the meekness of thy conversation; condescend to men of low estate, support the distressed, and patronize the neglected.—LAURENCE STERNE.

If we command our wealth, we shall be rich and free; if our wealth commands us, we are poor indeed. We are bought by the enemy with the treasure in our own coffers.—EDMUND BURKE.

By doing good with his money a man, as it were, stamps the image of God upon it, and makes it pass current for the merchandise of heaven.—JOHN RUTLEDGE.

It requires a great deal of boldness and a great deal of caution to make a great fortune; and when you have got it, it requires ten times as much wit to keep it.—MAYER A. ROTHSCHILD.

Excessive wealth is neither glory nor happiness. There is a fortune, a golden mean, which is the appropriate region of virtue and intelligence. Be content with that; and if the horn of plenty overflow, let its droppings fall upon your fellow-men; let them fall like the droppings of honey in the wilderness to cheer the faint and weary pilgrim.—WILLIAM WIRT.

Have the courage to appear poor and you disarm poverty of its sharpest sting.—ANNA JAMESON.

The wealth of a man is the number of things which he loves and blesses, and which he is loved and blessed by.—THOMAS CARLYLE.

Property has its duties as well as its rights.—BENJAMIN DISRAELI.

Wealth brings noble opportunities, and competence is a proper object of pursuit; but wealth, and even competence, may be bought at too high a price. Wealth itself has no moral attribute. It is not money, but the love of money, which is the root of all evil. It is the relation between wealth and the mind and the character of its possessor which is the essential thing.—HENRY W. HILLIARD.

In this world, it is not what we take up but what we give up that makes us rich.—HENRY WARD BEECHER.

No man can tell whether he is rich or poor by turning to his ledger. It is the heart that makes a man rich. He is rich according to what he is, not according to what he has.—HENRY WARD BEECHER.

Riches are not an end of life, but an investment of life.—HENRY WARD BEECHER.

Never respect men merely for their riches, but rather for their philanthropy; we do not value the sun for its height, but for its use.—PHILIP JAMES BAILEY.

Money is not required to buy one necessity of the soul.—HENRY DAVID THOREAU.

Money—the greatest god below the sky.—HERBERT SPENCER.

# WEALTH

Money alone is only a means; it presupposes a man to use it. The rich man can go where he pleases, but perhaps pleases himself nowhere. He can buy a library or visit the whole world, but perhaps has neither patience to read nor intelligence to see. . . . The purse may be full and the heart empty. He may have gained the world and lost himself; And with all his wealth around him . . . he may live as blank a life as any tattered ditcher.—ROBERT LOUIS STEVENSON.

Let the moment come when nothing is left but life, and you will find that you do not hesitate over the fate of material possessions.—EDWARD VERNON ("EDDIE") RICKENBACKER.

Mammon is the largest slaveholder in the world.—FREDERICK SAUNDERS.

He that will not permit his wealth to do any good to others while he is living, prevents it from doing good to himself when he is dead.—C. C. COLTON.

To value riches is not to be covetous. They are the gift of God, and, like every gift of his, good in themselves, and capable of a good use. But to overvalue riches, to give them a place in the heart which God did not design them to fill, this is covetousness. —H. L. WAYLAND.

Those who obtain riches by labor, care and watching, know their value. Those who impart them to sustain and extend knowledge, virtue and religion know their use. Those who lose them by accident or fraud know their vanity. And those who experience the difficulties and dangers of preserving them know their perplexities.—CHARLES SIMMONS.

There are two things needed in these days; first, for rich men to find out how poor men live; and second, for poor men to know how rich men work.—E. ATKINSON.

Property is a divine trust.—MALTBIE D. BABCOCK.

There is a burden of care in getting riches; fear in keeping them, temptation in using them, guilt in abusing them; sorrow in losing them; and a burden of account at last to be given concerning them.—MATTHEW HENRY.

# WEALTH

Wealth is not of necessity a curse, nor poverty a blessing. Wholesome and easy abundance is better than either extreme; better for our manhood that we have enough for daily comfort; enough for culture, for hospitality, for Christian charity. More than this may or may not be a blessing. Certainly it can be a blessing only by being accepted as a trust.—R. D. HITCHCOCK.

Fools can make money. It takes a wise man to tell how to spend it.—ENGLISH PROVERB.

The wealth of a state consists not in great treasures, solid walls, fair palaces, weapons and armor; but its best and noblest wealth, and its truest safety is in having learned, wise, honorable and well educated citizens.—ANONYMOUS.

The secret of making money is saving it. It is not what a man earns, not the amount of his income, but the relation of his expenditures to his receipts that determine his poverty or wealth.—ANONYMOUS.

> Dug from the mountainside, washed in the glen,
> Servant am I, or the master of men;
> Steal me, I curse you,
> Earn me, I bless you,
> Grasp me and hoard me, a fiend shall possess you;
> Lie for me, die for me, covet me, take me,
> Angel or devil, I am what you make me.
> —ANONYMOUS.

# WISDOM

There is a spirit in man: and the inspiration of the Almighty giveth them understanding.—JOB 32:8.

She is more precious than rubies: and all things thou canst desire are not to be compared unto her.

Length of days is in her right hand; and in her left hand riches and honor.

Her ways are ways of pleasantness, and all her paths are peace.—PROV. 3:15, 16, 17.

# WISDOM

He that winneth souls is wise.—Prov. 11:30.

Wisdom is better than weapons of war.—Eccles. 9:18.

The wisdom of this world is foolishness with God.—I Cor. 3:19.

Wisdom thoroughly learned, will never be forgotten.—Pythagoras.

What is the first business of one who studies philosophy? To part with self-conceit. For it is impossible for any one to begin to learn what he thinks he already knows.—Epictetus.

Wisdom does not show itself so much in precept as in life—in firmness of mind and mastery of appetite. It teaches us to do as well as to talk, and to make our words and actions all of a color.—Seneca.

He who learns the rules of wisdom without conforming to them in his life is like a man who ploughs in his field but does not sow.—As Saadi.

A fool doth know he is wise, but a wise man doth know himself to be a fool.—William Shakespeare.

> All places that the eye of heaven visits
> Are to a wise man ports and happy havens.
> —William Shakespeare.

The better part of valor is discretion.—William Shakespeare.

A little philosophy inclineth man's mind to atheism, but depth in philosophy bringeth man's mind about to religion.—Francis Bacon.

Wise men say nothing in dangerous times.—John Selden.

> How charming is divine philosophy!
> Not harsh and crabbed, as dull fools suppose,
> But musical as in Apollo's lute,
> And a perpetual feast of nectar'd sweets
> Where no crude surfeit reigns.
> —John Milton.

# WISDOM

> To know
> That which before us lies in daily life
> Is prime wisdom.
> > —JOHN MILTON.

> What in me is dark,
> Illumine, and what is low raise and support
> That to the height of that great argument
> I may assert eternal Providence,
> And justify the ways of God to men.
> > —JOHN MILTON.

The sublimity of wisdom is to do those things living which are to be desired when dying.—JEREMY TAYLOR.

Living in an age of extraordinary events and revolutions, I have learned from thence this truth which I desire might be communicated to posterity; that all is vanity which is not honest, and that there is no solid wisdom but in real piety.—JOHN EVELYN.

The wise man endeavors to shine in himself; the fool to outshine others. The first is humbled by the sense of his own infirmities; the last is lifted up by the discovery of those which he observes in other men. The wise man considers what he wants, and the fool what he abounds in. The wise man is happy when he gains his own approbation, and the fool when he recommends himself to the applause of those about him.—JOSEPH ADDISON.

> Be wise with speed;
> A fool at forty is a fool indeed.
> > —EDWARD YOUNG.

> Of all the causes which conspire to blind
> Men's erring judgment, and misguide the mind,—
> What the weak head with strongest bias rules,
> Is pride, the never-failing vice of fools.
> > —ALEXANDER POPE.

The truest wisdom is a resolute determination.—NAPOLEON BONAPARTE.

Wisdom is ofttimes nearer when we stoop than when we soar. —WILLIAM WORDSWORTH.

# WISDOM

Common sense in an uncommon degree is what the world calls wisdom.—Samuel Taylor Coleridge.

> Go where he will, the wise man is at home;
> His hearth the earth, his hall the azure dome.
> —Ralph Waldo Emerson.

Knowledge comes, but wisdom lingers. . . .—Alfred Tennyson.

A little group of wise hearts is better than a wilderness of fools.—John Ruskin.

Wisdom is the right use of knowledge.—Charles Haddon Spurgeon.

The wise man is he who knows the relative value of things.—Dean William Ralph Inge.

The intellect of the wise is like glass; it admits the light of heaven and reflects it.—Julius Charles Hare.

True wisdom is to know what is best worth knowing, and to do what is best worth doing.—Laurence Humphrey.

True wisdom, that from above, is teachable, moving on toward the goal of completeness through that which it learns.—E. D. Head.

Ours is not wisdom until it has become supreme and tolerant.—Anonymous.

Our chief wisdom consists in knowing our follies and faults, that we may correct them.—Anonymous.

# WOMAN

Who can find a virtuous woman? for her price is far above rubies.

The heart of her husband doth safely trust in her, so that he shall have not need of spoil.

She will do him good and not evil all the days of her life.

# WOMAN

She seeketh wool, and flax, and worketh willingly with her hands.

She is like the merchants' ships; she bringeth her food from afar.

She riseth also while it is yet night, and giveth meat to her household, and a portion to her maidens.

She considereth a field, and buyeth it: with the fruit of her hands she planteth a vineyard.

She girdeth her loins with strength, and strengtheneth her arms.

She perceiveth that her merchandise is good: her candle goeth not out by night.

She layeth her hands to the spindle, and her hands hold the distaff.

She stretcheth out her hand to the poor; yea, she reacheth forth her hands to the needy.

She is not afraid of the snow for her household: for all her household are clothed with scarlet.

She maketh herself coverings of tapestry; her clothing is silk and purple.

Her husband is known in the gates, when he sitteth among the elders of the land.

She maketh fine linen, and selleth it; and delivereth girdles unto the merchant.

Strength and honor are her clothing; and she shall rejoice in time to come.

She openeth her mouth with wisdom; and in her tongue is the law of kindness.

She looketh well to the ways of her household, and eateth not the bread of idleness.

Her children arise up, and call her blessed; her husband also, and he praiseth her.—Prov. 31:10-28.

Earth has nothing more tender than a woman's heart when it is the abode of piety.—Martin Luther.

'Tis beauty that doth oft make women proud;
'Tis virtue that doth make them most admired;
'Tis modesty that makes them soon divine.
—William Shakespeare.

# WOMAN

Kindness in women, not their beauteous looks,
Shall win my love.

—WILLIAM SHAKESPEARE.

Purity of heart is the noblest inheritance, and love the fairest ornament of woman.—MATTHIAS CLAUDIUS.

Unhappy is the man for whom his own mother has not made all other mothers venerable.—JEAN PAUL RICHTER.

Let France have good mothers and she will have good sons.
—NAPOLEON BONAPARTE.

There is one in the world who feels for him who is sad a keener pang than he feels for himself; there is one to whom reflected joy is better than that which comes direct; there is one who rejoices in another's honor more than in any which is one's own; there is one on whom another's trancendent excellence sheds no beam but that of delight; there is one who hides another's deformities more faithfully than one's own; there is one who loses all sense of self in the sentiment of kindness, tenderness and devotion to another; that one is woman.—WASHINGTON IRVING.

I have often had occasion to mark the fortitude with which women sustain the most overwhelming reverses of fortune. Those disasters which break down the spirit of a man and prostrate him in the dust seem to call forth all the energies of the softer sex, and give them such intrepidity and elevation to their character that at times it approaches sublimity.—WASHINGTON IRVING.

As the vine which has long twined its graceful foliage about the oak, and been lifted by it in sunshine, will, when the hardy plant is rifted by the thunderbolt, cling around it with its caressing tendrils, and bind up its shattered boughs, so is it beautifully ordered by Providence that woman who is the mere dependent and ornament of man in his happier hours, should be his stay and solace when smitten with sudden calamity; winding herself into the rugged recesses of his nature, tenderly supporting the drooping head and binding up the broken heart.—WASHINGTON IRVING.

Children, look into those eyes, listen to the dear voice, notice the feeling of even a single touch that is bestowed upon you by that gentle hand! Make much of it while yet you have that most precious of all good gifts,—a loving mother. Read the unfathomable love of those eyes; the kind anxiety of that tone and look, however slight your pain. In after life you may have friends, fond, dear friends, but never will you have again the inexpressible love and gentleness lavished upon you, which none but mother bestows.—THOMAS BABINGTON MACAULAY.

A woman's lot is made for her by the love she accepts.—GEORGE ELIOT.

When I see the elaborate study and ingenuity displayed by women in the pursuit of trifles, I feel no doubt of their capacity for the most herculean undertakings.—JULIA WARD HOWE.

The buckling on of a knight's armor by his lady's hand was not a mere caprice of romantic fashion. It is the type of an eternal truth that the soul's armor is never well set to the heart unless a woman's hand has braced it, and it is only when she braces it loosely that the honor of manhood fails.—JOHN RUSKIN.

The best woman has always somewhat of a man's strength; and the noblest man of a woman's gentleness.—DINAH M. MULOCK (MRS. CRAIK).

The deepest tenderness a woman can show to a man is to help him to do his duty.—DINAH M. MULOCK (MRS. CRAIK).

> Love droops; youth fades;
> The leaves of friendship fall;
> A mother's love outlives them all.
> —OLIVER WENDELL HOLMES.

Every man who is high up likes to think that he has done it all himself, and the wife smiles and lets it go at that.—SIR JAMES M. BARRIE.

Oh, what makes woman lovely? Virtue, faith and gentleness in suffering; an endurance through scorn or trial; these call beauty forth, give it the stamp celestial and admit it to sisterhood with angels.—CHARLES H. BRENT.

Educate a boy and you educate an individual; educate a girl and you educate a family.—JOHN CRUMPTON HARDY.

# WOMAN

The finest compliment that can be paid to a woman of sense is to address her as such. Next to God we are indebted to woman, first for life itself, and then for making it worth living.—C. N. BOVEE.

Woman is God's poem in whom the rhythm of righteousness and the beauty of holiness are expressed in the highest terms. —ROSALIE MILLS APPLEBY.

A beautiful and chaste woman is the perfect workmanship of God, and the true glory of angels, the rare miracle of earth, and the sole wonder of the world.—GEORGE HERMES.

There are a few things that never go out of style and a feminine woman is one of them.—JOBYNA RALSTON.

Virtue, modesty and truth are the guardian angels of woman. —C. C. COLTON.

The future of society is in the hands of mothers; if the world was lost through woman, she alone can save it.—LOUIS DE BEAUFORT.

Women are the poetry of the world in the same sense as the stars are the poetry of heaven. Clear, light-giving, harmonious, they are the terrestrial planets that rule the destinies of mankind. —WALTER CLARENCE HARGRAVE.

Frequently, when doubtful how to act in matters of importance, I have received more useful advice from women than from men. Women have the understanding of the heart, which is better than that of the head.—JOHN ROGERS.

Christianity has lifted woman to a new place in the world. . . . And just in proportion as Christianity has sway, will she rise to a higher dignity in human life. . . . What she has now, and all she shall have of privilege and true honor, she owes to that gospel which took those qualities which had been counted weak and unworthy and gave them a divine glory in Christ.—HERRICK JOHNSON.

Contact with a high-minded woman is good for the life of any man.—HENRY VINCENT.

# WOMAN

God has placed the genius of women in their hearts; because the works of this genius are always works of love.—ALFONSE DE LAMERTINE.

Woman was taken out of man—Not out of his head, to rule over him; nor out of his feet, to be trampled under by him; but out of his side, to be equal to him—under his arm, that he might protect her, and near his heart that he might love her.—MATTHEW HENRY.

The foundation of domestic happiness is faith in the virtue of woman.—WALTER SAVAGE LANDOR.

Too many women accept marriage at the altar as a paid-up bread ticket, never realizing that there is a price for them to pay perpetually. Getting a certain amount of leisure and able to make more by crowding the home duties ever into less and less time, they go in for "improvement," majoring in outside interests. They become self-centered, absorbed in their own cultivation. They become dull where their husbands are concerned. An absent-minded woman makes a mighty poor companion. An interested woman is always an interesting woman. The smartest woman—regardless of all else—is she who makes her home the pivot, herself necessary to her husband; who achieves a certain togetherness with him, a certain intimacy of companionship that could not be invaded by other undesirable interests.—ANNE SHANNON MONROE.

Blessed are the Mothers of the earth, for they have combined the practical and the spiritual into the workable way of human life. They have darned little stockings, mended little dresses, washed little faces, and have pointed little eyes to the stars, and little souls to eternal things.—WILLIAM L. STINGER.

The saddest thing that can befall a soul
Is when it loses faith in God and woman.
    Lost I these gems,
Though the world's throne stood empty in my path,
I would go wandering back into my childhood
    Searching for them with tears.
—ALEXANDER SMITH.

# WOMAN

If the time should ever come when women are not Christians and houses are not homes, then we shall have lost the chief cornerstones on which civilization rests.—A. B. WHITE.

# WORK

Six days shalt thou work, but on the seventh day thou shalt rest.—EXOD. 34:21.

What shall we do, that we might work the works of God?—JOHN 6:28.

The night cometh, when no man can work.—JOHN 9:4.

Toil is the sire of fame.—EURIPIDES.

Nothing is denied to well-directed labor; nothing is ever to be attained without it.—SIR JOSHUA REYNOLDS.

> Absence of occupation is not rest;
> A mind quite vacant is a mind distressed.
> —WILLIAM COWPER.

Pleasure soon exhausts us and itself also, but endeavor never does.—JEAN PAUL RICHTER.

Occupation was one of the pleasures of Paradise, and we cannot be happy without it.—ANNA JAMESON.

There is a perennial nobleness and even a sacredness in work. —THOMAS CARLYLE.

Labor, wide as the earth, has its summit in heaven.—THOMAS CARLYLE.

Blessed is the man who has found his work. Let him ask no other blessedness. Know thy work, and do it; and work at it like Hercules. One monster there is in the world—the idle man.— THOMAS CARLYLE.

> Let us then, be up and doing,
> With a heart for any fate;
> Still achieving, still pursuing,
> Learn to labor and to wait.
> —HENRY WADSWORTH LONGFELLOW.

# WORK

Do thy work, it shall succeed
   In thine or another's day;
And if denied the victor's mead,
   Thou shalt not lack the toiler's pay.
     —JOHN GREENLEAF WHITTIER.

I stood up straight and worked
My veritable work. And as the soul
Which grows within a child makes the child grow,
Or, as the fiery sap, the touch of God,
Careering through a tree, dilates the bark
And toughs with scale and knob, before it strikes
The summer foliage out in a green flame—
So life, in deepening with me, deepened all
The course I took, the work I did.
     —ELIZABETH BARRETT BROWNING.

It is not work that kills men; it is worry. Work is healthy; you can hardly put more upon a man than he can bear. Worry is rust upon the blade. It is not the revolution that destroys the machinery but the friction. Fear secretes acids; but love and trust are sweet juices.—HENRY WARD BEECHER.

It is not enough to be busy; so are the ants. The question is: What are we busy about?—HENRY DAVID THOREAU.

Toil is the true knight's pastime.—CHARLES KINGSLEY.

No man is born into the world whose work is not born with him. There is always work, and tools to work withal, for those who will; and blessed are the horny hands of toil.—JAMES RUSSELL LOWELL.

The moment a man can really do his work, he becomes speechless about it; all words are idle to him; all theories. Does a bird need to theorize about building its nest, or boast of it when it is built? All good work is essentially done that way—without hesitation; without difficulty; without boasting.—JOHN RUSKIN.

It is no man's business if he has genius or not. Work he must, whatever he is, but quietly and steadily; and the natural and enforced results of such work will always be the thing that God meant him to do, and will be his best.—JOHN RUSKIN.

# WORK

We are not sent into this world to do anything into which we cannot put our whole hearts. We have certain things to do for our bread, and that is to be done strenuously; other work to do for our delight, and that is to be done heartily; neither is to be done by halves or shifts, but with a will, and what is not worth this effort is not to be done at all.—JOHN RUSKIN.

The vocation of every man and woman is to serve other people.—LEO TOLSTOI.

The worst days of darkness through which I have ever passed have been greatly alleviated by throwing myself with all my energy into some work relating to others.—JAMES A. GARFIELD.

No true work since the world began was ever wasted; no true life since the world began has ever failed. Oh, understand those two perverted words, "failure" and "success" and measure them by the eternal, not the earthly standard.—FREDERICK W. FARRAR.

Toil is the love of life and its best fruits.—SIR LEWIS MORRIS.

If a man loves to labor at any trade, apart from any question of success or fame, the gods have called him.—ROBERT LOUIS STEVENSON.

> This is the gospel of labor—
>     Ring it, ye bells of the kirk—
> The Lord of Love comes down from above
>     To dwell with the men who work.
>                     —HENRY VAN DYKE.

> Let me but find it in my heart to say
> When vagrant wishes beckon me astray,—
> Of all who live, I am the one by whom
> This work can best be done in the right way.
>                     —HENRY VAN DYKE.

Nothing is really work unless you would rather be doing something else.—SIR JAMES BARRIE.

I believe in work, hard work, and long hours for work. Men do not break down from overwork, but from worry and dissipation.—CHARLES EVANS HUGHES.

# WORK

The greatest asset of any nation is the spirit of its people, and the greatest danger that can menace any nation is the breakdown of that spirit—the will to win and the courage to work.— GEORGE B. CORTELYOU.

The man who does not work for the love of work, but only for money is not likely to make money nor to find much fun in life. —CHARLES M. SCHWAB.

He who would really benefit mankind must reach them through their work.—HENRY FORD.

All growth depends upon activity. There is no development physically or intellectually without effort and effort means work. Work is not a curse; it is a prerogative of intelligence, the only means to manhood, and the measure of civilization.—CALVIN COOLIDGE.

On our national birthday it is well to remember that the rights to "Life, Liberty and the Pursuit of Happiness" are based on work.—LEIGH MITCHELL HODGES.

To love life through labor is to be intimate with life's inmost secret.—KAHLIL GIBRAN.

It is better to undertake a large task and get it half done than to undertake nothing and get it all done.—W. MARSHALL CRAIG.

Seeking to save society and to make the world a fit place in which to live is pagan philosophy and good work for a civic club. Seeking to save sinners and to make saints fit to live in God's world is Christian philosophy and the work of Christ, Christians and the Church. This world is not better and no worse than the people who live in it.—M. E. DODD.

A great deal of the joy of life consists in doing perfectly, or at least to the best of one's ability, everything which he attempts to do. There is a sense of satisfaction, a pride in surveying such work—a work which is rounded full, exact, complete in all its parts—which the superficial man, who leaves his work in a slovenly, slipshod, half-finished condition, can never know. It is this conscientious completeness which turns work into art. The smallest thing, well done, becomes artistic.—WILLIAM MATHEWS.

# WORK

Men are naturally tempted by the devil, but an idle man positively tempts the devil.—Spanish Proverb.

Joy hovers about the head of the man who loves his own occupation.—Anonymous.

# WORSHIP

Worship the Lord in the beauty of Holiness.—I Chron. 16:29.

It is written, Thou shalt worship the Lord thy God, and Him only shalt thou serve.—Matt. 4:10.

Words without thoughts never to heaven go.—William Shakespeare.

> First worship God.
>   He that forgets to pray
> Bids not himself good-morrow
>   Or good-day.
>     —Thomas Randolph.

The dullest observer must be sensible of the order and serenity prevalent in those households where the occasional exercise of a beautiful form of worship in the morning gives, as it were, the keynote to every temper for the day, and attunes every spirit to harmony.—Washington Irving.

What greater calamity can fall upon a nation than the loss of worship.—Thomas Carlyle.

The happiest man he is who learns from nature the lesson of worship.—Ralph Waldo Emerson.

Do not forget that even as "to work is to worship" so to be cheery is to worship also, and to be happy is the first step to being pious.—Robert Louis Stevenson.

> Let us put by some hour of every day
> For holy things—whether it be when dawn
> Peers through the windowpane, or when the noon
> Flames like a burnished topaz in the vault,
> Or when the thrush pours in the ear of eve

# WORSHIP

Its plaintive melody; some little hour
Wherein to hold rapt converse with the soul
From sordidness and self a sanctuary,
Swept by the winnowing of unseen wings
And touched by the White Light Ineffable.
                              —CLINTON SCOLLARD.

Man is a religious being; the heart instinctively seeks for a
God. Whether he worships on the banks of the Ganges, prays
with his face upturned to the sun, kneels toward Mecca, or, regarding all space as a temple, communes with the heavenly
Father according to the Christian creed, man is essentially devout.—WILLIAM JENNINGS BRYAN.

We must not forget to keep worship at the heart of life.—
HENRY T. HODGKIN.

The tongue blessing God without the heart is but a tinkling
cymbal; the heart blessing God without the tongue is sweet but
still music; both in concert make their harmony which fills and
delights heaven and earth.—R. VENNING.

Worship liberates the personality by giving a new perspective
to life, by integrating life with the multitude of life-forms, by
bringing into the life the virtues of humility, loyalty, devotion
and rightness of attitude, thus refreshing and reviving the spirit.
—ROSWELL C. LONG.

# YOUTH

Rejoice, O young man, in thy youth; and let thy heart cheer
thee in the days of thy youth, and walk in the ways of thine heart,
and in the sight of thine eyes; but know thou, that for all these
things God will bring thee into judgment.—ECCLES. 11:9.

Let no man despise thy youth.—I TIM. 4:12.

373

# YOUTH

As I approve of a youth that has something of the old man in him, so I am no less pleased with an old man that has something of the youth. He that follows this rule may be old in body, but can never be so in mind.—CICERO.

Bestow thy youth so that thou mayest have comfort to remember it when it hath forsaken thee, and not to sigh and grieve at the account thereof. While thou art young thou wilt think it will never have an end; but the longest day hath its evening, and thou shalt enjoy it but once; it never turns again; use it therefore as the spring time, which soon departeth and wherein thou oughtest to plant and sow all provisions for a long and happy life.—SIR WALTER RALEIGH.

The childhood shows the man
As morning shows the day.
—JOHN MILTON.

Our youth we can have but today; we may always find time to grow old.—BISHOP GEORGE BERKELEY.

The morning of life is like the dawn of day—full of purity, of imagery and harmony.—LORD CHESTERFIELD.

I love the acquaintance of young people, because, in the first place, I do not like to think myself growing old. In the next place, young acquaintances must last longest, if they do last.—SAMUEL JOHNSON.

To keep young, every day read a poem, hear a choice piece of music, view a fine painting, and if possible, do a good action. Man's highest merit always is, as much as possible, to rule external circumstances and as little as possible to let himself be ruled by them.—JOHANN WOLFGANG VON GOETHE.

The destiny of any nation, at any given time, depends on the opinions of its young men under five and twenty.—JOHANN WOLFGANG VON GOETHE.

Keep true to the dreams of thy youth.—FRIEDRICH SCHILLER.

Sweet childish days that were as long
As twenty days are now.
—WILLIAM WORDSWORTH.

# YOUTH

Naught cared this body for wind or weather
When Youth and I lived in it together.
—SAMUEL TAYLOR COLERIDGE.

In the lexicon of youth, which fate reserves for a bright manhood, there is no such word as "fail."
—OWEN MEREDITH.

The youth of a nation are the trustees of posterity.—BENJAMIN DISRAELI.

What is really wanted is to light up the spirit that is within the child. In some sense and in some degree there is in every child the material of good work in the world; not only those who are brilliant, not only those who are quick, but those who are stolid, and even those who are dull.—WILLIAM EWART GLADSTONE.

If I had the opportunity to say a final word to all the young people of America, it would be this: Don't think too much about yourselves. Try to cultivate the habit of thinking of others; this will reward you. Nourish your minds by good reading; discover what your life work is, work in which you can be happiest. Be unafraid in all things where you know you are right. Be unselfish. That's the first and final commandment for those who would be useful and happy in their usefulness.—CHARLES WILLIAM ELIOT.

The fairest flower in the garden of creation is a young mind, offering and unfolding itself to the influence of divine wisdom, as the heliotrope turns its sweet blossom to the sun.—JOSEPH RUSSEL SMITH.

Youth is the opportunity to do something and to become somebody.—T. T. MUNGER.

Unless a tree has borne blossoms in spring, you will vainly look for fruit on it in autumn.—JULIUS CHARLES HARE.

When we are out of sympathy with the young, then I think our work in this world is over.—GEORGE McDONALD.

# YOUTH

Those who enjoy the large pleasures of advanced age are those who have sacrificed the small pleasures of youth.—CHARLES E. CARPENTER.

In this is Youth most wonderful: that it knows not fear.—ANONYMOUS.

If our boys and girls are not so good as they were when you were a child their age, it may be that they had a much better mother and dad than your child has.—ANONYMOUS.

Every youth who is ambitious to grow to the full stature of noble manhood must make up his mind at the start that he has got to be bigger than the things that are trying to down him. If he doesn't he will go down with them.—ANONYMOUS.


# ZEAL

Whatsoever thy hand findeth to do, do it with thy might.—ECCLES. 9:10.

Look down from heaven, and behold from the habitation of thy holiness and of thy glory: where is thy zeal and thy strength, the sounding of thy heart and of thy mercies toward me? are they restrained?—ISA. 63:15.

Nothing can be fairer or more noble than the holy fervor of true zeal.—JEAN BAPTISTE MOLIÈRE.

Whether zeal or moderation be the point we aim at, let us keep fire out of the one and frost out of the other.—JOSEPH ADDISON.

Zeal for public good is the characteristic of a man of honor and a gentleman, and must take the place of pleasures, profits and all other private gratifications.—SIR RICHARD STEELE.

A zealous soul without meekness, is like a ship in a storm, in danger of wrecks. A meek soul without zeal is like a ship in a calm, that moves not so fast as it ought.—JAMES M. MASON.

# ZEAL

The heights by great men reached and kept
Were not attained by sudden flight,
But they while their companions slept
Were toiling upward in the night.
  —HENRY WADSWORTH LONGFELLOW.

This world is given as a prize for the men in earnest; and that which is true of this world is truer still of the world to come.—FREDERICK WILLIAM ROBERTSON.

False zeal may rise as high as true, and indeed much higher, because it is extremely apt to estimate its object above its intrinsic and comparative importance. Besides when a totally selfish heart is awakened into zeal, there is nothing in it to stem the tide of affection, which all unite and harmonize in the ardent pursuit of selfish ends. True zeal is a strong, steady, uniform, benevolent affection; but false zeal is a strong, desultory, boisterous, selfish passion.—NATHANIEL EMMONS.

All true zeal for God is a zeal for love, mercy and goodness.—R. E. THOMPSON.

Zeal is the fire of love, active for duty, burning as it flies.—W. R. WILLIAMS.

Zeal without knowledge is like fire without a grate to contain it; like a sword without a hilt to wield it by; like a high-bred horse without a bridle to guide him. It speaks without thinking, acts without planning, seeks to accomplish a good end without the adoption of becoming mean.—JULIUS BATE.

Experience shows that success is due less to ability than to zeal. The winner is he who gives himself to his work, body and soul.—CHARLES BUXTON.

Being everlastingly on the job beats carrying a rabbit's foot.—ANONYMOUS.

# INDEX

# INDEX

# INDEX

# INDEX

# INDEX

# INDEX

# INDEX

# INDEX

# INDEX

# INDEX

# INDEX

# INDEX

# INDEX

# INDEX

# INDEX

# INDEX

# INDEX

# INDEX

# INDEX

# INDEX

# INDEX

# INDEX

# INDEX

# INDEX